A Course of British and American Culture (2)

英美文化教程（下）

主　　审　张绍杰
主　　编　姜毓锋
副 主 编　甄艳华　刘　莉

分册主编　马艳辉　王　璐
编　　委　康晓芸　李　雪　袁妮娅　高英祺
　　　　　王开颜　徐红云　秦一竹

科 学 出 版 社
北　京

图书在版编目（CIP）数据

英美文化教程=A Course of British and American Culture. 下 / 姜毓锋主编. —北京：科学出版社，2009

ISBN 978-7-03-025064-3

Ⅰ. 英… Ⅱ. 姜… Ⅲ. ①英语–教材②英国–概况③美国–概况 Ⅳ. H31

中国版本图书馆 CIP 数据核字（2009）第 125548 号

责任编辑：朱 琳 / 责任校对：鲁 素
责任印制：徐晓晨 / 封面设计：无极书装

科学出版社出版
北京东黄城根北街 16 号
邮政编码：100717
http://www.sciencep.com
北京京华虎彩印刷有限公司 印刷
科学出版社发行 各地新华书店经销

*

2009 年 9 月第 一 版 开本：787×1092 1/16
2015 年 8 月第三次印刷 印张：12 1/2
字数：385 000

定价：32.00 元

（如有印装质量问题，我社负责调换）

前 言

《英美文化教程（下）》是一本关于美国社会与文化的教科书，旨在帮助读者了解美国社会与文化概貌，如地理、历史、政治、宗教、经济、教育、风俗和人物等。读者可通过课文学习和练习训练，丰富其目标语国家的文化背景知识，最终提高跨文化交际能力。本教程凝聚了哈尔滨理工大学、哈尔滨工业大学、北京语言大学、广州大学、湖南大学、哈尔滨医科大学和哈尔滨商业大学的专家、学者以及长期从事英美文化教学教师的辛勤汗水，特别要感谢的是，本教程还得到了东北师范大学副校长、英语博士生导师张绍杰教授的审阅以及美国专家的具体指导。本教程语言地道、原汁原味，内容新颖、通俗易懂，版式设计独特、图片丰富，可作为高校英语专业学生及非英语专业高年级学生英美文化课程教材，也可供具有同等英语水平的自学者使用。

为了帮助读者全面深入了解美国文化，增强整体观察和综合研究的能力，本教程讲述的基本内容采用了树状结构组合，横向展开，拓宽视野讨论美国社会的方方面面；纵向探索，追溯其运动轨迹和因果关系。本教程纵深和广度结合以相互补充，控制篇幅的同时保证信息量，达到兼容并蓄，提高可教性、可读性和参考性，满足多层次、多方位的不同需求。

本教程具有以下特点：

- 兼顾教学需求与自学需要，各章节配有要点提示；
- 各章生词当页标注，方便学生自主学习；各章注释以背景知识为主，复杂语法为辅；
- 各章配有精选练习题，提示本章复习要点；
- 设“名人”专章，凸显人文气息；
- 独有的大事年表以及所附的国旗、国歌、国花等知识为学习者提供方便。

诚然，一个民族的文化范畴包罗万象，大到政治、文化、经济、军事、历史、地理、宗教、民俗，小到民众的衣食住行，因此，一本教程很难详尽地细数美国文化的林林总总，只能择主干而弃枝叶。但编者希望，借此教程，将以往片面零星、散状分布的材料百川归海、上下贯串，呈献给读者一部脉络分明、内容全面、“整体性”强的美国文化教程。为此，编者力求做到尽善尽美、恰到好处，但定有不足和局限，望研究英美文化与国家概况的专家和读者批评指正。

编　者

2008 年 12 月于哈尔滨

目　录

Chapter 1

Geography

HIGHLIGHTS

introduction to the US — physiographic features — climate and natural disasters — natural resources

I. Introduction to the US

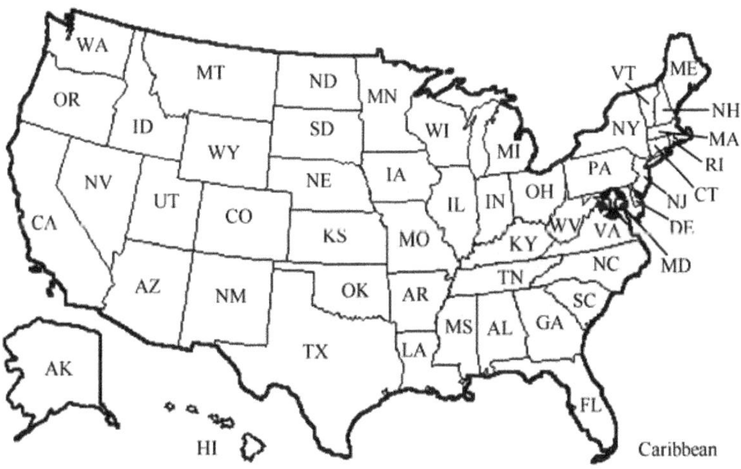

The United States is a country in the Western Hemisphere. It consists of 48 contiguous states on the North American continent; Alaska is an enormous **peninsula** (半岛) which forms the northwestern most part of North America, and Hawaii, an **archipelago** (群岛) in the Pacific Ocean. It also holds several United States territories in the Pacific and Caribbean. The country shares land borders with Canada and Mexico and a water border with Russia.

The official full name of the United States is usually referred to as the United States of America. It is often called the United States, the US, the US, the USA, or simply America, or the States in American spoken English. Its nickname is Yankee-land. It is a federal republic of

North America. It is divided into 50 federal states and the District of Columbia, which has developed from the original 13 states, and which secured their independence from Great Britain in 1783. Its currency is the US dollar of 100 cents. Its national day is on 4th of July (Independence Day).

1. The Land Area

The total land area of the USA is 9,372,615 square kilometers, the fourth largest country in the world after Russia, Canada and China. It stretches 2,575 kilometers from north to south and 4,500km from east to west. Of all the 50 states Alaska is the largest state in land area and Rhode Island the smallest. But on the mainland of the US, Texas, larger than France but half the size of Alaska, is the largest state in the country.

2. The Capital

Washington, D.C. is the capital of the United States of America. The city of Washington has the same boundaries as the District of Columbia (D.C.), a federal territory established in 1790 as the site of the new nation's permanent capital. Named after the first US president, George Washington, the city has served since 1800 as the seat of federal government. It is also the heart of a dynamic metropolitan region. During the 20th century, the Washington, D.C., metropolitan area grew rapidly as the responsibilities of national government increased, both at home and throughout the world.

3. The National Flag, Emblem and Anthem

The flag of the United States of America consists of 13 equal horizontal stripes of red (top and bottom) alternating with white, with a blue **rectangle** (长方形) in the canton bearing 50 small, white, five-pointed stars arranged in nine offset horizontal rows of six stars (top and bottom) alternating with rows of five stars. The 50 stars on the flag represent the 50 US states

and the 13 stripes represent the original 13 colonies that rebelled against the British Crown and became the first states in the Union. Nicknames for the flag include the Stars and Stripes, Old Glory, and the Star-Spangled Banner.

The bald eagle was chosen on June 20, 1782 as the **emblem** (徽章) of the United States of America because of its long life, great strength and majestic looks, and also because it was then believed to exist only on this continent.

On September 14, 1814, US soldiers at Baltimore's Fort McHenry raised a huge American flag to celebrate a crucial victory over British forces during the War of 1812. The sight of those "broad stripes and bright stars" inspired Francis Scott Key to write a poem which was later set to the tune of a popular British drinking song and renamed "The Star-Spangled Banner".

The Star-Spangled Banner was recognized for official use by the Navy in 1889 and the President in 1916, and was made the **national anthem** (国歌) by a congressional resolution on March 3, 1931, which was signed by President Herbert Hoover.

Lyrics:

O! say can you see by the dawn's early light
What so proudly we hailed at the twilight's last gleaming.
Whose broad stripes and bright stars through the perilous fight,
O'er the ramparts we watched were so gallantly streaming.
And the rockets' red glare, the bombs bursting in air,
Gave proof through the night that our flag was still there.
O! say does that star-spangled banner yet wave
O'er the land of the free and the home of the brave?
On the shore, dimly seen through the mists of the deep,
Where the foe's haughty host in dread silence reposes,
What is that which the breeze, o'er the towering steep,
As it fitfully blows, half conceals, half discloses?
Now it catches the gleam of the morning's first beam,
In full glory reflected now shines in the stream:
'Tis the star-spangled banner! Oh long may it wave
O'er the land of the free and the home of the brave!
And where is that band who so vauntingly swore
That the havoc of war and the battle's confusion,
A home and a country should leave us no more!
Their blood has washed out their foul footsteps' pollution.
No refuge could save the hireling and slave
From the terror of flight, or the gloom of the grave:
And the star-spangled banner in triumph doth wave
O'er the land of the free and the home of the brave!
O! thus be it ever, when freemen shall stand
Between their loved home and the war's desolation!
Blest with victory and peace, may the heav'n rescued land
Praise the Power that hath made and preserved us a nation.
Then conquer we must, when our cause it is just,
And this be our motto: "In God is our trust."
And the star-spangled banner in triumph shall wave
O'er the land of the free and the home of the brave!

4. National Flower, Stone and Bird

September 23, 1986, the House of Representatives passed a joint resolution naming the rose as the "national floral emblem" of the United States. The Senate passed the resolution in 1985. The **measure** (法案) then went to President Ronald Reagan. He signed the resolution into law on October 7, 1986 in a ceremony in the White House Rose Garden. On November 20, 1986, President Reagan signed *Proclamation 5574: The National Floral Emblem of the United States of America.*

The national stone of the United States is blue **sapphire** (蓝宝石) which represents planet Saturn mostly known for regular gains through mass labor industry and development of land. The blue color of sapphire is strongly linked with feelings of sympathy and harmony, friendship and loyalty.

The Founding Fathers of America wanted to choose an animal that was unique to the United States. For six years, the members of Congress engaged in a dispute over what the national emblem should be. As a result of the debate, the bald eagle was chosen because it symbolized strength, courage, freedom, and immortality. The bald eagle was made the national bird of the United States in 1782. The image of the bald eagle can be found in many places in the US, such as on the Great Seal, Federal agency seals, the President's flag, and on the one-dollar bill. The bald eagle is a large, powerful, brown bird with a white head and tail. The term "bald" does not mean that this bird lacks feathers. Instead, it comes from the word "piebald", an old word, meaning "marked with white".

II. Physiographic Features

1. Geographic Divisions

The eastern United States has a varied **topography** (地形). A broad, flat coastal plain lines the Atlantic and Gulf shores from the Texas-Mexico border to the New York City, and includes the Florida Peninsula. Areas further inland feature rolling hills and temperate forests. The Appalachian Mountains form a line of low mountains separating the eastern seaboard from the Great Lakes and the Mississippi River Basin. The five Great Lakes are located in the north-central portion of the country, four of them forming part of the border with Canada. The southeast states contain subtropical forests and, near the gulf coast, mangrove wetlands, especially in Florida. In the west of the Appalachians lie the Mississippi River Basin and two large eastern tributaries, the Ohio River and the Tennessee River. The Ohio and the Tennessee Valleys and the Midwest consist largely of rolling hills and productive farmland, stretching south to the Gulf Coast.

The Great Plains lie west of the Mississippi River and east of the Rocky Mountains. A large portion of the country's agricultural products are grown in the Great Plains. Before their general conversion to farmland, the Great Plains were noted for their extensive grasslands, from tallgrass **prairie** (大草原) in the eastern plains to shortgrass steppe in the western High Plains. Elevation rises gradually from less than a few hundred feet near the Mississippi River to more than a mile high in the High Plains. The generally low relief of the plains is broken in several places, most

notably in the Ozark and Ouachita Mountains, which form the US Interior Highlands, the only major mountainous region between the Rocky Mountains and the Appalachian Mountains. The Great Plains come to an abrupt end at the Rocky Mountains. The Rocky Mountains form a large portion of the Western US, entering from Canada and stretching nearly to Mexico. The Rocky Mountains generally contain fairly mild slopes and low peaks compared to many of the other great mountain ranges, with a few exceptions (such as the Teton Mountains in Wyoming and the Sawatch Range in Colorado). In addition, instead of being one generally continuous and solid mountain range, it is broken up into a number of smaller, **intermittent** (断断续续的) mountain ranges, forming a large number of series of basins and valleys.

In the west of the Rocky Mountains lies the Intermontane **Plateaus** (高原) (also known as the Intermountain West), a large, arid desert lying between the Rockies and the Cascades and Sierra Nevada ranges. The large southern portion, known as the Great Basin, consists of salt flats, drainage basins, and many small north-south mountain ranges. The Southwest is predominantly a low-lying desert region. A portion known as the Colorado Plateau, centered on the Four Corners region, is considered to have some of the most spectacular scenery in the world. It is accentuated in such national parks as **Grand Canyon** (大峡谷), Arches, and **Bryce Canyon** (布赖斯峡谷) among others. The Grand Canyon is among the most famous locations in the country.

The Intermontane Plateaus come to an end at the Cascade Range and the Sierra Nevada. The Cascades consist of largely intermittent, volcanic mountains rising prominently from the surrounding landscape. The Sierra Nevada, further south, is a high, rugged, and dense mountain range. It contains the highest point in the contiguous 48 states, Mount Whitney. These areas contain some spectacular scenery as well, as evidenced by such national parks as **Yosemite** (约塞米蒂国家公园) and Mount Rainier. West of the Cascades and Sierra Nevada is a series of valleys, such as the Central Valley in California and the Willamette Valley in Oregon. Along the coast is a series of low mountain ranges known as the Pacific Coast Ranges. Much of the Pacific Northwest coast is inhabited by some of the densest vegetation outside of the Tropics, and also the tallest trees in the world (the Redwoods).

Alaska contains some of the most dramatic and untapped scenery in the country. Tall, prominent mountain ranges rise up sharply from broad, flat tundra (冻土地带) plains. On the islands off the south and southwest coast are many volcanoes. Hawaii, far to the south of Alaska in the Pacific Ocean, is a chain of tropical, volcanic islands, popular as a tourist destination for many from East Asia and the mainland United States.

2. Rivers in the US

The United States of America has over 250,000 rivers. The longest river in the USA is the Missouri River, but the biggest in terms of water volume is the deeper Mississippi River.

1) The Missouri River

The Missouri River is 4,090km long. It rises in southwest Montana and joins the Mississippi at St. Louis. Over its course it typically is a broad, silt-laden river, giving rise to its nickname "Big Muddy". The vast drainage basin of the Missouri and its tributaries covers an area of about 1,502,200 sq km. Many dams were built on the river for flood control, hydroelectric power, and irrigation.

2) The Mississippi River

The Mississippi River is the most important river in the country. It flows about 3,730km from its northwestern source in the Rockies to the Gulf of Mexico. It drains all the central area of the USA and has a wide **delta** (三角洲), and many tributaries. Before America completed her railway system, the Mississippi had been the most important artery of transportation in the country.

The river was named by the Indians the Mississippi, meaning "Father of Waters", or the "Old Man River". On the river there is a famous town of Hannibal where the noted American writer Mark Twain was raised. His most popular and important writings are concerned with this area. His book *The Adventures of Huckleberry Finn* tells the story of how the boy Huckleberry Finn and his black friend Jim, a runaway slave, sailed down the Mississippi on a raft.

3) The Ohio River

The Ohio River, 1,579km long, is the major eastern tributary of the Mississippi. The river had great significance in the history of the Native Americans. It was a primary transportation route during the westward expansion of the early US. It runs from the rainy east and joins the Mississippi at Cairo, Illinois, and finally reaches the Great Lakes area. Its drainage basin, including all tributaries, is about 490,603 sq km.

4) The Colorado River

The Colorado River rises in the snow-capped Rocky Mountains, flowing 2,330km through Colorado, Utah, Arizona and north Mexico into the Gulf of California. It drains an area of 629,100 sq km, and slashes its way through a wilderness of mountains, plateaus, and deserts, which offer some of the most dramatically beautiful scenery to be found anywhere in the world. The river is cliff-bound nine tenths of its way and travels 1,600km through deep canyons.

5) Rio Grande

The Rio Grande River is another large river in southwest America. It runs about 3,034km which, for much of its length, forms the border between Texas and Mexico. It rises in the southern Rocky Mountains in Colorado and flows to the Gulf of Mexico. The economic importance of the river is restricted to areas in northern New Mexico and Southern Texas. The deserts and plains remain for the most part unaffected by the river.

6) The Columbia River

The Columbia River, about 2,000km long, rises in British Columbia on the western slope of the Rocky Mountains. It flows first northwestward, then generally southward through British Columbia and Washington, and finally westward to the Pacific Ocean. In its lower course it forms the border between Washington and Oregon. The volume of the Columbia's flow is second only to that of the Mississippi, among US rivers.

7) Other Rivers

The Potomac River is famous not only because Washington D.C. is located on its bank but also because it is the dividing line between the South and the North.

The Hudson River is famous because New York stands at its estuary. It is connected with Lake Erie by a canal and New York City owed much to this connection for its prosperity in the 19th century.

3. Lakes in the US

The most important lakes in America are the Great Lakes which include five big lakes: Lake Superior, Lake Michigan, Lake Huron, Lake Erie, and Lake Ontario. Only Lake Michigan is wholly in the United States; the other four are shared with Canada. The Great Lakes and their connecting channels form the largest fresh surface water system on the Earth. The Great Lakes, in their current state, are actually one of the youngest natural features on the North American continent. Covering more than 764,000 sq km and draining more than twice as much land, these "Freshwater Seas" hold an estimated six quadrillion gallons of water, about one-fifth of the world's fresh surface water supply and nine-tenths of the US supply.

Lake	Surface Area (km^2)	Characteristics	Fun Facts
Lake Superior	82,413	Superior has the largest surface area of any freshwater lake in the world. Lake Superior has a surface area of 82,413 sq km. Its shoreline is nearly 4,387km long. Superior is also the coldest and deepest of the five Great Lakes. Average depths are close to 147m; the deepest point in the lake reaches 406m.	Lake Superior's volume is so large that it could contain all the other Great Lakes plus three additional lakes the size of Lake Erie.
Lake Huron (including Georgian Bay)	59,596	Lake Huron is the second largest of the Great Lakes by volume, holding nearly 3,540 km^3 of water. The shores of Huron extend more than 6,157km and are characterized by shallow, sandy beaches and the rocky coasts of Georgian Bay. Lake Huron is 245km wide and approximately 332km from north to south. Home to many ship wrecks, the lake averages a depth of 59m.	Lake Huron has the longest shoreline of the Great Lakes, counting the shorelines of its islands.
Lake Michigan	58,016	Lake Michigan, ranked the third largest of the Great Lakes according to volume, is the only Great Lake entirely within the United States. Averaging 85m deep, the lake reaches 281m at its deepest point. Lake Michigan is approximately 190km wide and 494km long and boasts more than 2,633km of shoreline, including many sandy beaches.	The world's largest freshwater sand dunes (沙丘) line the shores of Lake Michigan. Lakes Michigan and Huron are actually "one" Great Lake, separated by the Straits of Mackinaw. The Mackinac Bridge (the "Mighty Mac") spans the straits, connecting Michigan's upper and lower peninsulas.

Continued

Lake	Surface Area (km^2)	Characteristics	Fun Facts
Lake Erie	25,745	Lake Erie is the shallowest of the Great Lakes and overall the smallest by volume. Erie is also exposed to the greatest effects from urbanization and agriculture. Lake Erie measures 388km wide and 92km from north to south, and has 4385km of shoreline. Because it is not as deep as the other lakes, Erie warms rapidly in the spring and summer and is frequently the only Great Lake to freeze over in winter.	Lake Erie is the warmest and most biologically productive of the Great Lakes. Built in 1822, Marblehead Lighthouse on Lake Erie is the oldest active light tower on the Great Lakes.
Lake Ontario	19,529	Lake Ontario is a much deeper lake, averaging 86 m deep. Comparing their volumes, Lake Ontario holds almost four times more water than Lake Erie. Ontario ranks the fourth among the Great Lakes in maximum depth, but its average depth is second to Lake Superior.	Lake Ontario lies 99m below Lake Erie, at the base of Niagara Falls. The oldest light-house on the US side of the Great Lakes was set up at Fort Niagara in 1818 to aid navigation.

In northwest Utah lies the Great Salt Lake, the largest inland salt lake in North America, rather rectangular in shape. In an average year the lake covers an area of around 4,400 sq km, but the lake's size fluctuates substantially due to its shallowness. Its average depth is 4m. The Great Salt Lake is several times more **saline** (咸的) than seawater. It contains about 4.4 billion tons of minerals. Approximately three fourths of this total is common table salt.

4. Mountains in the US

There are two mountain ranges — The Rocky Mountains, running slightly from the northwest to southeast, and the Appalachian Mountains, running slightly from the northeast to southwest.

The Rocky Mountains Ranges

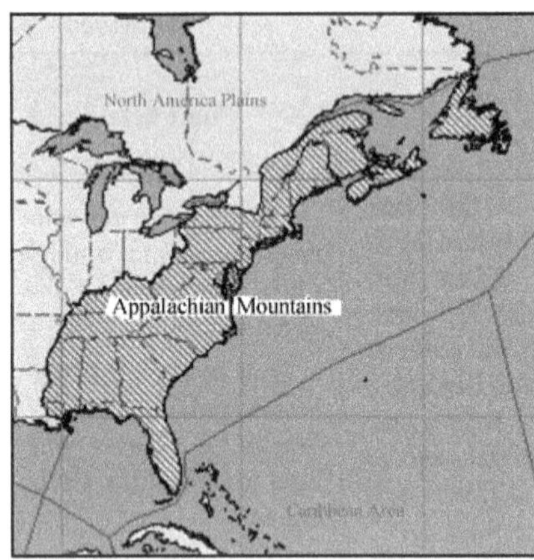

The Appalachian Mountains Ranges

The Rocky Mountains, or the Rockies, as the backbone of the North American continent, is a chain of mountains in the west of North America, running from the border of the US and Mexico up to Canada. Several peaks are 4,000m high. It is the north-south line of North American continent's great mountain backbone, known as the Continental Divide, separating the major river systems of the United States. The rivers from the eastern slopes of the Rockies flow into the Mississippi and the Gulf of Mexico. Those that begin on the western slopes of the Rockies flow to the Pacific Ocean and the Gulf of California.

The eastern part of North America is dominated by another set of mountain range called the Appalachian Mountains, or the Appalachians, or the Appalachian Highlands. This range of mountains in eastern North America, extend south-west from Quebec in Canada to Alabama in the USA. Its highest peak is Mountain Mitchell, 2,038m. Good transportation and an abundance of raw materials have helped make certain valleys of the Appalachian Highlands highly developed industrial regions. The area is also noted for forests and mines.

Ⅲ. Climate and Natural Disasters

1. Climate

Taken as a whole, the climate of the United States can be classified as temperate with some mild **subtropical zones** (亚热带), the southern Florida and Hawaii being tropical. The United States is mainly situated in the northern temperate zone, but has different types of climate in different areas.

The climate of New England is relatively cold. The winters are long and hard. In many parts of Maine, there is snow on the ground from early November to late May. The summers are short and warm. The fall, however, is a beautiful time of year. In the fall, the leaves of trees turn into different colors, giving the hills and woods a bright look. This change of color is a memorable sight, and many people visit New England at this time of year just to ride through the woods and enjoy their beauty.

The climate of the Middle Atlantic States region is generally pleasant. There are four definite seasons. The winters are cold and snowy, and the springs are warm, with plenty of rain to help the growth of crops. Summers are short and hot but pleasant, while the falls are cool.

The South enjoys a warm climate and abundant rainfall. Many of its states lie within the band that stretches across the entire southern nation known as the Sun Belt. The climate, however, varies with the geographical position of each state. Virginia and North Carolina have a temperate climate like that of Maryland. In southern Florida, on the other hand, the climate is almost tropical. Georgia, Alabama, Mississippi, and Louisiana all have warm climates with almost no cold or winter weather. Some states in this region are sometimes harassed by the disaster of **hurricanes** (飓风).

Since the Great Plains stretch from the Canadian border to Texas, the climate in this region varies widely. North Dakota has extreme temperatures, strong winds, and low **precipitation** (降水量). Oklahoma, on the other hand, has a more temperate climate. The open treeless, unbroken land offers little protection against storms or against the rapid changes of weather that occur in this area. In winter, snow piles up to six meters high in some places. In summer, in these same places, both plants and animals may die from the extreme heat. In many parts of the plains there is little rain. Water in such areas becomes more important than land. For thousands of farmers, a few inches more or a few inches less of rain during the growing season may make the difference between success and failure. Extended periods of very hot weather during a summer without rain may not only destroy crops but also turn the land into dust. This dust often turns into the **infamous** (声名狼藉的) dust storms of this area，destroying farms and farm buildings and leaving the land bare of all fertile soil.

The climate of the Midwest is temperate. The region lies in a great valley between the Allegheny Mountains to the east and the Great Plains and Rocky Mountains to the west. This is a largely open country, and the wind blows freely, often bringing sudden and extreme changes in temperature. Midwest summers are sometimes very hot; winters are sometimes extremely cold.

The states west of the Rocky Mountains have sharply different climatic conditions. This is largely because of the effects of the mountain ranges and the Pacific Ocean. Winds from the Pacific bring plenty of rain, yet these winds are conditioned by the mountains along the coast. Generally speaking, the western slopes of the Coastal Mountains are cool, rainy, and cloudy. The part of Washington near the Pacific Ocean has the largest rainfall in the country. But after crossing these mountains, very little rain falls and deserts appear.

2. Natural Disasters

The United States is affected by a large variety of natural disasters yearly. Although severe drought is rare, it has occasionally caused major problems, such as during the Dust Bowl (1931–1942), which coincided with the **Great Depression** (大萧条). More recently, the western US experienced widespread drought from 1999 to 2004, and signs of a major, long-term drought across the Great Plains have developed. The Great Plains covers much of the central United States, portions of Canada and Mexico.

The United States also experiences, by a large margin, the most frequent and powerful tornadoes (龙卷风) in the world. The Great Plains and Midwest, due to the contrasting air masses, sees frequent severe thunderstorms and tornado outbreaks during spring and summer.

Hurricane Katrina hits Gulf Coast.

Another natural disaster that frequents the country are hurricanes, which can hit anywhere along the Gulf Coast or the Atlantic Coast as well as Hawaii in the Pacific Ocean. Hurricane season runs from June 1 to November 30, with a peak from mid-August through early October. Some of the more devastating hurricanes have included the Galveston Hurricane of 1900, Hurricane Andrew in 1992, and Hurricane Katrina in 2005.

Like drought, widespread severe flooding is rare. Some exceptions include the Great Mississippi Flood of 1927, the Great Flood of 1993. Localized flooding can, however, occur anywhere, and mudslides from heavy rain can cause problems in any mountainous area, particularly the Southwest.

The West Coast of the continental United States and areas of Alaska (including the Aleutian Islands, the Alaskan Peninsula and southern Alaskan coast) make up part of the Pacific Ring of Fire, an area of heavy **tectonic** (地壳构造的) and volcanic activity that is the source of 90% of the world's earthquakes. The American Northwest sees the highest concentration of active volcanoes in the United States, especially in Washington, Oregon and northern California along the Cascade Mountains. There are several active volcanoes located in the islands of Hawaii, including Kilauea in ongoing eruption since 1983, but they do not typically adversely affect the inhabitants of the islands.

IV. Natural Resources

The United States is a land rich in natural resources. Some of these resources, such as coal, **copper** (铜), lead, **molybdenum** (钼), **phosphates** (磷酸盐), **uranium** (铀), **bauxite** (矾土), gold, iron, mercury, **nickel** (镍), **potash** (碳酸钾), silver, **tungsten** (钨), zinc, petroleum, natural gas, **timber** (木材), are especially plentiful in the country.

America has a large deposit of **iron ore** (铁矿石). The nation produces more than 80 million tons of iron a year. For many years, iron ore came primarily from the Great Lake region of Minnesota and Michigan, but the mines were severely depleted during the two World Wars. The richer ores are exhausted, though large amounts of lower-grade materials remain and form the basis of a thriving industry. Iron ores are also mined in Missouri, New York, Utah and Wyoming.

Coal is another major natural resource found in large quantities in the US which can last for hundreds of years. Coal deposits are widely distributed in the country. Most of coal reserves are to be found in the Appalachians, the Central Plain, and the Rockies.

America, very rich in oil, was once the largest oil producing country in the world. Oil wells in the United States produce more than 3,200 million barrels of petroleum a year. The production, processing and marketing of such petroleum products as gasoline and oil make up one of America's largest industries. Most domestic production of oil and natural gas comes from offshore areas of Louisiana and Texas, and from onshore areas of Texas, Oklahoma, and California.

Although the oil production in the US is very large, the big consumption has also made America insufficient in oil supply. The shortage of domestic supplies of energy was forcefully publicized by the Arab oil **embargo** (禁运) of 1973 to 1974. Until this embargo most Americans did not realize that the United States does not have enough energy to meet its evergrowing needs.

Other basic metals and minerals mined on a large scale in America include zinc, copper, silver, and phosphate rock.

America enjoys abundant water resources. Today the rivers and streams of America furnish 63% of the water supply for cities, towns and farmlands, 93% of the water is used by industry, and almost all of the water is used to create electric power. Unlike some other countries, America as a whole has little trouble as caused by the shortage of fresh water.

America also has plenty of fertile soil. Farmlands in the United States make up about 12% of the **arable lands** (耕地) in the world, and they are among the richest and most productive ones. Of the 2.3 billion acres of land in the 50 states an estimated 300 million acres are planted annually. The country's very large acreage of highly productive farmlands could be expected to continue to supply the nation generously, with substantial **surplus** (剩余的) for export.

1. **the Dust Bowl**（1931–1942）：20 世纪 30 年代的沙尘暴。
2. **tornado**：龙卷风，一种纵向的气旋，伴随有倒漏斗形的积雨云，涡流直径达几百码，以每小时 500 英里（800 公里）的速度移动，其旋转具有极大的毁坏性。
3. **hurricane**：飓风，一种猛烈的热带风暴，形成于大西洋或加勒比海赤道地区，从形成地向北、西北或东北移动，通常携有大量雨水。
4. **tsunami**：海啸，由海底地震或火山喷发而引起的巨大海浪。

▶▶ I. Multiple Choice

1. The United States has altogether _______ states.
   A) forty-eight B) forty-nine C) fifty D) fifty-one

2. _______ is the Largest state in land area and _______ the smallest.
   A) Alaska; Rhode Island B) New York; Rhode Island
   C) Hawaii; Rhode Island D) Texas; Rhode Island

3. Before their conversion to farmland, the Great Plains were noted for their _______.
   A) forests B) industry
   C) agriculture D) extensive grasslands

4. The longest river in America is _______.
   A) Missouri River B) Mississippi River
   C) Yellowstone River D) Colorado River

5. _______ has the largest surface area of any freshwater lake in the world.
   A) Lake Superior B) Lake Michigan
   C) Lake Huron D) Lake Erie

6. The climate of the United States, as a whole, can be classified as _______.
   A) tropical B) temperate C) subtropical D) monsoonal

7. The Great Plains and Midwest, due to the contrasting air masses, sees frequent severe _______ during spring and summer.
   A) drought B) hurricanes
   C) thunderstorms and tornado outbreaks D) flooding

8. One natural disaster that frequents the country are _______, which can hit anywhere along the Gulf Coast or the Atlantic Coast as well as Hawaii in the Pacific Ocean.
   A) drought B) hurricanes
   C) thunderstorms and tornado outbreaks D) flooding

9. The American _______ sees the highest concentration of active volcanoes in the United States, in Washington, Oregon and northern California along the Cascade Mountains.
   A) Northwest　　B) Northeast　　C) Southwest　　D) Southeast

10. America has plenty of fertile soil. Farmlands in the United States make up about _______ of the arable lands in the world, and they are among the richest and most productive ones.
    A) 20%　　B) 12%　　C) 18%　　D) 16%

▶▶ II. Sentence Completion

1. The United States shares land borders with _________ and _________, and a water border with _________.
2. The United States secured its independence from Great Britain in _________.
3. The United States ranks as the fourth largest country in the world after _________, _________ and _________.
4. The five Great Lakes are located in the _________ portion of the country, _________ of them forming part of the border with Canada.
5. Hawaii, far to the south of Alaska in the Pacific Ocean, is a chain of _________, _________, popular as a tourist destination for many from East Asia and the mainland United States.
6. The Mississippi River, which means _________ or _________, flows from its northwestern source in _________ to _________.
7. Of all the US rivers, _________ ranks the first for its volume, and _________ comes the next.
8. The most important lakes in America are _________ which include five big lakes: _________, _________, _________, _________ and _________. Only _________ is wholly in the United States; the other four are shared with _________.
9. The Rocky Mountains, or the Rockies, as the backbone of the North American continent, is a chain of mountains, in _________ of North America, running from the border of _________ and _________ up to _________.
10. Some states in the South of America are sometimes harassed by the disaster of _________.

SUMMARY

The United States is a country in the Western Hemisphere, whose official full name is the United States of America. The total land area of the USA is 9,372,615 square kilometers. Washington, D.C. is the capital. Its currency is the US dollar of 100 cents.

Its national day is July 4 (Independence Day). On September 23, 1986, the House of Representatives passed a joint resolution naming the rose as the "national floral emblem". The bald eagle was chosen on June 20, 1782, as the national bird because of its long life, great strength and majestic looks. The national anthem of US is the famous *The Star-Spangled Banner* which was created on September 14, 1814, by a lawyer and amateur poet.

The United States is commonly divided into five major regions, which have over 250,000 rivers and rich natural resources. The Great Lakes are very important, covering more than 764,000 sq km and hold an estimated six quadrillion gallons of water.

The Rocky Mountains and the Appalachian Mountains are two major mountain ranges in America. The United States is often affected by a large variety of natural disasters every year. Taking as a whole, the climate of the United States can be classified as temperate with some mild subtropical zones and the southern Florida and Hawaii being tropical.

Chapter 2

History

HIGHLIGHTS

colonial period — War of Independence — westward expansion era — American Civil War — US imperialism — America in WWI and WWII — America after WWII

I. Colonial Period

American history is generally agreed to have begun in 1607 when the first group of the British colonists went to America and started to build their settlement there.

The period of colonization covered the years from 1607 to 1776, that is, from the first settlement of English colonists to the independence of America.

1. American Indians

The earliest inhabitants in North and South Americas were the American Indians, who had lived and labored there for thousands of years before Christopher Columbus, an Italian navigator, discovered the New World in 1492. Some scientists believe that they had come over from Asia about 25,000 years ago when Asia and North America, separated by the Bering Strait today, were tied together by a land bridge and it was possible to walk from Asia to America because much ocean water was frozen in **glaciers** (冰河) and the sea level was lower than it is today. The grass-eating animals were among the first to leave Asia, followed by flesh-eating animals, and thus, in search of their food supply, the hunters tracked the animals across northern Alaska into Canada and south along the Mackenzie River. They then followed the animals south along the eastern edge of the Rocky Mountains, and gradually spread all over North and South Americas. For these early immigrants, America was no melting pot. The American Indians were divided into hundreds of tribes, enormously varied in physical appearance, language and civilization. Some tribes made their living by hunting, others by fishing, farming or gathering rye seeds. Later, the sea covered the land bridge from Asia to America and separated the two Americas from the rest of the world. The Indians and the people of the rest of the world knew little about each other until the New World was discovered in 1492.

2. Discovery of America

By the end of 15th century, the modern European world was to be formed. Its formation was marked by the growth of trade and commerce, the rise of the middle class, the evolution of national states, the reformation of the Christian church, and the development of representative government. These changes, gradually developing over many years, led directly to the effective discovery and the settlement of the New World.

In the mid 15th century, a great number of long ocean voyages took place. History will always remember two names — Christopher Columbus and Amerigo Vespucci. It was they who discovered and identified the new continents.

Christopher Columbus and his men, financed by the King and Queen of Spain, set out on August 3,1492 on three small ships. On October 12, they reached a group of islands which now are called the Bahamas. Columbus named the island he landed on San Salvador, meaning "Holy Savior". Columbus, however, mistook these islands for part of India and so called the people there Indians. The three ships visited some other islands, one of which is now known as Cuba. Then he headed back to Spain. Columbus made three more voyages between 1493 and 1504 and in his third voyage in 1498, he discovered the mainland of South America. The great discoverer died in 1506, never realizing that he had discovered a new continent. Another important figure in the process of the discovery of the New World was Amerigo Vespucci. He was not the discoverer of the new continents, but it was he who first confirmed the fact that a new continent rather than Asia had been discovered. Vespucci made his first voyage in 1499 and the second in 1500. He also made another two but unimportant voyages later. He was for a time regarded as the discoverer of the new land because he wrote many letters in which the new continents were described in great details and the letters were most quickly published and widely spread. Thus a false impression was created that it was Vespucci rather than Columbus who first discovered the New World, so in 1507 the New World was named after him, the Latin form of his Christian name, Amerigo.

3. Colonization of North America

The New World was a great and rich land. North and South Americas together made up an area almost as large as Africa and Europe combined. In the New World there were all these resources necessary for agricultural and industrial development: fertile land, seas full of fish, great forests, all the essential metals, and minerals, huge coal and oil supplies, and rivers rich in water power.

The ruling class of Europe fell upon this rich land greedily. Only 50 years after Columbus' first voyage, the Spanish and Portuguese had overrun the vast land of what is now called Latin America. For about 100 years after Columbus' crossing of the Atlantic, only explorers and traders visited North America. But at the beginning of 17th century, European settlers began to arrive. Portugal set up colonies in Brazil, while Spain explored and colonized much of South America and Mexico.

The settling of present United States and Canada by the English and French went more slowly, though quite cruelly. During the reign of Queen Elizabeth Ⅰ (1588–1603), the English in growing numbers realized that the New World was their best place to make their fortunes, and to worship and live according to their beliefs. Some of them might move to America to leave oppressive political institutions, to escape burdensome church duties, to acquire large landholdings or merely to change their general pattern of living. Of course, material gain was a common factor.

In April 1607, three ships with 104 English settlers arrived off the Virginia coast. They built the first successful settlement called Jamestown. This region was soon to develop a flourishing economy from its tobacco crop, which found a ready market in England. In 1620 the first group of Puritans arrived from England. They were so called because they represented the rising **bourgeoisie** (资产阶级) of the time and wished to "purify" the Church of England, the established church, with the King as its head. In order to escape from religious **persecution** (迫害) at home, a group of Puritans set sail for America on a ship called the *Mayflower*. This group of "pilgrims", as they called themselves, went to the New World in search of religious freedom. They began their journey in September with 102 men, women and children on board. Before they landed, they signed an agreement called the *Mayflower Compact*, in which they promised to obey the rules and laws of the colony. This was the beginning of the US democracy. During the first icy winter in the dwelling place called Plymouth, the Pilgrims suffered much hardship and about half of them died. When spring came, the Indians began to help them. The Indians showed them how to hunt, fish, and plant. The Pilgrims had a fine harvest of corn in fall. They were thankful. They made a feast and invited the Native Americans who had helped them. This was the first Thanksgiving in North America.

The Mayflower

Later more Puritans arrived in the nearby areas of Massachusetts. By 1679 they set up four New England colonies: Massachusetts, Rhode Island, Connecticut, and New Hampshire. The colonies of New York, New Jersey, Maryland, Pennsylvania, and Delaware were called the Middle Colonies. Some of them were not started by the English colonists. New York and New Jersey were first founded by the Dutch, and Delaware was first settled by the Dutch and the Swedish. These three colonies were taken by the English in 1664. The Southern Colonies included Virginia, North and South Carolina and Georgia. North and South Carolinas were settled by pioneers from other colonies, and Georgia, the last colony, was founded in 1733, which was named after the English King George II.

By the mid 18th century North America had been actually divided out among the European colonists. Most of the east coast, south of the St. Lawrence River, north of Florida and stretching inland as far as the Appalachians in the west were in the hands of the British.

4. Thirteen Colonies

By the time when Georgia was set up, the 13 colonies had had a population of 629,000. By 1750 it increased to 1,171,000. In terms of their political administration, the 13 colonies could be divided into three types: the proprietary colonies, which belonged to a person or a group of persons; the Royal colonies, those controlled directly by the King of England and the English Government; and self-governing colonies, which were ruled by the colonists living in them. Most of the proprietary colonies soon became Royal ones. Only Connecticut and Rhode Island were self-governing colonies.

Later, owing to geographical, economic and social factors, the 13 colonies developed in different directions. The New England colonies, where the soil was thin and poor, were not suitable for farming. So the Yankee farmer in New England was forced to become jack-of-all-traders. The New England colonies soon became a center for fishing and shipbuilding, and the successful merchants and prosperous shipbuilders laid the foundation for the later appearance of the American big bourgeoisie. The Middle Colonies known as the breadbasket had a more favorable climate and soil and thus became the most productive area for general farming. This colonial breadbasket produced wheat and potatoes as the major **staple** (主要产品). The Southern Colonies developed a plantation system, with the exploration of slave labor. Tobacco was the main crop in the South. Other crops were rice and **indigo** (靛青), a blue dye taken from various plants. Much later, cotton became important. In the beginning, plantation workers were **indentured** (契约的) servants, white as well as black. Later planters used the black slaves instead.

Society in the 13 British colonies was like a pyramid, the top of which was made up of foreign merchants and landlords, and the base refugees from Europe, black slaves from Africa and the American Indians. The Africans were **out-and-out** (完全的) slaves, who were sold like animals. As for the Indians, they would not put up with slavery. If any Indian was enslaved, his fellow tribe members would fight to free him. So the colonists soon gave up the attempt to use them as slave labor. Instead they seized the land of the Indians and drove them away or killed them. Slaves, indentured servants and workers who found themselves unable to bear their conditions used to run away to the frontier where they cleared the forests and opened up farms of their own. Uprisings or rebellions often took place against the Royal Government of the colonies.

II. War of Independence

1. Britain's Policy Toward American Colonies

The American population grew rapidly, from about 500,000 in 1713 to 4 million in 1775. This new people, many of them of non-Anglo-Saxon origin, felt stronger ties to their local area than to the distant authority of the Crown. Increasingly, the restrictions and controls imposed from London were seen as irrelevant and **onerous** (繁重的). Furthermore, the Seven Years' War had cost huge sums of money, and it was felt by London that the colonists themselves should bear the **brunt** (主要的压力) of the cost of the American **garrison** (驻军) of 8,000 British soldiers. The following measures had been adopted by the British Government:

1763 *Royal Order*, forbidding the colonists to buy any more land from the Indians in the west beyond a certain line, and vesting in the Crown the sole power to hold and dispose of such lands.

1764 *Sugar Act*, imposing import duties on non-English goods to the American colonies in order to raise more money for supporting British Government in the colonies.

1764 *Currency Act*, forbidding the colonies to issue paper money.

1765 *Stamp Act*, taxing numerous articles and transactions in America to help pay the costs of British Government in the colonies.

1765 *Quartering Act*, requiring colonists to help house and feed British regular troops stationed in the colonies.

1766 *Declaratory Act*, asserting the supremacy of the British Parliament in making laws for the colonies.

1767 *Customs Collecting Act*, establishing British commissioners in the colonies to collect customs and other duties.

1767 *Revenue Act*, laying taxes on lead, paint and other articles imported into the colonies.

1767 *Tea Act*, regulating importation of tea in British dominions in America in favor of the British East India Company.

Thus it was in 1770 that the unpopularity of British methods led to violent street disturbances, and troops fired on a **rioting mob** (无秩序的民众), killing five — the Boston Massacre. After the event, Boston was in an **uproar** (骚动). By 1772, Samuel Adams had organized the Committee of Correspondence, which made possible the cooperation of colonists all over the 13 colonies. In 1773, as a response to the *Tea Act*, the Boston Tea Party saw British-monopolized tea thrown into the harbor in a gesture of contempt for the taxation system. As a result, Boston was closed to shipping, and generous trade **concessions** (承认) were given to the newly integrated French Canadians in Quebec.

As a punishment on the Boston people, several laws were passed by the English Parliament. As they were intolerable, they were called *Intolerable Acts*, two of which were most notorious. One was the *Boston Port Act*, declaring the close of the harbor. The other was about the deprivation of self-government for the Massachusetts people. These acts aroused much stronger **indignation** (愤怒) within all the colonial people.

2. Unity of the Colonies

The contradiction between England and her 13 colonies became more acute, and the colonies began to unite.

In September 1774, 55 representatives from all the colonies except Georgia held a meeting in Philadelphia to talk about their troubles with their mother country. The meeting was called the First Continental Congress. At the meeting the majority of representatives still thought they could settle their quarrel with the British by peaceful means. They agreed to refuse to buy British goods, hoping in this way to force the British Government to give in to their demands. They also agreed to raise a volunteer army to protect the colonies if Britain used force to break the **boycott** (联合抵制). Neither Parliament nor King George listened to the **petition** (请愿) of the First Continental Congress. Matters grew rapidly worse as England planned to send more soldiers to enforce the laws. Some of the colonies began to collect arms and ammunition, to have their **militia** (民兵) trained and to organize a number of "minute men".

3. The Outbreak of War and the *Declaration of Independence*

In April 1775 General Thomas Gage, the commander officer of the garrison at Boston, was assigned there to enforce the laws. He mounted a **sortie** (出击) to seize a stockpile of arms and powder at Concord, promptly became involved in a running fight, and, in retreating to Boston, suffered severe losses at Lexington. The affair quickly escalated and colonial militia began to **entrench** (挖壕沟) themselves enthusiastically around Boston Harbor, overlooking the British garrison. In June Gage's newly arrived replacement, Sir William Howe, launched a successful frontal assault against the American earthworks on Breed's Hill and Bunker Hill, which cost the British over 1,000 casualties, 40% of the attacking force, and was a serious blow to their pride, **morale** (士气), and capability for offensive operations.

The news of Lexington and Concord flew from one local community to another, from Maine to Georgia. It was here in Lexington that the first shot in the American War of Independence was fired.

Immediately after this, in May 1775, the Second Continental Congress was held with representatives from all the 13 colonies. This Congress agreed to take steps to organize and equip an American army and appointed George Washington, a Virginian, commander in chief of the American forces. The Congress also provided for asking help from other countries, especially France which was a rival of Britain.

At the beginning of 1776, Thomas Paine, an American patriot published a **pamphlet** (小册子) entitled *Common Sense*. In his pamphlet, he blamed the King George III for colonies' problems and urged Americans to declare their independence. Finally a committee, composed of Thomas Jefferson, Benjamin Franklin, John Adams and some other members, was appointed to draw up a *Declaration of Independence*. After three weeks of discussion, the committee prepared the famous document which was formally adopted on July 4, 1776, a day which has been celebrated each year as Independence Day or National Day in US.

The *Declaration of Independence* was a masterpiece of bourgeois political philosophy. It examined the problem of American independence from the angle of human rights, convincingly proved the justice of the Revolution by defining the rights of men, raised **unequivocally** (不含糊地) the slogan of equality and freedom for all human beings, and **denounced** (公然抨击) the feudal privileges for a small group of nobles. Its influence spread far beyond American boundaries.

4. Progress of the War

The War of Independence started in 1775 and ended in 1783, lasting about eight years.

The war did not go well for Americans at first who suffered repeated setback. At that time, the British army was the finest and strongest in the world. The British had a navy to control the sea and a highly-developed industry and commerce to keep the army well supplied, while the American army was composed mainly of farmers, craftsmen, and small traders, who were poorly trained and equipped. What is more, there was no strong central government to raise money to support the American army. As a result, they were constantly driven back.

It was under such unfavorable circumstances that George Washington, with his intelligence and determination, won a great victory in the battle of Trenton.

George Washington had taken Boston in May 1775, but then he had to move his army to New York. Later, he was forced to withdraw from the city, too, with the British army following closely behind. By the middle of December 1776, the Revolution seemed lost. Then, on Christmas night, Washington led a surprise attack. He and his soldiers crossed the freezing Delaware River while the **mercenary** (雇佣的) Hessian troops under the British command were celebrating the holiday in their winter camp at Trenton. The Americans won a brilliant victory, defeating enemy forces much bigger than their own.

A Committee Drafting the *Declaration of Independence*

The victory at Trenton raised the spirit of American people. In October 1777, the Americans won another great victory at Saratoga. In this battle the British troops suffered very heavy losses and about 6,000 British soldiers were forced to surrender. The victory at Saratoga was the turning point of the war. But then the American army was still not strong enough to beat the British; it won some battles but lost others. Washington withdrew his army to Valley Forge, Pennsylvania, where, in spite of the bitter conditions, he went ahead with military training.

Finally in 1781, the Americans, with the help of the French navy, won a decisive victory at Yorktown in Virginia. On October 19, the same year, the British general Cornwallis was forced to surrender, and the war came to end. A peace negotiation was held and the final treaty was signed in Paris on September 3, 1783. According to the treaty, the territory of America was granted from the Atlantic Ocean to the Mississippi River in the west and from the Great Lakes in the north to Spanish Florida in the south. The navigation of the Mississippi was declared to be open to Americans and British subjects.

5. The Significance of the War

The American War of Independence was of great historical importance and influence. A new republic emerged, which marked a new beginning of American history. It told the world that a just cause would sooner or later win while the evil cause would certainly lose. The victory of the American people also greatly encouraged the people in the colonies ruled by the Spanish and promoted the national liberation struggle of the other colonies in the world.

6. The Constitutional Convention

After America won her independence in 1783, there appeared new problems for the newly independent states to deal with, such as founding their country and government.

Before and during the Independent War, the US had not been named yet, but near the end of the war, a committee was appointed to draw up a constitution which was to **stipulate** (规定) how the US should be governed. It resulted in the *Articles of the Confederation* and in 1781 it was accepted by all the states. Thus the US were officially founded.

But the *Articles of the Confederation* gave too little power to the central government, so a series of attempts to organize a movement to outline and press reforms **culminated in** (达到顶点) the Congress calling the Philadelphia Convention in 1787. The work of the Convention was to draw up a constitution and frame a central government. That is, they had to seek common ground between the states. After many heated debates and countless compromises, the delegates found a satisfactory solution. Congress should be made up of two houses, a House of Representatives and a Senate. The big states had more members in the House of Representatives than the small ones, but all states had the same number in the Senate. Finally, the *Constitution* took its shape and won its **ratification** (认可) in 1788.

The appearance of the *American Constitution* was a great event in American history. It established the federal system which was the first in the world at that time, making the birth of the US possible. In 1791, the first ten amendments, known as *Bill of Rights*, were put into the *Constitution*. Among the more important rights guaranteed to the US citizens are freedom of religion, freedom of speech, freedom of the press, the right to assemble, and the right to petition for what a citizen may think is needed from the government.

III. Westward Expansion Era

1. The New Government and Louisiana Purchase

After the *Constitution* was ratified by the states, the nation began to organize her first Federal Government. As had been expected, Washington was elected the first President of the US by a **unanimous** (全体一致的) vote which has never happened again in this country. Washington took action to establish the Executive Branch of the US Government. Congress passed the *Judiciary Act* of 1789, which established the entire federal judiciary, including the Supreme Court. Washington's Administration achieved much success. His vice president John Adams succeeded him in presidency. Adams was a member of the Federalist Party. However, the

Federalists became divided after Adams sent a peace mission to France despite ongoing disputes with that nation. Thomas Jefferson, a Democratic-Republican, defeated Adams for the presidency in the 1800 election.

The most glorious achievement of Jefferson as President was the Louisiana Purchase. The Louisiana Purchase, in 1803, gave western farmers use of the important Mississippi River waterway, removed the French presence from the western border of US, provided the US farmers with vast expanses of land, and furthered American leaders' vision of creating a "Great Nation".

2. The War Against England (1812–1814)

After James Madison, the fourth President of the country, was elected to the office, he was confronted with a very serious situation abroad. Relations with England were tense and a second war was on the way.

Britain was not **reconciled to** (无可奈何地接受) the loss of their 13 colonies. British warships were often placed outside American harbors to keep a watch on shipping that came and went. At the same time, in order to find more men for the crews of its large navy, Britain began to **impress** (强迫男子服海军役) great numbers of sailors from seized American ships. Also Indians in the Northwest were stirred up by the British to oppose America. Congress, therefore, had to declare war against British in June, 1812.

The war continued for about three years without decisive victory for either side. Then both sides agreed to negotiate a peace settlement and signed the *Peace Treaty of Ghent* on the Christmas Eve of 1814. The War of 1812 had been called the Second War of Independence, which not only greatly influenced the American history, but also promoted the development of economy. It was only after this war that US completely got rid of the British control and began a new period of rapid development from a semi-colonial economy to an independent and self-reliant capitalist economy.

3. American Expansion

(1) The Territorial Expansion

On December 2, 1823, President James Monroe delivered to Congress his annual message in which he announced his *Monroe Doctrine*, which proclaimed the US' opinion that European powers should no longer colonize or interfere in the Americas. This was a defining moment in the foreign policy of the US. The essence of the *Doctrine* was "America for Americans", which later became a cornerstone of the US foreign policy.

In 1845, the US **annexed** (侵吞) the Mexican territory of Texas after the US settlers there had first formed an "independent government" with Washington's support. Further the US provocations on the border resulted in the Mexican-US War (1846–1848). In consequence of the Mexican War, the US added to itself a territory of approximately 2,446,000 square kilometers, embracing the present state of Texas, California, Arizona, Nevada, Utah, New Mexico, Colorado, and part of Wyoming.

In the same year, the US forced England to **cede** (割让) the Oregon region, which includes the present states of Oregon, Washington, Idaho, and part of Montana and Wyoming.

In 1867, the US purchased from Czarist Russia the territory of Alaska and the off-lying Aleutian Islands for $ 7.2 million. This territory is twice as large as the original 13 colonies.

By the middle of 19th century, the national territory of the US had reached over nine million sq km, about 10 times the size of the total area of the original 13 colonies.

(2) The Economic Expansion

After the War of Independence the American national economy was growing rapidly. Its industrial revolution began in 1807 with its textile industry. New equipment and technology were introduced from Europe, and modern industries were established. Its total value of the industrial production in 1860 was increased by about 10 times that of 1810.

In the 1820s there came a flood of new immigrants from Europe to the US because labor was needed with the rapid development of industry in America and most European countries were in a very bad state. The immigrants played an important role in promoting the rapid expansion of the American capitalist economy.

(3) Economic Antagonism Between North and South

As a rapid growth of capitalism, the center of the American economy had definitely shifted from the **agrarian** (农业的) areas to the industrial centers in the North by the time Andrew Jackson came to presidency in 1829. In the north, the capitalist economy developed rapidly and industrial production advanced at an amazing speed. The output value of manufacture increased almost three times from 1840 to 1869. Coal and iron production were greatly increased. Transportation was also improved. Many canals were dug and thousands of miles of railways were built. All this stimulated the further development of industry. By 1860, American industry had ranked fourth in the world.

But in the South things were quite different. The South was agricultural and had a large number of plantations, which were making huge profits out of tobacco and cotton with slave labor. The South insisted that slavery be kept, and furthermore, that more states in the Union be turned into slave states. Meanwhile the South exported each year plenty of cotton to England and

Europe and imported a large quantity of manufactured goods from abroad. So the southerners wished to have a low tariff, as a high tariff would raise the prices of imported goods. On the contrary, the North had a different view. The northern industrialists wanted a high tariff to protect the industries in the North.

In sum, two different social-economic systems existed side by side in the United States. In the South slavery was the foundation of the economic system while in the North industry and commerce were the main character of its economy. The swiftly growing industries in the North required the restriction of slavery as well as an expanding territory in order to provide capitalist production with raw materials, markets and an abundant labor supply. The slave economy in the South was an obstacle to industrial growth and expansion. This economic **antagonism** (对抗) finally led to the outbreak of the Civil War.

IV. The American Civil War

1. Causes of the War

In the middle of 19th century, white Americans of the North and South were unable to reconcile fundamental differences in their approach to government, economy, society and African American slavery. The issue of slavery in the new territories was settled by the *Compromise of 1850* brokered by Whig Henry Clay and Democrat Stephen Douglas. The *Compromise* included admission of California as a free state and the passage of the *Fugitive Slave Act* to make it easier for masters to **reclaim** (收回) runaway slaves. In 1854, the proposed *Kansas-Nebraska Act* **abrogated** (废止) the *Missouri Compromise* by providing that each new state of the Union would decide its stance on slavery. After Abraham Lincoln won the 1860 election, 11 southern states **seceded from** (退出) the Union between late 1860 and 1861, establishing a rebel government, the Confederate States of America, on February 8, 1861. They were South Carolina, Mississippi, Florida, Alabama, Georgia, Louisiana, Texas, Virginia, Arkansas, Tennessee, and North Carolina; Jefferson Davis was its first and only President.

By 1860, there were nearly four million slaves residing in the US, nearly eight times as many from 1790; within the same period, cotton production in the US boomed from less than 1,000 tons to nearly one million tons per year. There were some slave rebellions, including by Gabriel Prosser (1800), Denmark Vesey (1822), and Nat Turner (1831), but they all failed and led to tighter slave oversight in the South. White abolitionist John Brown tried and failed to free a group of black slaves in Harpers Ferry, Virginia and was therefore executed for his actions. Harriet Beecher Stowe, daughter of Minister Lyman Beecher, published her novel *Uncle Tom's*

Cabin in 1852 in response to the passage of the *Fugitive Slave Act*. The novel intended to express her views of the cruelty of slavery and nearly 300,000 copies were sold during its first year of publication. Numerous slaves also escaped their masters through the Underground Railroad, a term defining secret routes where abolitionists confidentially transported runaway slaves to "free state" territory; its most famous leader was Harriet Tubman.

2. Progress of the War

The Civil War began when Confederate General Pierre Beauregard opened fire upon Fort Sumter, in the Confederate State of South Carolina. The war lasted four years from 1861 to 1865.

In material resources, the North enjoyed a decided advantage. Twenty-three states with a population of 22 million confronted the South 11 states with a population of 9 million. The industrial superiority of the North even exceeded its advantage in manpower. Unlike the rural South, the northern states had abundant facilities for manufacture of arms and ammunition, clothing, and other supplies. Over two thirds of railroad **mileage** (里程) of the country was in the North, and most of the merchant marines and the navy remained in the Union's hands. Moreover, the wealth of the North was many times as great as that of the South, and the Federal Government was better able to borrow money to help pay for the war.

The Battle of Gettysburg

Strong as the North was, the South also had advantages, most of them military. For several months before the attack on Fort Sumter, it had been actively preparing for war and was in possession of many federal forts and **arsenals** (军械库). In addition, the South had the advantage of superior military leadership. About one third of the regular army's officers were from the South, including General Robert E. Lee, who was regarded as a military genius. The South also had the advantage of fighting on its own soil.

There were two main arenas of war, the Eastern Arena and the Western Arena. The basic battleground for the Eastern Arena was Virginia. The Western Arena included the areas west to the Appalachian Range and the Mississippi River area.

On the whole, the Confederate army won many battles on the Eastern Arena while they were defeated again and again on the Western Arena.

In a succession of bloody attempts to capture Richmond, the Confederate capital, the Union forces were repeatedly thrown back. In July, 1861 there was a great battle on a stream called Bull

Run, not far from Washington. The Union was beaten. When George McClellan, the General, led the army, things became even worse, because he was incompetent. In the seven days' battles from June 25 to July 1, 1862, the Union troops led by McClellan were driven steadily backward. Later, in a bloody battle at Chancellorsville, the Union forces suffered a severe defeat. As yet, none of the Confederate victories had been decisive. General Lee believed that his chance had come after the Battle of Chancellorsville. So he struck northward into Pennsylvania. But his march was **intercepted** (阻止) at Gettysburg, where, after a three-day battle, Lee's veterans, with crippling losses, fell back to the Potomac. The Union forces won a great victory at Gettysburg and this greatly encouraged the Union Army.

In the Mississippi Valley, the Union forces won an almost uninterrupted series of victories. They began by breaking a long Confederate line in the Tennessee, thus making it possible to occupy almost all the western part of the state. After the important port of Memphis on the Mississippi was taken, the Union troops could advance some 320km into the heart of the Confederacy. General Grant, an excellent and **tenacious** (不屈不挠的) general, then pushed slowly but steadily southward. On July 4, 1863, Grant captured the town of Vicksburg, together with the surrender of the strongest Confederate army in the West. The Mississippi River was now entirely in the Union's hands. The Confederacy was broken into two, and it became almost impossible to bring supplies from Texas and Arkansas.

A Union fleet, headed by David Farragut, sailed into the mouth of the Mississippi, where he forced the surrender of New Orleans, the largest city in the South. In another battle, he captured a Confederate **ironclad** (装铁甲的) vessel.

Grant's slow but **inexorable** (不屈不挠的) advance on Richmond in 1864 **foreshadowed** (预示) the end of the war. From all sides northern troops **closed in** (包围), and on February 1, 1865, General Sherman's western army began a march northward from Georgia. General Lee's army eventually surrendered at Appomattox, Virginia. This was on April 9, 1865. The war ended. The South was finally defeated.

In order to change the situation and win the war, several measures were taken by Lincoln's Administration in 1862: (1) in May 1862, Congress passed the *Homestead Act*, under which the land problem was solved in the interests of the small farmers; (2) on September 22, 1862, Lincoln issued the *Emancipation Proclamation*, which liberated some four million black slaves in the South. After it went into effect on January 1 of the following year, there were more slave revolts and strikes than ever in the South and as many as half a million black slaves fled the plantation, thus seriously disrupting production in the South; (3) black slaves were allowed to serve in the Union Army from August 1862. A large number of black slaves joined the Union Army. They fought bravely and many gave their lives to the cause of their people's emancipation.

3. The Significance of the War

The Civil War is of great significance in American history, which preserved the Union and solved the agrarian problem. It destroyed the feudal slavery-plantation system, which had been an obstacle on the path to the development of capitalism, so that America developed at a higher speed after the war. In this sense, it is, therefore, also called the Second American Bourgeois Revolution.

The Civil War, in fact, was a struggle of life and death between two social systems, between the progressive and the backward, between the one that could push history forward and the one that would drag history to the old times.

The Civil War also extended its far-reaching influence to the European revolutions. Lenin pointed that the war had "the greatest, world historical, progressive and revolutionary significance".

V. The US Imperialism and WWI

1. Formation of US Imperialism

1) Industrialization

The period from the Civil War to the beginning of the 20th century was a period of rapid industrial growth and urban development. Towards the end of 19th century US had already become a highly developed capitalist country and reached the stage of imperialism. Machinery steadily replaced the use of hand labor in the manufacturing of goods. Railways extended from coast to coast. Ships were built. Transportation and communications were greatly improved to meet the needs of an industrial society. Investments in business grew larger, and corporations replaced small privately owned firms in many industries. By 1894, America had become the world leading industrial country. Its total industrial production of manufactures was almost sevenfold more than that of 1860, accounting for one third of the world total.

2) Concentration of Capital

The rapid concentration of capital was also accelerated after the Civil War. The small and medium enterprises were swallowed up by the bigger ones. Big monopolies first appeared in the heavy industries. Industrial **barons** (工业巨头), such as the Vanderbilts, Rockefellers, Morgans and Fords, controlled 80% to 95% of national railways and the production of oil, steel and automobiles. The light industries went through a similar process of concentration. The development of big capitalist farms also placed the monopolists in control of farm production and prices. All these showed that US capitalism had grown into **full-fledged** (成熟的) imperialism.

3) Working-class Movement

A rising working-class movement accompanied the growth of monopoly capital. The first labor organization came into being in the 1870s. Strikes often took place in the industrial cities in those days. The Pennsylvania railway workers' strike of 1877 was the first large-scale struggle of its kind in the American history. On May 1, 1886, hundreds of thousands of workers went on simultaneous strikes in Chicago, Washington, New York and other large cities. They fought for an eight-hour working day, higher wages and better working conditions. Two days later, the police opened fire on the strikers at Chicago's Haymarket, **inflicting** (加害于) many casualties. To **pay tribute to** (表示敬意) the Haymarket martyrs, the Second International Meeting in Paris in 1889 adopted a resolution designating May 1 as International Labor Day to be observed by the workers of the world. The US working class movement had a new **upsurge** (高潮) at the turn of the century. On March 8, 1909, women workers in Chicago launched a big struggle for freedom and equal rights with men. Their efforts won the recognition of the Second International Congress of women socialists which decided in 1910 that March 8 each year was to be observed as International Working Women's Day.

4) Overseas Expansion

With the emergence of industrial America came the emergence of imperial US and US as a world power. The growing industrial might of the nation was reflected clearly in the US mad policy of aggression and expansion abroad.

(1) US-Spanish War

The US-Spanish War broke out in April, 1898, lasted for only 70 days and ended with US as the victor. A peace treaty was signed in December 1898 in Paris. As a result of the war, Spain was forced to cede her former colonies Cuba, Puerto Rico, Guam and the Philippines to US; US agreed to pay 20 million dollars for them in an attempt to **put a good face on** (对……表现勇气) its foreign expansion. Cuba remained a US "protectorate" for some years, while the Philippines were not granted its independence until after the end of WWI. US seized Hawaii from Spain after the US-Spanish War.

The US-Spanish War was the first imperialist war for redividing the world. It marked a new stage in which the US transformed into an imperialist power. From that time the US began its modern history.

(2) Theodore Roosevelt's Policy

By the early years of 20th century, Theodore Roosevelt who became President in 1901 carried out the aggressive policy in a most faithful and open manner. **Wielding** (使用) the *Big Stick* in the name of *Monroe Doctrine*, he carried out the policy in Latin America and brought most of the Caribbean countries under US control. During Theodore Roosevelt's Administration, he got the control of Panama Canal. In 1906, US put down the Cuban uprising. All those showed that US was exercising a policy of domination.

2. America in WWI

WWI took place primarily in Europe between 1914 and 1918. It came as an inevitable explosion of the major contradictions racking the capitalist world. The war was **waged** (开始) between two groups of imperialist powers, Allies and the Central European Power. The Allies or the Entente consisted of England, France, Russia, US and other countries. The central European Powers consisted of Germany, Austria Hungary, and later Turkey and Bulgaria. The basic causes of the war lay in the political, economic and colonial rivalries of the great powers, stretching back into the late 19th century.

(1) American Diplomacy of Neutrality

Since the beginning of WWI in 1914, US, under President Woodrow Wilson, had maintained strict neutrality. Even in May 1915, when a German submarine sank the British ocean liner Lusitania, killing 128 US citizens out of total 1,200 dead, US, though in uproar, remained neutral. In 1916, Wilson was reelected after running largely on a platform of antiwar, pro-neutrality rhetoric.

(2) America's Entrance into the War

There might be a number of factors which contributed to America's entrance into the war. After about three years' fighting, the war at the beginning of 1917 showed signs of German's winning the war. Germany had a large submarine fleet and its use seemed to offer a way to victory. In the meantime, the February Revolution took place in Russia. The US Government thought that Russia might withdraw from the war and the Entente might be defeated, and this would greatly harm the interests of American capitalists who had invested a huge deal of capital in the Entente Allies. As the war went on, Germany would be bold enough to announce that submarines were to be used to sink all ships, including neutral ones, going to England. This would greatly harm the American trade. That the Germans attempted to interest Mexico in going to war against US, which was revealed by the British, was also a factor. Wilson broke off diplomatic relations with Germany in February. Then in March, five American ships were sunk and that became the direct cause for its entrance into the war.

America's participation of the war helped to end it sooner or later. Its troops were sent to Europe just at the time when the Central and Allied Powers had been greatly weakened in the conflict. The entry of US into the war quickened Germany's defeat. By November 1918 the Allied forces had compelled the Germans to seek an **armistice** (停战). US was a fully recognized world power at that time.

(3) Peacemaking in Paris

The drafting of peace terms went ahead. It was time for the winners to divide up spoils. President Wilson sailed for Europe in December and was given as enthusiastic reception. Encouraged, Wilson was determined to impose a kind of peace settlement he wanted. In January 1918, Wilson proposed his *Fourteen Points* as a basis of peace negotiation. It had been designed to weaken the Germans and counter the Russians, including freedom of seas, removal of trade barriers, adjustment of colonial claims, reduction of **armaments** (军备) and organization of a League of Nation, etc. In his *Fourteen Points*, Wilson **flaunted** (挥动) the banner of peace, liberty, justice and humanism. However, his attempt to secure the world peace was, in essence, to establish the US domination in the world.

After the close of war, 27 victorious nations attended the Paris Conference on June 18, 1919. It was, in fact, a meeting to divide the spoils and to redivide the old colonies. The conference was manipulated by a few powers like America, England, France, Italy and Japan. They saw the peace meeting as an opportunity to get revenge on Germany and to enact many of the secret treaties that had already been formulated. The *Treaty of Versailles* was signed in June 1919. Almost all the points Wilson proposed were rejected. Only the League of Nations was established, but England and France controlled the body, instead of US. The Congress of US just refused to ratify the treaty. Nor did it agree to join the League of Nations.

Representatives Signing the *Treaty of Versailles*

3. America in Post-WWI

Between WWI and WWII, there were two decades — the 1920s and 1930s. The 1920s was noted for the so-called prosperity, while the 1930s was characterized by the Great Depression and the *New Deal*.

(1) False Prosperity in the 1920s

During most of the 1920s, US enjoyed a period of unbalanced prosperity: farm prices and wages fell, while industrial profits grew. The boom was fueled by a rise in debt and an inflated stock market.

The expression of "roaring twenties" is often used to describe the period of American life. The roaring twenties **ushered in** (开辟) an exciting time of social change and economic prosperity, as the recession at the end of WWI was quickly replaced by an unprecedented period of financial growth. The stock market soared to unimaginable heights because of the so-called Second Industrial Revolution at the turn of the 20th century, which saw the development of new inventions and machines that changed American society drastically. For example, industry leader Henry Ford developed the assembly line, which enabled mass production of the automobile. The automobile helped give rise to suburban America, as thousands of middle-class Americans left the congested cities for nicer communities in the city outskirts. The airplane, radio, and motion picture ranked with the automobile as popular new inventions of the time. At the same time, a new age of American literature blossomed in the 1920s.

(2) The Great Depression (1929–1933)

The post-war industrial boom and the prosperity were soon to vanish. In 1929, a deep, worldwide economic crisis broke out. The first outward sign of the depression was the collapse of the stock market in October 1929, followed by the closing of thousands of plants and banks. At least 13 million workers, and possibly as many as 15 million, were out of work. At least two thirds of the nation's banks had been closed down. The production of coal, iron, steel, and automobiles dropped by 40% to 80%. The farm crisis, in existence since 1921, was worse than ever.

(3) Roosevelt's New Deal

Franklin D. Roosevelt was elected as the US President in 1932. Immediately after taking the oath of office, Roosevelt set out to provide relief, recovery and reform in his package of programs known as the New Deal. Taking a calculated risk, Roosevelt structured the New Deal policies around the untested theories of British economist John Maynard Keynes, who believed that planned deficit spending by the federal government could "prime the economic pump" and **jump-start** (启动) the economy again.

At home, many public projects were launched to create employment through a huge increase in government responsibility. Crops were destroyed and agricultural production was cut down to stabilize the falling prices. The big industries were also compelled to make reforms.

At abroad, Roosevelt took efforts to consolidate the old markets and to conquer new ones under the cloak of the Good Neighbor Policy.

Roosevelt also took measures of Social Security, paying pensions to the old, the unemployed and the injured.

The New Deal program had some initial remedial effect, but it failed to produce recovery, and solve the problem of unemployment. The crisis continued to deepen until a change was brought about by the outbreak of the Second World War.

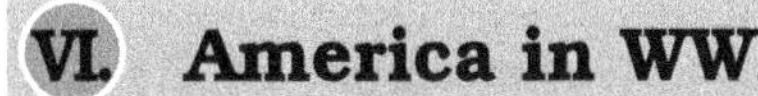

VI. America in WWII

1. From Isolation to Intervention

With the German and Italian fascists bent on war, the world situation was **deteriorating** (恶化) rapidly when Roosevelt was reelected President in 1936. But US still remained neutral. As with World War I, US did not enter World War II until after the rest of the active Allies had done so.

The US' first contribution to the war was simultaneously to cut off the oil and raw material supplies desperately needed by Japan to maintain its offensive in Manchuria, and to increase military and financial aid to China. Its first contribution to the Allies came in September 1940, when US gave Britain 50 old destroyers in exchange for military bases in the Caribbean. This was followed in December 1940, when US began a *Lend-Lease Program* with Britain, supplying much needed military equipment.

On December 7, 1941 Japan launched a surprise attack on the US naval base in Pearl Harbor, citing US' recent trade **embargo** (限制) as justification. The following day, Franklin D. Roosevelt successfully urged a joint session of Congress to declare war on Japan, calling December 7, 1941 "a date which will live in **infamy** (声名狼藉)". Four days after the attack on Pearl Harbor, on December 11, Nazi Germany declared war on US, drawing the country into a two-theater war.

2. Battle Against Germany

Upon entering the war, US and its Allies decided to concentrate the bulk of their efforts on fighting Hitler in Europe, while maintaining a defensive position in the Pacific until Hitler was

Normandy Landing

defeated. The US' first step was to set up a large airforce in Britain to concentrate on bombing raids into Germany itself.

The American army's first ground action was fighting alongside the British, Australian and New Zealand armies in North Africa. By May 1943, the British Eighth Army had expelled the Germans from North Africa and the Allies controlled this vital link until the end of the war. The American navy also played an active role in the Atlantic arena, protecting the **convoys** (船队) and bringing vital American war material to Britain.

After immense preparations, on June 6, 1944, or D-Day, the first **contingents** (分遣队) of US, British and Canadian invasion armies, protected by a greatly superior air force, landed on the beaches of Normandy and began the penetration of Western Europe that eventually overthrew Hitler and Nazi Germany. Following the landing at Normandy, the Americans contributed greatly to the outcome of the war, with **dogged** (顽强的) fighting in the Battle of the Ardennes and the Battle of the Bulge resulting in Allied victories against the Germans. The battles took a heavy toll on the Americans, who lost 19,000 men during the Battle of the Bulge alone. The Allied bombing raids on Germany increased to unprecedented levels after the D-Day invasion, with over 70% of all bombs dropped on Germany occurring after this date. On April 30, 1945, with Berlin completely overrun and with Russian forces and his country in tatters, Adolf Hitler committed suicide. On May 8, 1945, the war with Germany was over, following its unconditional surrender to the Allied forces.

3. Battle Against Japan

Due to the US' commitment to defeating Hitler in Europe, the first years of the war against Japan was largely a defensive battle with the US Navy attempting to prevent the Japanese Navy from asserting dominance of the Pacific region. Initially, Japan won the majority of its battles in a short period of time. Japan quickly defeated and created military bases in Guam, Thailand, Malaya, Papua New Guinea, Indonesia and Burma. This was done virtually unopposed and with quicker speed than that of the German **Blitzkrieg** (闪电战) during the early stages of the war. This was important for Japan, as it had only 10% of the homeland industrial production capacity of US.

The turning point of the war was the Battle of Midway in June 1942. The Americans began by selecting smaller, lesser defended islands as targets as opposed to attacking the major Japanese **strongholds** (要塞). During this period, they **inadvertently** (偶然地) triggered what would become their most comprehensive victory in the entire war.

The Battle of Midway

The Pacific War became the largest naval conflict in history. The American Navy emerged victorious after at one point being stretched to almost breaking point with almost complete destruction of the Japanese Navy. The American forces were then poised for an invasion of the Japanese mainland, to force the Japanese into unconditional surrender. On April 12, 1945, President Franklin D. Roosevelt died and Vice President Harry S. Truman was sworn in as the 33rd President of US. The decision to use nuclear weapons to end the conflict has been one of the most controversial decisions of the war. Supporters of the use of the bombs argued that an invasion would have cost enormous numbers of lives, while opponents argued that the large number of civilian casualties resulting from the bombings were still unjustified. The first bomb was dropped on Hiroshima on August 6, 1945, and the second bomb was dropped on Nagasaki on August 9. On August 15, 1945, the Japanese surrendered unconditionally.

VII. America After WWII

World War II upset the balance of power by reducing the influence of France and the United Kingdom. US and the Soviet Union became the world's only remaining superpowers, and their relations were not exactly friendly. The two nations were never actually engaged in military conflict, so the hostilities became known as the Cold War.

1. Truman and the Cold War

(1) The Truman Doctrine

Harry S. Truman announced the *Truman Doctrine* in 1947, which shaped US foreign policy for four decades.

After World War II, Truman worked tirelessly to establish a new international order. He helped create the World Bank and the International Monetary Fund (IMF) and funded the reconstruction of Japan under General Douglas MacArthur. Truman in 1947 also outlined the *Marshall Plan*, officially the *European Recovery Program*, which set aside more than $10 billion for the reconstruction and reindustrialization of Allied Countries of Europe, and repelling Communism after the Second World War.

In order to check Soviet influence abroad and prevent the further spread of Communism, in 1947, Truman incorporated the desire for **containment** (抑制) into his *Truman Doctrine*. In a special address to Congress on March 12, 1947, Truman announced that US would support foreign governments resisting "attempted **subjugation** (征服) by armed minorities or by outside pressures", that is, Communist revolutionaries or the Soviet Union. He then convinced Congress to agree to give military and economic aid to Greece and Turkey in their fight against Communism.

In 1949, Truman also convinced the Western European powers to join the North Atlantic Treaty Organization (NATO), so that they might mutually defend themselves against the danger of Soviet invasion. Threatened, the Soviet Union sponsored a similar treaty of its own in Eastern Europe, called the *Warsaw Pact*, in 1955.

2. The Eisenhower Doctrine

Eisenhower's election in 1952 ushered in an unprecedented era of economic growth and prosperity in US. The post-war "baby boom" also contributed to population growth.

After taking office in 1953, he devised a new foreign policy tactic to contain the Soviet Union and even win back territory that had already been lost. Devised primarily by Secretary of State John Foster Dulles, this so-called "New Look" at foreign policy proposed the use of nuclear weapons and new technology rather than ground troops and conventional bombs, all in an effort to threaten "massive **retaliation** (报复)" against the Soviet Union for Communist advances abroad.

In 1957, in order to protect American oil interest in the Middle East, Eisenhower announced the *Eisenhower Doctrine*. It contained the points of instant and massive retaliation, avoidance of getting involved in frustrating wars of containment, such as the one in Korea, meeting "aggression" vigorously at places, with means of America's own choosing. The *Doctrine* was based upon the fact that US had overwhelming superiority in nuclear weapons and in the means of delivering them.

The Vietnam War was a long-time suffering for US. The US involvement in Southeast Asia, originally, began with the Cold War perspective in foreign affairs. The Vietnam War was an example of American imperialism for the benefit of the US corporate and military interests. The war started under Eisenhower and was continued by Kennedy and Johnson. When Nixon was elected President, about 10,000 people gathered in Washington, opposing the Vietnam War, and appealed to their government to withdraw from it. Eight million students from more than 600 universities and colleges and 360 high schools held a national students' strike in protest against the US' armed involvement in Cambodia.

In 1955, Dr. Martin Luther King, Jr., a black social reformer and clergyman, organized a boycott of the bus service in Montgomery, Alabama, which went on for more than a year until public transportation was desegregated. "Sit-ins" were used at white-only lunch counters in the South. African Americans who were refused service simply remained in their seats and were replaced by others when the police came to arrest them. In 1963, more than 200,000 people, led by King, marched to the Lincoln Memorial in Washington, D.C. where King addressed the public "his dream". King's philosophy of nonviolence demonstrations was widely adopted in the rapidly growing civil rights movement in 1950s and 1960s. King was honored for his effort to fight discrimination.

3. The Bay of Pigs Invasion and the Cuban Missile Crisis

On April 17, 1961, President John F. Kennedy launched an attack on Cuba, using 1,500 Central Intelligence Agency (CIA) trained Cuban exiles. The exiles were to invade Cuba through the Bay of Pigs in southwestern Cuba. The forces made many mistakes, and at the last moment, Kennedy was advised not to send air support, and he did not. The invasion was a complete failure and within days, Cuban forces crushed the US troops. Kennedy never trusted military or intelligence advice again, and the Soviet Union concluded that Kennedy was a weak leader. The invasion also angered many Latin-American nations.

In 1962, the Soviet Union was desperately behind US in the arms race. Soviet missiles were only powerful enough to be launched against Europe but US missiles were capable of striking the entire Soviet Union (missiles were located in Turkey). In late April 1962, Soviet Premier Nikita Khrushchëv conceived the idea of placing **intermediate-range missiles** (中程导弹) in Cuba. A deployment in Cuba would double the Soviet strategic arsenal and provide a real **deterrent** (威慑) to a potential US attack against the Soviet Union.

Meanwhile, Fidel Castro was looking for a way to defend his island nation from an attack by US. Ever since the Bay of Pigs invasion failed, Castro felt a second attack was inevitable. Consequently, he approved of Khrushchëv's plan to place missiles on the island. In the summer of 1962 the Soviet Union worked quickly and secretly to build its missile installations in Cuba.

The crisis began on October 15, 1962 when a *U-2* **reconnaissance** (侦查) photographs revealed Soviet missiles under construction in Cuba. The next morning, Kennedy was informed of the missile installations. Immediately the Executive Committee made up of 12 of his most important advisers was formed to handle the crisis. After seven days of guarded and intense

The Cuban Missile Crisis

debate, Executive Committee concluded that it had to impose a naval **quarantine** (隔离) around Cuba, which would prevent the arrival of more Soviet offensive weapons on the island.

On October 22, Kennedy announced the discovery of the missile installations to the public and his decision to quarantine the island. He also proclaimed that any nuclear missile launched from Cuba would be regarded as an attack on US by the Soviet Union and demanded that the Soviets remove all of their offensive weapons from Cuba.

On October 26, Executive Committee heard from Khrushchëv in an **impassioned** (充满激情的) letter. He proposed the removing of Soviet missiles and personnel if US would guarantee not to invade Cuba.

October 27 was the worst day of the crisis. A *U-2* was shot down over Cuba and Executive Committee received a second letter from Khrushchëv demanding the removal of US missiles in Turkey in exchange for Soviet missiles in Cuba. Attorney General Robert Kennedy suggested ignoring the second letter and contacted Soviet Ambassador Anatoly Dobrynin to tell him of the US agreement with the first.

Tensions finally began to ease on October 28 when Khrushchëv announced that he would **dismantle** (拆卸) the installations and return the missiles to the Soviet Union, expressing his trust that US would not invade Cuba. Further negotiations were held to implement the October 28 agreement, including a US demand that Soviet light bombers be removed from Cuba, and specifying the exact form and conditions of US assurances not to invade Cuba.

4. Situation from President Johnson to President Reagan

In January 1964, the new President Johnson made a series of proposals which he called the *Great Society* and began a "war on poverty". He signed many programs into law that helped Americans in poverty, that is, those who do not make enough money to survive. During this time two of the most important programs signed into law were *Medicare* and *Medicaid*. *Medicare* provided cheap health insurance to senior citizens and *Medicaid* provided health insurance for the poor. Cities and schools also received boosts with the creation of the Department of Housing and Urban Development and the signing of the *Elementary and Secondary Education Act* of 1965.

Protests were growing in the 1960s. Blacks and whites in high schools and colleges in the South and the North staged sit-ins, protests that are accomplished by sitting down and not being productive or letting people pass.

Another kind of protest was growing in the South. In 1961, groups of African Americans began riding buses from Washington, D.C. that were bound for New Orleans to make sure that the Rosa Parks Supreme Court decision was being enforced. These bus riders were known as "freedom riders". The rides went smoothly until the buses reached Alabama, where the freedom riders would be greeted with violence from angry whites.

Nixon, the former Vice President, had quietly been nominated by the Republicans as their candidate. Nixon claimed to represent the "silent majority" in America, that is, those that had begun to take on a more conservative approach to politics and disliked the "hippie" and civil rights movements. Nixon also promised to end the war in Vietnam, although he never said he would win it. In his most surprising reversal of foreign policy goals, Nixon opened door to China. Domestically, Nixon was less successful. His largest problem was an economy threatened by inflation and by increasing deficits in the balance of payments. Yet his fatal trouble was the disclosure of the Watergate Scandal. In the presidential election year 1972, five men of the Committee for the Reelection of the President broke into the Democratic national headquarters at the Watergate Hotel, Washington, D.C., where they planted **bugs** (窃听器) in order to get information for the Committee. But unfortunately they were arrested. Although it was never approved that Nixon planned the Watergate break-in or that he ever knew about it beforehand, he was eventually forced out of office because he was found guilty for his effect to avoid the investigation and disclosures. Faced with impeachment, Nixon resigned on August 9, 1974.

Jimmy Carter became President in 1977, whose Administration experienced an eventful period. On the economy, Carter's Administration's initial focus on unemployment was soon replaced by concern with the highest inflation rates. The inflation was caused mainly by rises in Organization of Petroleum Exporting Countries (OPEC) oil price, wage boosts, and large budget deficits. Carter won approval of a treaty giving Panama sovereign control over the Panama Canal by 2000 A. D. On the foreign affairs, he succeeded in his mediation efforts to settle long-standing differences growing out of the 1973 Arab-Israeli War. However, his failure in dealings with the hostage crisis of the American embassy in Teheran spoiled his image among the American public. In the general election of 1980, Carter was defeated by his opponent, Ronald Reagan.

In the years before and following Reagan's election, a conservative movement grew which complained that the government spent too much money and collected too many taxes. So,

Reagan decided to cut taxes and spending. Reagan's policy of supply-side economics (increasing supply and services to stimulate the economy) soon became known simply as "Reaganomics". Reagan made progress in other areas too. He made up for Carter's general indecision by resolving an air traffic controller's strike quickly and cleanly.

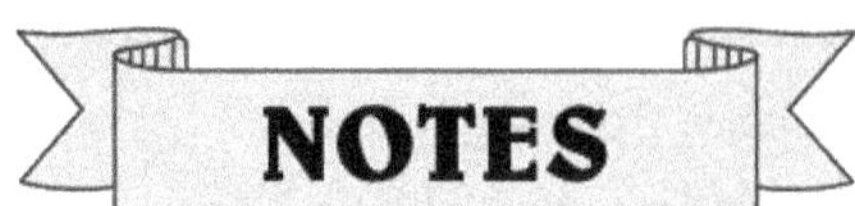

1. **Yankee**：新英格兰居住者。
2. **jack-of-all-traders**：博而不精的人。
3. **the Seven Years' War**：七年战争。1756—1763 年，由欧洲主要国家组成的两大交战集团（英国与法国，以及普鲁士的侵略政策与奥地利和俄国的国际政治利益发生冲突）在欧洲、北美洲、印度等广大地域和海域进行的争夺殖民地和领土的战争。
4. **minute men**：一分钟人。独立战争期间，"一分钟人"在北美享有盛誉，它指的是反抗英军、追求自治的民兵游击战士，他们出则为兵，入则为民，来无影、去无踪，四处袭扰英军，让英国人在整个战争期间吃尽了苦头。
5. **Hessian**：黑森人。在 18 世纪的德国，黑森士兵是黑森-卡塞尔地区唯一的资产。他们的传奇历史不过百年，但他们成功地塑造了自己的声誉：如果你要进行战争，黑森士兵是你可以用金钱买到的最优秀的军队。而黑森-卡塞尔，这个弱小的邦国以国家的形式进行雇佣兵交易，从中获得的利益则用于支撑这个小邦国的生存。
6. ***Kansas-Nebraska Act***：《堪萨斯-内布拉斯加法案》。此法案是 1854 年美国国会通过的取消限制奴隶制扩展到西部新开发地区的法案。19 世纪以后，美国领土迅速扩张，在密苏里河以西的堪萨斯-内布拉斯加地区，前往垦殖的人日益增多，他们要求建立新州。按密苏里协议（1820）规定，该地区在北纬 36°30′以北，应以自由州加入联邦，但奴隶主凭借在政府和参议院中的优势，力图在这一地区扩大种植园、畜牧业，主张实行奴隶制。
7. ***The Missouri Compromise***：《密苏里协议》。1820 年，争执不下的南北双方终于达成了《密苏里协议》，约定密苏里州以自由州身份并入联邦，并且约定在密苏里北部边界以北奴隶制为非法，在此线以南任何地区都可以继续实行蓄奴制。
8. **Robert E. Lee** (1807−1870)：罗伯特·爱德华·李。美国职业军人，为南北战争期间联盟国最出色的将军。他最终以总司令的身份指挥联盟国军队。战后，他积极推动重建，在其生命的最后数年担任一所大学校长。

9. ***Lend-Lease Program***：租借法案。此法案是美国国会在第二次世界大战初期 1941 年 3 月通过的。该法案授权总统可以通过出售、转让、交换或租借的方式，向总统认为其防务对美国国防至关重要的任何国家提供国防物资。战争期间，美国据此向外国提供了价值高达 500 亿美元的租借物资。租借法案的通过，使美国处于非交战状态，是美国积极干预反法西斯战争的重要里程碑。租借法案对盟军在二次大战中取得胜利有直接影响。
10. **D-Day**：第二次世界大战中盟国西欧的登陆日。
11. ***Marshall Plan***：马歇尔计划。此计划又称欧洲复兴计划，是二战后美国对被战争破坏的西欧各国进行援助、协助重建的计划，对欧洲国家的发展和世界政治格局产生了深远的影响。该计划因时任美国国务卿乔治・马歇尔而得名。
12. **International Monetary Fund (IMF)**：国际货币基金组织。
13. **North Atlantic Treaty Organization (NATO)**：北大西洋公约组织。其简称为北约组织或北约，是美国与西欧、北美主要发达国家为实现防卫协作而建立的一个国际军事集团组织。1949 年 4 月 4 日美国与加拿大、英国、法国、比利时、荷兰、卢森堡、丹麦、挪威、冰岛、葡萄牙、意大利共 12 国在华盛顿签订了《北大西洋公约》，标志着北约正式成立。公约于 1949 年 8 月 24 日生效。北约的目的是与前苏联为首的东欧集团国成员相抗衡，若某成员国一旦受到攻击，其他成员国可以及时做出反应、联合进行反击。但这一条款在“9・11”事件之前，一直未曾付诸实施。及至前苏联解体，华沙公约组织宣告解散，北约遂成为一个地区性防卫协作组织。
14. **United Nations Security Council (UNSC)**：联合国安全理事会。
15. **Central Intelligence Agency (CIA)**：中央情报局。
16. ***U-2***：U-2 侦察机。U-2 侦察机是由美国洛克希德・马丁公司研制开发，首飞为 1955 年。美国空军和 CIA 用来侦察敌后方战略目标，如今可作为战术侦察机。几十年来曾征战全球，但是也有十几架在敌国的领空被击落。

I. Multiple Choice

1. Of the 13 British colonies only _______ were self-governing colonies.
   A) Massachusetts and Connecticut
   B) Connecticut and Rhode Island
   C) Massachusetts and Rhode Island
   D) New Hampshire and Connecticut

2. The First Continental Congress was attended by the representatives from all the colonies EXCEPT _______.
   A) Delaware
   B) Pennsylvania
   C) Massachusetts
   D) Georgia

3. The victory of _______ was the turning point of the War of Independence.
   A) Saratoga
   B) Gettysburg
   C) Trenton
   D) Yorktown

4. When the Second War of Independence broke out in 1812, the US President was _______.
   A) Thomas Jefferson
   B) James Madison
   C) John Adams
   D) James Monroe

5. The Mexican territories annexed by US as a result of the Mexican War include the following present states EXCEPT _______.
   A) Oregon
   B) Texas
   C) California
   D) Arizona

6. Which of the following is NOT the measure taken by Lincoln's Administration in 1862 to change the situation and win the Civil War?
   A) The passage of the Homestead Act.
   B) The issuing of the *Emancipation Proclamation*.
   C) The allowance of Negroes to join the Union Army.
   D) The ordering of the Union Army to take over Richmond.

7. The US imperialism was marked by all the following EXCEPT _______.
   A) highly developed industry
   B) high concentration of capital
   C) free business competition
   D) overseas territorial expansion

8. When the First World War began, President Wilson immediately called upon the American people to _______.
   A) be ready for the war
   B) observe strict neutrality
   C) give financial help to Allies
   D) end the trade relations with Germany

9. The Post-WWII program of economic assistance to Western Europe was known as _______.
   A) containment policy B) *Truman Doctrine* C) *Marshall Plan* D) Communist prevention

10. Dr. Martin Luther King, Jr. advocated the philosophy of _______.
   A) economic equality B) nonviolence C) military protest D) black power

▶▶ II. Sentence Completion

1. In 1620 the first group of __________ arrived from England. They were so called because they represented the rising bourgeoisie of the time and wished to "purify" the Church of England, the established church, with the King as its head. In order to escape from _________ persecution at home, a group of Puritans set sail for America on a ship called the _________.
2. A committee, composed of __________, Benjamin Franklin, John Adams and some other members, was appointed to draw up a _________. After three weeks of discussion, the committee prepared the famous document which was formally adopted on July 4, 1776, a day which has been celebrated each year as Independence Day or _________ in the US.
3. On December 2, 1823, President James Monroe delivered to Congress his annual message in which he announced his __________, which proclaimed the US' opinion that European powers should no longer __________ or __________ in the Americas.
4. As a rapid growth of capitalism, the centre of the American economy had definitely shifted from the __________ areas to the __________ centers in the North by the time came to presidency in 1829.
5. __________, daughter of Minister Lyman Beecher, published her novel __________ in 1852 in response to the passage of the *Fugitive Slave Act*. The novel intended to express her views of the cruelty of _________ and nearly 300,000 copies were sold during its first year of publication.
6. Franklin D. Roosevelt was elected as the US President in __________. Immediately after taking the oath of office, Roosevelt set out to provide relief, _________ and reform in his package of programs known as the _________.

▶▶ III. Term Explanation

1. the First Continental Congress

____

____

2. Louisiana Purchase

____

____

3. US-Spanish War

____

____

4. roaring twenties

____

____

5. Watergate Scandal

____

____

SUMMARY

American history is a short one, about 400 years from 1607 to the present. Throughout the history, the population and the economy of US have changed dramatically. The nation has developed from a small English colony into a great nation with diverse cultures.

The Indians living in America originated from Asia some 25,000 years ago. After the discovery of the New World by Columbus in 1492, the European powers sent many explorers to the new continents and they began to compete against each other in occupying the New World. That England exercised stricter polices upon the colonial people led to the American War of Independence (1775—1783). After 1840s, America initiated its vast territorial and economic expansion. The Civil War (1861—1865) broke out due to the antagonism in social-economic system between the North and the South. The period from the Civil War to the beginning of 20th century was a period of rapid industrial growth and urban development. With the emergence of industrial America came the emergence of imperial US and US as a world power. US policy toward WW I was from strict neutrality to involvement and US' participation of the war helped to end the war. Between WW I and WW II, there were two decades of striking contrast — the prosperous 1920s and the depressed 1930s. World War II upset the balance of power by reducing the influence of France and the United Kingdom. The United States and the Soviet Union became the World's only remaining superpowers and their hostile relations caused the Cold War. Harry S. Truman announced the *Truman Doctrine* in 1947, which shaped US foreign policy for four decades. Eisenhower's election in 1952 ushered in an unprecedented era of economic growth and prosperity in US. The Vietnam War was an example of US imperialism for the benefit of the US corporate and military interests. Dr. Martin Luther King, Jr.'s philosophy of nonviolence demonstrations was widely adopted in the rapidly growing civil rights movement in 1950s and 1960s.

In 1960s and 1970s, the American domestic and foreign policies underwent some important changes. Up to now, the United States is still one of the developed capitalist countries in the world.

Chapter 3

Government and Politics

HIGHLIGHTS

Constitution — Congress — Presidency — Supreme Court — Election — party system — foreign affairs — super power

I. Political Structure

The United States is one of the youngest countries in the world and yet it has the world's oldest written Constitution. This is often attributed to the political wisdom of the founding fathers of the Republic. And, it is also said to have demonstrated the vitality and flexibility of the US *Constitution*, upon which the nation is based.

1. The American Constitution

The Constitution of the United States of America is the supreme law of the United States. It provides the framework for the organization of the United States Government. The document defines the three main branches of the government: the legislative branch with a **bicameral** (两院制) Congress, an executive branch led by the President, and a judicial branch headed by the Supreme Court. Besides providing for the organization of these branches, the *Constitution* carefully outlines which powers each branch may exercise. It also reserves numerous rights for the individual states, thereby establishing the United States' federal system of government. It is the shortest and oldest written constitution of any major **sovereign** (统治的) state.

The Constitution of the United States is the oldest written constitution in the world today. One of the reasons for its **longevity** (长期使用) is that the founding fathers used broad enough language to allow room for interpretation. The US Supreme Court has become the ultimate decision maker when it comes to deciding what the 7,000 words in the *Constitution* mean and how they should be applied. But the views of the justices of the Supreme Court have changed over time as society has changed. Because the principles of the *Constitution* are broadly expressed, the Supreme Court has been able to apply those principles to meet the needs of new generations. Because of its flexibility and adaptability, the *Constitution* is often referred to as a "living constitution".

(1) The Articles of Confederation

When the War of Independence ended, the United States was not one unified nation as it is today. Instead, it was a group of 13 former colonies called states. Each has its own government and was organized very much like an independent nation. Each made its own laws and handled all of its internal affairs. During the war, the 13 colonies had agreed to work together and formed a national congress under the *Articles of Confederation*.

The Articles of Confederation was the first governing constitution of the United States of America. *The Articles* were created by the chosen representatives of the states in the Second Continental Congress out of a perceived need to have a plan of confederacy for securing the freedom, sovereignty, and independence of the United States.

Although serving a crucial role in the victory in the American Revolutionary War, a group of reformers, known as "federalists", felt that the *Articles* lacked the necessary provisions for a sufficiently effective government. Fundamentally, a federation was sought to replace the confederation. The key criticism by those who favored a more powerful central state was that the government lacked taxing authority; it had to request funds from the states. Also various federalist **factions** (党派) wanted a government that could impose uniform **tariffs** (关税), give land grants, and assume responsibility for unpaid state war debts. Another criticism of the *Articles* was that they did not strike the right balance between large and small states in the legislative decision making process. Due to its one-state, one-vote **plank** (政策), the larger states were expected to contribute more but had only one vote. The *Articles* were replaced by the United States *Constitution*.

(2) The Constitutional Convention

The Constitutional Convention **convened** (聚集) in Philadelphia, then the country's largest city in 1787. State legislatures chose 74 delegates to the convention; 55 attended. They met at the Pennsylvania State House — now Independence Hall — in the same room where some of them had signed the *Declaration of Independence* 11 years before. Delegates came from every state except Rhode Island. That state was controlled by farmers and debtors who feared that the convention would weaken states' powers to relieve debtors of their debts.

The delegates were distinguished by their education, experience, and **enlightenment** (启蒙). Benjamin Franklin, of Pennsylvania, was the best-known American in the world. At 81 he was the oldest delegate. George Washington, of Virginia, was the most respected American in the country. He was chosen to preside over the convention. The presence of men like Franklin and Washington gave the convention **legitimacy** (合法性). The delegates quickly determined that the *Articles* were hopeless. Rather than revise them, as instructed by Congress, the delegates decided to start over and draft a new constitution.

Despite disagreements, the delegates did see eye to eye on the most fundamental issues and designed a new form of government for the new nation. The plan for the government was written in very simple language in a document called *The Constitution of the United States*. They agreed that the government should be a republic in which people could vote for at least some of the officials who would represent them. This was the only form of government they seriously considered. They also agreed that the national government should be supreme over the state governments. The *Constitution* also called for the election of a national leader, or President. At the same time, they thought the government should be limited, with checks to prevent it from exercising too much power. They agreed that the national government should have three separate branches to exercise separate powers. They thought both the legislative and executive branches should be strong.

To guarantee separation of power, the Founders built in overlapping powers called checks and balances. Madison suggested, "The great security against a gradual concentration of the several powers in the same department consists in giving those who administer each department the necessary constitutional means and personal motives to resist encroachments by the others. Ambition must be made to counteract ambition." To that end, each branch was given some authority over the others. If one branch abused its power, the others could use their checks to **thwart** (挫败) it.

(3) Ratification of the *Constitution*

The **ratification** (批准), or adoption, of the *Constitution* took place between September of 1787 and July of 1788. The Federal Convention, which had drafted the *Constitution* between May and September in 1787, had no authority to impose it on the American people. Article VII of the *Constitution* and resolutions adopted by the convention on September 17, 1787, detailed a four-stage ratification process: (1) submission of the *Constitution* to the Confederation Congress, (2) transmission of the *Constitution* by Congress to the state legislatures, (3) election of delegates to conventions in each state to consider the *Constitution*, and (4) ratification by the conventions of at least nine of the 13 states.

Ratification was not guaranteed, however. The Confederation Congress might reject the *Constitution*, rewrite it, or refer it to a second general convention, claiming that the first had violated its limited mandate to suggest **amendments** (修正案) to the *Articles*. On September 28, 1787, after three days of bitter debate, the Confederation Congress sent the *Constitution* to the states with neither an **endorsement** (认可) nor a **condemnation** (指责).

The struggle for ratification of the *Constitution* was both a direct, unabashed contest for votes and a complex, impressive argument about politics and constitutional theory. It was the first time that the people of a nation freely determined their form of government. It was also the first national political controversy in American history; the people of all 13 states for the first time debated and decided the same issue.

Ratification of the US *Constitution* in several important states would not have occurred if the Federalists had not assured the states that amendments to the *Constitution* would be passed to protect individual liberties against **incursions** (入侵) by the national government. Many of the recommendations of the states ratifying conventions included specific rights that were considered later by James Madison as he labored to draft what became the *Bill of the Rights*. It is commonly viewed as consisting of the first 10 articles of *Amendments to the Constitution* of the United States of America, which lay out the basic rights that all citizens shall enjoy. These amendments give all Americans rights to believe in any religion; to speak, write and publish as they like; to gather together peacefully and to petition the government; to be secure in their homes without fear of unreasonable searches and **seizure** (没收) of persons and property; and to receive fair and just treatment in courts of law.

The *Constitution* went into effect in March 1789. The *Bill of Rights* was added in 1791. Other amendments have been added over the years, but the political system created by the *Constitution* and the *Bill of the Rights* is basically the same today as it was in 1790.

2. Three Branches of the American Government

The federal government has three branches: the legislative, executive, and judicial. Through a system of separation of powers and the system of "checks and balances", each of these branches has some authority to act on its own, some authority to regulate the other two branches, and has some of its own authority, in turn, regulated by the other branches. The policies of the federal government have a broad impact on both the domestic and foreign affairs of the United States. In addition, the powers of the federal government as a whole are limited by the *Constitution*.

(1) The Legislative Branch

Legislature is a type of representative assembly with the power to create and change laws. The legislative branch in the United States is bicameral. It is made up of elected representatives from all of the states and is the only branch that can make federal laws, levy federal taxes, declare

The United States Capitol

war or put foreign treaties into effect. It consists of a Congress that is divided into two groups called houses: the **Senate** (参议院) and the **House of Representatives** (众议院).

According to the *Constitution*, each state must have two Senators to represent the people. They must be at least 30 years of age, citizens of the US for at least nine years, and residents of the state from which they are chosen. Once they are selected, they serve a six-year term. With one third of the members elected every two years, the Senate does not select its members at the same time. Nominally, the Vice President presides over the Senate; he has, however, no part in its deliberations and no vote either except when it is necessary. With such a minor role, the Vice President does not like to attend the routine sessions very much.

The other chamber of Congress is the House of Representatives. Different from Senators, the Representatives can be younger. They must be at least 25 years old, citizens of the US for at least seven years, and residents of the states from which they are elected. The number of each state's Representatives is calculated according to the state's population. However small the population of a state may be, it must have at least one Representative. Also different from Senators, each Representative serves a two-year term of office. He can continue if he is re-elected.

As said above, the primary duty of Congress is to make laws for the country. However, the law-making process is a very complicated one. For any **bill** (法案) to become a law, it must go through a **labyrinthine** (曲折的) procedure. The first step is coming up with the idea for a new law or changing the current law. Anyone can come up with the idea, but it must be introduced by someone from the legislature in its proper form. This is called bill drafting. It is read, studied in committees, commented on and amended in the Senate or House chamber in which it was introduced. It is then voted upon. If it passes, it is sent to the other house where a similar procedure occurs. Groups who try to persuade Congressmen to vote for or against a bill are known as "lobbies". Once the exact wording is agreed upon by both houses, the bill goes to the President for his approval or veto. Only when the President signs the bill does it become a law. If the bill is rejected by the President, it may be dead or resurface some other time.

(2) The Executive Branch

The chief executive of the United States is the President, who, together with the vice

President, is elected to a four-year term. Under a *Constitutional Amendment* passed in 1951, a President can be elected to only two terms. Except for the right of succession to the presidency, the vice President's only Constitutional duties are to serve as the presiding officer of the Senate. As the chief executive of the government, the President has definite and important powers over both international and national affairs.

White House

The President has the authority to appoint federal judges as vacancies occur, including members of the Supreme Court. All such court appointments are subject to confirmation by the Senate. Within the executive branch, the President has broad powers to issue regulations and directives regarding the work of the federal government's many departments and agencies. He is commander-in-chief of the armed forces. The President appoints the heads and senior officials of the executive branch agencies; the larger majority of federal workers, however, are selected through a non-political civil service system. The major departments of the government are headed by appointed secretaries who collectively make up the President's cabinet. Each appointment must be confirmed by a vote of the Senate.

Under the *Constitution*, the President is primarily responsible for foreign relations with other nations. The President appoints ambassadors and other officials. He also formulates and manages the nation's foreign policy. The President often represents the United States abroad in consultations with other heads of state through his officials, and negotiates treaties with other countries. Such treaties must be approved by a two thirds vote of the Senate. Presidents also negotiate with other nations less formal "executive agreements" that are not subject to Senate approval.

As a law maker, the President has the right to veto or sign any bills passed by Congress. He may call Congress into a special session and recommend some legislation to solve a particular problem. If it does not respond to him, he may call upon the people directly for support through the press, radio and television. His annual "State of the Union Message" and other special messages to Congress have often become the basis of legislative activities.

As Commander-in-chief, the President can call into Federal service the state units of the National Guard and he may send the US armed forces to any part of the world. He has the right to appoint and dismiss all the top-ranking military officers. He may make undeclared wars for a period of 60 days without Congressional approval. Furthermore, he is the only person who has the authority to order the use of nuclear weapons.

(3) The Judicial Branch

The judicial branch is headed by the Supreme Court, which is the only court specifically created by the *Constitution*. In addition, the Congress has established 12 federal courts of appeal and, below them, 94 federal district courts. Federal judges are appointed for life or voluntary retirement; and can only be removed from office through the process of **impeachment** (弹劾) in the Congress.

The Supreme Court

The district courts are trial courts. There are 94 trial courts, based on population but with at least one in each state. They have a number of judges, although a single judge or jury decides each case. The courts of appeals are intermediate **appellate courts** (受理上诉的法庭). There are 12 courts of appeals, based on regions of the country.

The Supreme Court is the ultimate appellate court. Although it can hear some cases that have not proceeded through the lower courts first, in practice it hears nearly all of its cases on appeal. A group of nine justices decides its cases. The district courts conduct **trial** (审判). The courts of appeals and Supreme Court do not; they do not have juries or witnesses to testify and present evidence. Rather than determine guilt or innocence, these courts evaluate arguments about legal questions arising in the cases.

The state judiciaries have a structure similar to the federal judiciary. In most states, though, there are two **tiers** (等级) or trial courts. The lower tier is usually for criminal cases involving minor crimes, and the upper tier is for criminal cases involving major crimes and for civil cases. In about three-fourths of the states, there are intermediate appellate courts, and in all of the states there is a supreme court.

Jurisdiction is the authority to hear and decide cases. According to the *Constitution*, the federal courts exercise jurisdiction over cases in which the subject involves either the US *Constitution*, statutes, or treaties; **maritime** (海运) law; or cases in which the litigants include either the US government, more than one state government, one state government and a citizen of another state, citizens of more than one state, or a foreign government or citizen. The state courts exercise jurisdiction over the remaining cases. These include most criminal cases because the state has authority over most criminal matters and pass most criminal laws.

Despite this dividing line, some cases begin in the state courts and end in the federal courts. These involve state law and federal law, frequently a state statute and federal constitutional right.

For these cases there are two major paths from the state judiciary to the federal judiciary.

When Americans talk about their three-part national government, they often refer to what they call its system of "checks and balances". This system works in many ways to keep serious mistakes from being made by one branch or another. Here are a few examples of checks and balances:

If Congress proposes a law that the President thinks is unwise, the President can veto it. That means the proposal does not become law. Congress can enact the law despite the President's views only if two thirds of the members of both houses vote in favor of it.

If Congress passes a law which is then challenged in the courts as unconstitutional, the Supreme Court has the power to declare the law unconstitutional and therefore no longer in effect.

The President has the power to make treaties with other nations and to make all appointments to federal positions, including the position of Supreme Court justice. The Senate, however, must approve all treaties and confirm all appointments before they become official. In this way the Congress can prevent the President from making unwise appointments.

3. Two-party System

The United States has two major political parties, which have a long tradition dating back to the 1790s. The function and character of these political parties, as well as the emergence of the Two-party system itself, have much to do with the unique historical forces operating from this country's beginning as an independent nation. This development can be attributed to three major factors: the election system, the centralizing influence of the presidency, and the general division of interests into two camps.

(1) Why a Two-party System?

In the United States, under the single-member-district system, whether it be a Congressional district, a state, or the nation, it elects only one individual at a time. To win an election, a candidate needs more votes than any other candidate to be elected. There is only one representative from a congressional district. Thus there is a tendency for some groups within a district to form **coalitions** (联合), or to combine forces, so that together they can elect that official. This tightens the development of political organization. As more coalitions are formed, there are fewer parties.

To elect a presidential candidate, the political party tries to band together as many different groups as possible. This requires a vast coalition of interests throughout the country. Those interests that oppose the groups in one party flock to the opposing party. The nation thus tends to split into two major parties. Interests that are too small ever to elect a president of their own selection can influence the selection of a candidate who may be successful in obtaining a majority. A president elected with coalition support is somewhat responsive to the demands of each interest within the coalition.

There tends to be a polarization of interests on any problem in this country. Even prior to the adoption of the *Constitution*, there was a natural **polarization** (分化) of the country into two camps along economic and political lines.

(2) Structures and Traditional Images of the Two Parties

All of these factors have contributed to shaping the modern Democratic and Republican parties with an elephant and a donkey as their symbols. Established and supported by those with wealth and power, both have ruled the nation alternatively for different lengths of time. This system is the well-known Two-party system practiced in the US.

The Democratic and Republican parties are structured to resemble the American federal system, with national committees, national conventions, 50 state committees, and more than 3,000 country committees with city, ward, and **precinct** (区域) level organizations under their supervision. But there is no real hierarchy of authority in American parties. City and country organizations operate quite independently.

Both of the parties have voluntary membership. There is neither admittance procedure nor any party **dues** (党费). All the party expenditures are covered by **donations** (捐献) from their party members. It is not rare that a Democrat votes for a Republican candidate or vice versa. Any person has the liberty to decide which party he would like to be in and he can also change his membership at any time.

The Democrats have been considered a party of less **affluent** (富有) people, more liberal-minded, and played an active role for the federal government in the economic and social sectors, particularly where rights of minority groups are involved. The Democratic Party is said to enjoy their greatest advantage on issues like helping the poor, the elderly, and the homeless; handling unemployment; dealing with the environment and improving health care.

The Republican Party has generally been a party of more affluent and conservative voters. It has favored free economic principles, and prefers state and local government power to federal power. The Republican Party is said to be better at managing foreign policy, dealing with national defense and holding down taxes.

4. Elections

The focal point of American political life is the presidential election. More citizens participate in this process than in any other aspect of civic life, and their choice has enormous significance for the nation and, indeed, for the world. In the United States, the President is not directly elected by the people but by a body established under the *Constitution* called the **Electoral College** (美国总统选举团). Its members are supposed to mirror the wishes of the voters in their state.

(1) Who Runs for President?

Most people have little chance of becoming a president: they are unknown to the public; they do not have the financial resources or contacts to raise the money needed for a national campaign; they have jobs, so they could not leave to run a serious campaign; their friends would probably **ridicule** (取笑) them for even thinking of such a thing. But a few people are in different position. Most candidates for president are, in fact, senators or governors. Vice presidents also frequently compete for the position.

(2) How a Candidate Wins the Nomination?

Presidential candidates try to win a majority of delegates at their party's national nominating convention in the summer preceding the November election. Delegates to those conventions are elected in **state caucuses** (政党选举候选人预备会议), conventions, and primaries. Candidates must campaign to win the support of those who attend caucuses and conventions.

Normally, candidates formally announce their candidacies in the year proceeding the presidential election year. Then their aim is to persist and survive the long primary and caucus season that begins in February of election year and continues until only one candidate is left.

(3) The Electoral College

All planning for the campaign has to take into account the peculiar American institution of the Electoral College. The United States does not have a direct election of the President, although this may surprise those who thought they voted for Bush or Obama. In fact they voted for Bush's or Obama's electors who formed part of the Electoral College.

The Electoral College is devised as a compromise between having president elected by Congress or by popular vote. It is a body that elects the president and vice president. Each state is represented by the same number of members as in its congressional delegation. In another word, each has as many electors as the total representation in Congress (House plus Senate). The smallest state (and the District of Columbia) has three, whereas the largest state — California — has 53. The voters vote for electors who will cast their ballots in the Electoral College. The distribution of electoral votes among the states can vary every 10 years depending on the results of the US **Census** (人口调查).

With the exception of Maine and Nebraska, which divide their Electoral College votes according to who wins in each congressional district, all other states' electoral votes go to the candidate winning the most votes in that state. If one candidate wins a majority of the electors voting across the United States, that candidate wins. If no candidate wins a majority, the election is decided in the House of Representatives, where each state has one vote and a majority is necessary to win.

Because of the winner-take-all feature of the Electoral College, the system gives an advantage to large states and their urban populations. The 11 largest states have a majority (270) of the 538 votes. Candidates concentrate their efforts on these states. The Electoral College is based on states, so it encourages campaigns designed to win "states".

II. Foreign Policies

As the US entered the 21st century, it is the only superpower in the world. The country continues to play a leading role in the international politics. We are going to examine the heritage, ideology and the future of the US foreign policies.

1. Heritage

The foreign policy of the US is the policy by which the United States interacts with foreign nations. The US foreign policy is highly influential on the world stage, as it is the only remaining superpower. The global reach of the United States is backed by a 13 trillion dollar economy, the largest in the world.

There are two overall visions of American foreign policy. The first one, which dominated in the 19th century, is the vision of America as Promised Land. Modest and restrained, it embraces three broad principles: in addition to an aversion to entangling alliances, the *Monroe Doctrine* (this doctrine regards any attack upon the territory of an American state as the threat to all American nations), and the notion of Manifest Destiny. This vision emphasized American **exceptionalism** (例外论) in the world at large. The experience of intervention in Europe during the two world wars led Americans to believe that they were the people who were chosen to extend peace and stability to the four corners of the earth. Their faith has now been shaken, but they are still building foreign policy on that traditional belief.

The officially stated goals of the foreign policy of the United States, as mentioned in the Foreign Policy Agenda of the US Department of State, are "to create a more secure, democratic, and prosperous world for the benefit of the American people and the international community". In addition, the United States House Committee on Foreign Affairs states as some of its jurisdictional goals: "export controls, including nonproliferation of nuclear technology and nuclear hardware; measures to foster commercial intercourse with foreign nations and to safeguard American business abroad; International commodity agreements; international education; and protection of American citizens abroad and expatriation". US foreign policy has been the subject of much debate, criticism and praise both domestically and abroad.

2. Ideological Elements

Foreign policy ideas rise and fall in popularity, come back to life, and mingle with others over time. But the recurring debates over American grand strategy, including the *Bush Doctrine*, can all be connected to the following ideological elements.

(1) Exceptionalism

Americans have never been more **unanimous** (一致同意) than the founders were in their belief that America had a special place in the world. Even such rivals as Alexander Hamilton and Thomas Jefferson, who disagreed about almost everything else, could concur that America was the "City on the Hill" and that its people were blessed with civil and religious liberty. They also shared the conviction that their nation might one day grow into what Jefferson called an "Empire for Liberty". But it would not do so by force. Perhaps the fullest elaboration of the policy implications of this conviction came in John Quincy Adam's Fourth of July speech in 1821: "American does not go abroad in search of monsters to destroy. She is the well-wisher to the freedom and independence of all. She is the champion only of her own."

(2) Unilateralism

The founding fathers were equally committed to unilateralism, a principled **wariness** (谨慎) about any obligations to other nations. The phrase "no entangling alliances" came from Jefferson's inaugural address, but the idea was first articulated in George Washington's farewell message: "It is our true policy to steer clear of permanent alliances with any portion of the foreign world...," Washington declared, adding that the nation could **prudently** (慎重的) enter "temporary alliance for extraordinary emergencies". Indeed, when James Madison took the nation to war against Britain in 1812, he resisted the temptation to ally with France.

(3) Expansionism

The 19th century journalist John O'Sullivan coined the phrase "Manifest Destiny" in an 1839 article. It conveyed the belief in the divinely conferred right of the republic to expand westward and bring more of the continent into "the great experiment of Liberty and Federated self-government". But Americans had been acting upon that conviction much earlier, starting with their insistence that Britain cede all lands of the Mississippi at the end of the Revolutionary

War. *The Northwest Ordinance* of 1787 and Jefferson's 1803 Louisiana Purchase confirmed that expansionist ambition. President James Polk saw Manifest Destiny as clear justification of the war he provoked with Mexico. That struggle secured favorable borders for the new state of Texas and wrested California and much of the southwest from a defeated Mexico, but it also elicited an unprecedented wave of criticism from Ralph Waldo Emerson, Henry David Thoreau, and other writers of the day. The spread of slavery into the new territories was certainly a great concern, but another was the conviction that imperial acquisitions violated the spirit of the nation's republican ideals.

1. **is attributed to**：归因于。
2. **impose uniform tariffs**：征收统一的关税。
3. **The presence of men like Franklin and Washington gave the convention legitimacy.**
   此句中 gave the convention legitimacy 意为"使得此次会议合法化"。
4. **see eye to eye**：达成一致。
5. **checks and balances**：监督与制衡。
6. **routine sessions**：例会。
7. **approval or veto**：批准或否决。
8. **Democratic national convention**：民主党全国大会，这个大会上将正式宣布民主党总统候选人，候选人将接受推选，正式宣布总统竞选开始。
9. **Promised Land**：理想中的乐土。
10. **no entangling alliances**：不与任何国家纠结为盟。

▶▶ I. Sentence Completion

1. The *Constitution of the United States of America* is the __________ of the United States. It provides the framework for the organization of the United States Government.
2. When the War of Independence ended, the United States was not one unified nation as it is today. Instead, it was a group of 13 former colonies called states. During the war, the 13 colonies had agreed to work together and formed a national congress under __________.
3. They agreed that the government should be a __________ in which people could vote for at least some of the officials. They also agreed that the national government should be supreme over the __________ governments. The *Constitution* also called for the election of a national leader, or __________.
4. The __________, or adoption, of the *Constitution* took place between September of 1787 and July of 1788.
5. The *Constitution* went into effect in March 1789. The __________ was added in 1791. Other __________ have been added over the years.
6. The federal government has three branches: the legislative, __________, and judicial. Through a system of separation of powers and the system of "__________", each of these branches has some authority to act on its own, some authority to regulate the other two branches, and has some of its own authority, in turn, regulated by the other branches.
7. Legislature is a type of representative assembly with the power to create and change laws. The legislative branch in the United States is __________. It consists of a Congress that is divided into two groups called houses: __________ and __________.
8. The chief executive of the United States is the __________, who, together with the Vice President, is elected to a four-year term. Under a __________ passed in 1951, a president can be elected to only __________ terms.
9. The judicial branch is headed by the __________, which is the only court specifically created by the *Constitution*.
10. All of these factors have contributed to shaping the modern __________ and __________ parties with an elephant and a donkey as their symbols.

11. In the United States, the President is not directly elected by the people but by a body established under the *Constitution* called __________. Its members are supposed to mirror the wishes of the voters in their state.

▶▶ II. Term Explanation

1. *American Constitution*

____

____

2. *Bill of Rights*

____

____

3. jurisdiction

____

____

4. Electoral College

____

____

5. Manifest Destiny

____

____

▶▶ III. True or False

1. *The Constitution of the United States* is the oldest written Constitution in the world today.
2. The Congress can not override a presidential veto of its legislation.
3. The American political system created by the *Constitutions* and the *Bill of Rights* is basically the same as it was in 1790.
4. The admittance procedure for obtaining Democratic membership is very complex and almost all the party members are loyal to the Party.
5. The United States has a direct election of the President.
6. The President may make undeclared wars for a period of 60 days without Congressional approval.
7. The Vice President's Constitutional duties are to serve as the presiding officer of the House of the Representatives.
8. The *Constitution* was immediately ratified by the US Federal Convention after its completion.

9. Interest groups represent people before the government and help educate their members.
10. Alexander Hamilton and Thomas Jefferson disagreed about almost everything in their political beliefs.

▶▶ IV. Questions for Discussion

1. Why was it necessary to change the *Articles of Confederation* and write a new Constitution?
2. What are the major powers of the three branches of the US Government? How are the three branches supposed to check and balance each other?

SUMMARY

The federal government of the United States is the central United States governmental body, established by the United States *Constitution*. Vertically, this chapter has provided a historical perspective on how American government was formed, and horizontally, it has examined the division of power in the American political system and the way in which the system actually operates.

The government of the United States is composed of three branches: Congress — the legislative branch which makes the law; the President who represents the executive branch and enforces the laws; and the system of courts or the judicial branch which explains the law. To prevent any of the three branches from being too powerful the *Constitution* implies that they are all equal but separate. If the federal government is to function smoothly, the three branches must work together harmoniously.

There is one more very important part of the American political scene which is not part of any formal written document: the political party system. Today, the United States has two major political parties: the Democratic Party and the Republican Party. The former is more liberal, while the latter is more conservative.

The distinction of the American experience, its geographic isolation, its political system, its humanitarianism, and its basic belief all have combined to frame the unique national style of American foreign policy, which featured in exceptionalism, unilateralism and expansionism.

The core issue of American politics concerns the relation of state and society, or a dichotomy of the government and the people. Most Americans have rooted beliefs that liberty and equality are the nation's founding principles and the people should have civil rights to protect themselves from any forms of governmental oppressions. Idealistic as these beliefs are, most Americans still find the conflict over the balance between the government and the people at the heart of American politics.

Chapter 4

Religion

HIGHLIGHTS

Christian — non-Christian — freedom, diversity — fundamentalist — cyber church — secularization

I. Major Groups

The role played by religious thought and practice is of great importance to a full understanding of American life. It is **paradoxical** (自相矛盾的) that America, as the most materialistic and highly industrialized nation in the world is also one of the most religious. The following statistics from a recent Gallop Poll are impressive in terms of America's religiousness: 86% of Americans say they believe in God; 44% claim they are born-again or **evangelical** (福音的) Christians; 46% attend church every week or almost every week; 63% think that religion can answer all or most of today's problems; 68% claim that they are a member of a local church.

Although the *Constitutio*n declares the separation of Church and State, religion has always pervaded American political life. During **inaugural** (就职) ceremonies, US presidents take the oath of office on the *Bibl*e. Almost all American presidents have claimed affiliation with an established church. Every session of Congress opens with a prayer. The motto of the seal of the US carries the biblical words, "Rebellion to tyrants is obedience to God." American currency bears the inscription "In God We Trust."

The fate of America has from the very beginning been closely linked to notions of religious destiny. Using *Genesis* and *Exodus* in the *Bible*, the Puritans presented themselves as God's Chosen People, searching for the Promised Land. Puritanism had begun to lose its energy by the end of the 17th century, but it passed on to subsequent American culture a sense of the importance of God's purpose for the nation.

The great diversity of ethnic backgrounds has produced religious pluralism; almost all major religions practiced around the world could be found in the US Today, the majority of Americans attend a Christian church or a non-Christian church. **Protestants** (新教徒), **Catholics** (天主教徒), and Jews can communicate within a shared cultural universe in the US.

Religion in the United States has a history of diversity, due in large part to the nation's multicultural **demographic** (人口) makeup. The largest religion in the US is Christianity, practiced by the majority of the population (nearly 76.5% in 2001).

(1) Protestants

Americans are largely protestant and belong to a few major **denominations** (教派)—Baptist, Methodist, Lutheran, Presbyterian, and Episcopalian.

(2) Roman Catholics

Roman Catholicism is by far the largest unified religious body. More than 50 million Americans are of the Roman Catholic faith, and the majority of them are descendants of immigrants from Ireland, Italy and Poland.

(3) Eastern Orthodox Churches

There are more than five million members of the Eastern Orthodox churches in the United States, mainly descendants of people who migrated from Russia, or Greece or from other parts of Orthodox Eastern Europe.

II. Distinctive Characteristics

From the very beginning as a nation, American people enjoyed complete religious freedom guaranteed by the *Constitution*. Americans are free to practice or not to practice religion, whichever they choose. This constitutional guarantee of religious freedom encouraged religious enthusiasm among the public.

1. Freedom and Toleration

It is a popular notion that each **dissenting** (意见不同的) group that came to colonial America wanted religious freedom for itself. However, few were prepared to grant religious liberty, or even toleration, to all other **sectarian** (宗教教派的) movements. Freedom and toleration were only very gradually established in the face of the rival imperialism of sectarian groups, each holding **staunchly** (坚定的) to its own cherished version of the true faith, and, in most cases, utterly impatient of dissent. Indeed, intolerance pervaded the early period of intense religious interest and

internecine (血腥的) religious competition. Aside from the early efforts of Roger Williams and other dissidents to establish toleration, there was no initial commitment to a religious freedom.

Gradually, however, religious freedom and toleration were brought about. Major factors in the rise of religious freedom and toleration include the following: there was no **cleavage** (分裂) between two or a few opposing religious groupings; there was only a fragmented diversity of numerous small sects. So, in-group solidarity was diffused and conflict could not be massive; no one religious grouping had the opportunity to seize a dominant political position; due to the circumstances of settlement, there was no prior established church common to all the colonies, and, therefore, no vested **ex-ecclesiastical** (教会的) interests in property, office, and institutional prestige; outside the solid centers of intense religious orthodoxy, there was much public indifference to organized religion in the late 19th century. Besides, expanding economic and social opportunities tended to distract men from religion; the dissenting varieties of Protestantism had the incipient principle of toleration: since the individual believer had direct access to Divine truth through the *Bible*, valid religious experience could be approached by divergent paths; settlers were needed to provide labor, to aid in military security, and to increase capital gains, and the colonies accepting immigrants of various faiths could foresee tangible economic advantages. These factors are sufficient to indicate how power considerations, economic interest, religious organization, and creeds converged to produce religious freedom in the United States.

At any rate, religious liberty, once established as an official national doctrine, reinforced the continuing forces of a pluralistic society until the broad principle had worked deeply into the whole cultural **fabric** (结构). Intolerance and conflict still occur in very substantial proportions, but they are opposed to, and not supported by, the dominant institutions.

2. Pluralism and Diversity

The American traditions of individual freedom and tolerance have accommodated a remarkable variety of religious practices and beliefs. Although about four of five Americans identify themselves as Christian, even this majority encompasses many denominations, among them Catholic, Baptist and Lutheran—some of which have further divided into subgroups even as movements like **fundamentalism** (原教旨主义) and **evangelicalism** (福音主义) transcend denominational differences. Other religions, including Judaism, Hinduism and Buddhism thrive in the United States. About 8% of Americans describe themselves as nonreligious, secular or atheist.

Most of the denominations are quite small. Religious bodies with 50,000 or more members account for more than 90% of church memberships, whereas the remaining less than 10% is scattered through more than 200 groupings. Relations between religions and denominations often are cooperative and close. On Christmas Day 2005, hundreds of Jewish and Hindu volunteers took the place of Christian workers at Washington hospitals and other nonprofit organizations, allowing the Christians to spend their holiday with family.

Given the atmosphere of religious freedom, it is not surprising that a number of denominations originated in the United States. The formation of cults and sects constitutes a fascinating and important social and cultural problem. They are more likely to arise out of rapid social change, the disturbance of value-system, and conditions of religious liberty produced by religious **heterogeneity** (多样性). Where there is marked social cleavage between classes, nationalities, or races, sects expressing the separate aspirations of contending groups or **strata** (层) tend to solidify the existing cleavages. Hence, the main denominational cleavages in the US have not been based primarily upon doctrinal religious differences, but upon political and economic bases.

Whatever reason that may have brought about denominations, what is certain is that one of the dominant aspects of American religious history is the "religious proliferativeness" of American society. The resulting mosaic of diverse religious bodies is an important and integral part of loose, experimental, pluralistic motif running through the total pattern of American culture.

3. Prospects

(1) The Fundamentalist Revival

Fundamentalism refers to a belief in, and strict adherence to, a set of basic principles. It was originally coined to describe a narrowly defined set of beliefs that developed into a movement within the Protestant community of the United States in the early part of the 20th century.

In the US, the growth in church membership has not kept pace with the growth of the general population. Some churches have actually lost members. Others, however, have gained many members. Those churches that have registered large gains tend to be smaller, less established religious groups. They are also the more conservative groups. Among them are various fundamentalists. In contrast to mainline Protestants, fundamentalists emphasize a literal interpretation of everything in the *Bible*.

The revival of fundamentalist is a reflection of the conservative trend in society. It is also a **culmination** (巅峰) of a number of factors. The social changes of the last two decades have driven many conservative people into fundamentalist churches. The highly personal style of worship in fundamentalist churches tends to attract the casualties of this fast-changing, high-tech age individuals who are socially isolated, alienated and dehumanized by modern society.

(2) The Popularity of the Cyber Church

New telecommunication technologies and general trends towards the privatization of religion would boost cyber churches as well in the 21st century—especially among professionals, baby boomers, and perhaps large segments of the elderly in the US.

Today, one can find religious news and chat groups abound on the internet. Currently, Christian denominations, especially Roman Catholics, dominate cyberspace, accounting for almost 80% of the 10 million or so websites devoted to religion. Today, according to Zaleski, the writer of *The Soul of Cyberspace*, "It takes only the click of a mouse to jump from one temple, one **mosque** (清真寺), or one church to the next."

Recently, an increasing number of religious organizations are using computer technology to spread their message via the Internet to people everywhere in the world. Pope John Paul II has termed this technological trend the "new evangelism".

1. **It is paradoxical that America, as the most materialistic and highly industrial nation in the world is also one of the most religious.**
   此句中"It is paradoxical that..."意为"自相矛盾的是……"。
2. **the separation of Church and State**：政教分离。
3. **Puritans**：清教徒。16 世纪出现于英国，该派要求以加尔文学说为依据改革英国国教会，承认《圣经》为唯一权威，反对国王和主教的专制。主张清除国教会所保留的天主教旧制度，简化仪式，提倡过勤俭清洁的生活，故此得名。后又分为长老派与独立派。在英国国内遭受迫害时期曾大量逃亡到北美建立殖民地。
4. **Protestants**：新教，基督教三大教派之一。16 世纪欧洲宗教改革后分化出来而不属于天主教的各宗派之统称。中国人则称之为基督教或耶稣教，新教一词通用于学术界。
5. **Roman Catholics**：天主教，是基督教的主要教派之一。广义的天主教是指所有正统的基督教，狭义的天主教是指罗马天主教会。多数情况下天主教都是指狭义的天主教，从而将其同东正教和新教相区别，如无特别说明，天主教都是指罗马天主教会。
6. **Eastern Orthodox Churches**：东正教，或称东方正教是基督教中的一个派别，主要是指依循由东罗马帝国（拜占庭帝国）所流传下来的基督教传统的教会。是与天主教、基督新教并立的三大派别之一。
7. **in-group solidarity**：教派内部的团结一致。
8. **religious heterogeneity**：宗教多样性。

I. Sentence Completion

1. Although the *Constitution* declares the separation of ___________, religion has always pervaded American political life.
2. During inaugural ceremonies, US presidents take the oath of office on the __________. Almost all American presidents have claimed affiliation with an established church. Every session of Congress opens with a __________.
3. __________ refers to a belief in a set of basic principles. It was originally coined to describe a narrowly defined set of beliefs that developed into a movement within the _________ community of the United States in the early part of the 20th century.
4. Whatever the reasons may be, modern American experience seems to suggest that there has appeared growing of __________ both religious beliefs and religious practices over the past century.
5. The social changes of the last two decades have driven many conservative people into __________.
6. Recently, an increasing number of religious organizations are using computer technology to spread their message via the Internet to people everywhere in the world. Pope John Paul II has termed this technological trend the __________.

II. Term Explanation

1. fundamentalism

____

____

2. religious pluralism

____

____

3. cyber church

____

____

▶▶ III. True or False

1. New telecommunication technologies and general trends towards the privatization of religion boosted cyber churches.
2. The Protestant denominations such as Methodist, Baptist, and Presbyterian are all part of the Roman Catholic Church.
3. No single church has become the center of religious life in the United States because the emphasis is on the individual, not a particular church.
4. Fundamentalism refers to a belief in, and strict adherence to, a set of basic religious principles.
5. It seems that there is no sign of secularization in terms of religious belief and religious practices over the past century in the United States.
6. Because America is the most materialistic and highly industrial nation in the world, it is also one of the least religious.
7. The great diversity of ethnic backgrounds has produced religious pluralism.
8. Although there is cultural diversity in the United States, there is no religious diversity.

▶▶ IV. Questions for Discussion

1. What are the major religious groups in the United States?
2. How has religion influenced the American society?
3. Do you think the Internet will boost religion in the United States by making the religion more accessible?

SUMMARY

From the beginning of its history, religion has played an important role in the United States. Many early colonial settlers came to America to avoid religious persecution in Europe. They wanted to practice their belief in God in their own way in the new world. To ensure this religious freedom, Americans laid down in the Constitution the separation of church and state. The government was forbidden to establish a national church and no denomination was to be favoured over the others.

Religion in the United States has a history of diversity, due in large part to the nation's multicultural demographic makeup. The largest religion in the US is Christianity, practiced by the majority of the population.

In Christian world, many countries in the West have experienced declines in religious observance and increase in secularization. On the contrary, America not only has a greater number of religious believers, but also enjoys a much higher church attendance. The majority of Americans believe in God, life after death and nine out of ten owned a *Bible*.

There is already a great deal of diversity in US religion. Yet the diversity continues to increase. We see this in a number of new religious trends, including the fundamentalist revival, the proliferation of religious branches, and the popularity of cyber church.

In conclusion, religion has permeated every aspect of American culture. It was the way that early Americans saw life. Their lives, laws, and other aspects of the culture all reflected their religious belief. Today, for Americans, religion provides a personal identity, social contacts, and important rituals; religion provides the customs and ceremonies that mark life's most important occasions. God remains an honorary citizen in the US.

Chapter 5

Economy

HIGHLIGHTS

colonial economy — new nation's economy — gilded age — economic growth in 20th century — traditional industries — service industries

From a holistic point of view, the United States has a capitalist mixed economy, which is fueled by abundant natural resources, high productivity and a well-developed infrastructure. In 232 years of development after the War of Independence, the United States has grown into a huge, integrated, industrialized and the world's largest national economic power, making up over a quarter of the world economy.

I. A Historical Overview

The United States is a highly industrialized and monopolized country. The historical development of the US economy can be traced back to the **quest** (寻求) of European settlers for economic gain in the 16th, 17th, and 18th centuries. After experiencing a marginally successful colonial economy before the 1770s, the New Nation then progressed from a small, independent farming economy to a highly complex industrial economy, and, eventually, to powerful capitalism characteristic of trust corporations or imperialism — the last stage in the capitalist development, in which process government involvement has gradually increased. This **evolution** (演变) has helped make the United States the first country in the world to enter the "post-industrial" society with the service sector contributing 79.2% of GDP. Indeed, with a per capita GDP of US$48,000 in 2008, the United States has arguably the largest and most technologically powerful economy in the world.

1. Pre-historical Economy: Colonial Era

Colonial economy was on a large scale characterized by traditional agriculture and home handicraft, though colonial prosperity resulted basically from **trapping** (捕捉) and trading in furs. People relied primarily on small farms and were self-sufficient throughout this period of time. Households produced their own daily necessities, such as cloth, candles and other domestic goods, grew crops and tobacco and processed food. In the few small cities and among the larger plantations of South Carolina, their products of tobacco, rice, and indigo were even exported for some necessities and virtually all luxuries. As the colonies grew, supportive industries emerged and developed. The fishing industry was prosperous and considered to be a source of wealth. A variety of specialized operations, such as sawmills and **gristmills** (磨坊) began to appear. Shipyards were opened to build fishing fleets and, in time, the basic merchant marine, while small iron manufacturing was also set up.

By the 18th century, regional patterns of development had become clear and stable with the New England colonies relying on shipbuilding and sailing to generate wealth, plantations in the South (particularly in Maryland, Virginia, and the Carolinas) growing crops of tobacco, rice and indigo, the middle colonies of New York, Pennsylvania, New Jersey, and Delaware shipping general crops and furs. Except for slaves, standards of living were generally high — higher, in fact, than in the dominative England itself, which prepared the North American colonies, both economically and politically, to become part of the emerging self-government movement in English politics since the time of James I (1603–1625), which led to the ultimate result of independence and the creation of a new nation.

2. The Birth of the United States: The New Nation's Economy

The year 1787 has witnessed the adoption of the *US Constitution* after the independence of 13 states in the north, which together established their nation as a unified "common" market, with no internal **tariffs** (关税) or taxes on interstate commerce. In spite of disputes, the extent of federal government's power included regulating commerce with foreign nations and among the states, fixing uniform bankruptcy laws, creating money and regulating its value, establishing post offices and roads, etc..

Alexander Hamilton, one of the nation's founding fathers took a very broad view as the first secretary of the treasury, advocating that the United States should pursue economic growth through diversified shipping, manufacturing and banking. He urged a means of economic development strategy in which the federal government would nurture infant industries by providing overt subsidies and imposing protective tariffs on imports — an essential part of American foreign policy up till today. Additionally, he also sought and achieved congressional authority, in 1791, to set up the first national bank of the United States to facilitate the flow of currency and to assume the public debts that the colonies had incurred during the Revolutionary War.

When Thomas Jefferson, who had always been opposing a strong central government, took the presidency office in 1801, he promoted an economic policy in favor of small farmers rather than wealthy and political classes, and he particularly praised small farmers as "the most valuable citizens". Jefferson, together with his successor James Madison, then turned to adopt a more decentralized and **agrarian** (代表农业利益的) democracy, as was called Jeffersonian Democracy, with the basic philosophy to protect the common man from political and economic tyranny.

3. The Gilded Age: Economic Development and Growth

Throughout the 19th century, the United States greatly grew and expanded drastically in all aspects conceivable for the development of a country with several historic movements and revolutions.

Massive westward movements, to most Americans, were not only the best depiction of the **legacy** (遗产) of individualism, but also a big boost to the economic growth. Small farmers from the South frequently moved farther west to open up vast stretches of new territory for development, and whole villages in the East sometimes uprooted and established new settlements in the more fertile farmland of the Midwest. The US federal government was actively involved in the westward expansion either in the form of land-granting or in the form of constructing roads, canals and waterways. At any rate, an internal system of transportation was ready in form, which not only opened new and huge markets, but also laid a solid base for the industrialization that followed.

The United States was quickly and thoroughly baptized by the Industrial Revolution soon after its debut in Europe in the late 18th and early 19th centuries. The invention of the **cotton gin** (轧棉机), the establishment of cotton-to-cloth textile mills in Massachusetts, and finally the application of the steam-powered manufacturing overtaking water-powered manufacturing allowed the industry to widely spread. By the time of 1860, when Abraham Lincoln was elected president, 16% of the US population lived in urban areas, and a third of the nation's income came from manufacturing. When the conflicts between the industrialized North and slavery-protective South had been upgraded to civil warfare, the industrial advantages of the North helped secure a Northern victory, which sealed the destiny of the nation and its economic system.

The rapid economic development following the Civil War laid the **groundwork** (地基，根基) for the modern US industrial economy. By 1900s, or even earlier, the United States had overtaken Britain as the world's greatest industry-dominated nation with the most powerful economy.

4. Economic Growth in the 20th Century

By the dawn of the 20th century, the United States had become increasingly industrialized and urbanized, with huge wealth and mainstream capitalism concentrated in urban areas. The crucial change came with the emergence of the trust corporations, which appeared first in the railroad industry and then elsewhere. Large corporations had centralized capital and established ownership over the means of production and the United States had entered the last stage in the development of capitalism — imperialism, though the economy still included a competitive free market sector.

Business elites who amassed vast financial empires were idealized by the general public and assumed the status of tycoons. They usually laid the success in seeing the long-range potential for a new service or product, as John D. Rockefeller did with oil, J. Pierpont Morgan banking, and Andrew Carnegie steel. Henry Ford, in 1913, introduced the continuous assembly in his automobile empire and then a better variation of the "moving assembly" line, which made possible a major saving in labor costs. However, while most people, esp. the middle class, embraced this Americanized dream and success, they sought for open competition and free market anyhow, rather than monopoly. A series of laws were passed to regulate and prevent large firms from controlling a single industry, and many of American present-day regulatory agencies, such as Federal Trade Commission, Food and Drug Administration, were created to watch over business of every kind, which helped break up the monopoly. Government involvement in the economy, a practice the previous political leaders were reluctant to do in the early years of American history, increased most significantly in the 1930s, when America was hit by the Great Depression (1929–1933). President Franklin D. Roosevelt proposed the New Deal to alleviate serious economic dislocation in the nation's history. As a result, New Deal legislation extended federal authority in all fields, notably banking, agriculture, social security and public welfare.

In the wake of World War II, **pent-up** (被压抑的) consumer demand fueled exceptionally strong economic growth in the United States. The economy jumped 56% from 1940 to 1945 in five years of wartime, and the GNP (nation's Gross National Product) rose from about $200,000 million in 1940 to $300,000 million in 1950 and to more than $500,000 million in 1960. This period of time was a golden era of American capitalism and the stimuli came from every source of economic life. The automobile industry successfully converted back to producing cars, and new industries, arising from national defense such as aviation and electronics, grew by leaps and bounds. A housing boom, stimulated in part by easily affordable mortgages for returning members of the military, added to the expansion. Coupled with the widespread ownership of cars and growing demand for single-family homes, Americans migrated from central cities to suburbs. Business patterns began to change as well. Shopping centers multiplied, the "baby boom" increased the number of consumers, and then many industries soon followed, leaving cities for less crowded sites. More and more Americans joined the middle class with the number of labors providing services growing to surpass the number producing goods, a majority of workers were employed in white-collar jobs from the 1950s and onwards, and thus the United States ushered in what Daniel Bell called "post-industrial society".

In the late 1960s it was apparent that this juggernaut of prosperity was slowing down, and it began to become visibly apparent in the early 1970s, when **stagflation** (滞胀) eventually gripped the nation. The over-production but less-competitive ability problems of farms and the poverty problems of the black and urban poor underlying the previous prosperous decade, increasing military spending on the Vietnam War, and soared federal **deficits** (赤字) and trade deficit accumulated and gradually plunged itself into a long period of economic recession till 1983. The recovery that built up steam since then was not without its problems. Up till 1990s, a new president, Bill Clinton (1993–2000), was brought into office, under whose administration the US economy turned in an increasingly healthy performance as time progressed. During this decade, GDP rose by 69% and real output increased; combined with manageable inflation and low unemployment, strong profits sent the stock market surging, known as the Dot-com Boom. In 1998, the government posted its first **surplus** (盈余) in 30 years. Americans ended the 1990s with a restored sense of confidence. By the end of 1999, the economy had grown continuously since March 1991, the longest peacetime economic expansion in history. In the meantime, the US economy was more closely intertwined with and integrated into the global economy than ever before. Facing the traditional European competitors and the newly rising Asia, American policy-makers had to weigh global economic conditions for their economy to excel.

During the first 200 years or so of the nation's existence, Americans were never forced to change their great optimism about economy and affluence, and they viewed the material wealth of the United States as an ever-expanding pie. It is, however, difficult to predict the economic future. More and more, Americans find themselves competing in a global economy, and there will continue to be cycles of upturns and downturns. But in conclusion, the US economy has shown signs of steady and sometimes vigorous growth. The United States still remains and will remain the most dynamic economy in the world.

II. Sectors of the U.S. Economy

The US economy is highly diversified. As a leading economic power in the world, the United States owns the most successful traditional industries as the most efficient agriculture, the most advanced industry and manufacturing, and it has also developed a tertiary industry or service industry unparalleled by any other country in the world. As calculated by sector, according to *The World Factbook*, agriculture has estimatively accounted for 1.2% of the national GDP in the year 2008, industry 19.6% and service 79.2%.

1. Agriculture

From the US earliest days, farming and agriculture have held an essential and significant place in the country's economy. The United States is blessed with generosity of the nature, from vast piece of land, fertile soil to a good climate all satisfactory for agriculture. In what is now the continental United States, there are more than three million square miles of land. When the European settlers first arrived, most of this land was rich, fertile farmland with abundance of trees and animals. Such undeveloped natural resources, together with the determination and hard work of American people, the United States became a wealthy nation soon after its foundation. Today, about 47% of the land area of the United States is devoted almost equally to crops and livestock.

A wide range of agricultural products in the United States include corn, wheat, soybeans, cotton, rice, tobacco, tomatoes, potatoes, peanuts, and more diversified farming are extended to diary cattle, meat of chicken, pig, turkey. Most of the important crop-growing areas in the United States are in the central plain region between the Appalachians and the Rockies. Corn tops the list as No. 1 cash crop by value of production and there is the wide Corn Belt south of the Great Lakes. The wheat-land is mostly in the prairie region and the state of Kansas leads the whole country in production volume. Cotton and tobacco are the legacy economic crops in the South. As listed earlier in this part, the high yield of American agriculture makes up 1.2% of the national GDP.

However, high farming costs (for example, tractors, fertilizers and pesticides) and low product prices have made it hard for individual and small farmers to make a profit, and thus the farm population has decreased over the years and smaller farms are vanishing. As of 2008, according to the United States Department of Agriculture statistics, approximately only 2% to 3% of the population is directly employed in agriculture. However, this does not mean any less efficiency. As a matter of fact, agricultural reforms and innovations have always been the theme in history as accompanied by any industrial progress ever since the Industrial Revolution. The readiness of farmers to adopt new tools, skills and technologies has been one of the ever-lasting strengths of American agriculture. Computers are but the latest in a long time innovations that have helped agriculture to cut costs and improve productivity.

Since agriculture in the United States is highly mechanized and widely operated on a large scale, both farming and stock-raising have developed into an industry. The modern US agriculture is, by any standard, big business, or "agribusiness" as is often referred to. The coinage of this term is factually to reflect the large-scale nature of agricultural enterprises of present-day US economy. As such, agribusiness is the entire complex of farm-related businesses, compromising individual farm producers, farming cooperatives, rural banks, shoppers of farm products, commodity dealers, firms that manufacture farm equipment, food processors, grocery chains and many other businesses. In many ways, this agribusiness vividly depicts changes in the US agriculture in the second half of 20th century.

2. Industry and Manufacturing

From a historical perspective, the Industrial Revolution has brought about the birth of modern US industry; by 1870s, the total value of industrial products in the United States had, for the first time and ever since, surpassed that of its agricultural products; and the 20th century has seen the rise and decline of a succession of industries.

Modern economists generally apply the term "the secondary sector of the economy" to refer to industry in traditional sense. This sector takes the output of the primary sector (agriculture and fishing) and creates a finished, usable product: manufacturing and construction. Manufacturing has always been the wealth-producing industry in the US economy, and the main and important sectors are transportation, automobiles, aircrafts, munitions, iron and steel, coal mining, petroleum, natural gas, machinery, telecommunications, electronic and electric equipment, high-tech hardware, chemicals, textile and consumer goods.

The US industrial and manufacturing heartland is the Northeast region, which lies to the north of the Ohio River and the Potomac River and to the east of the Mississippi River. With 95% of the nation's iron and steel and machine making industries, it is the oldest and key industrial region in the United States. Other main industries include ship building, coal mining, textile, and chemicals. Many industrial big cities such as New York, Philadelphia, Boston, Detroit, Pittsburgh, Baltimore and Chicago are located in the region. But other industrial regions have grown in the Southwest (California) and Northwest with high-tech industry, aircraft manufacture and oil refinery concentrated heavily in big cities as Los Angeles and San Francisco. The West is at present the most rapidly growing section of the country.

Though not the cradle, the United States can be regarded as the most profound and thorough beneficiary of the two Industrial Revolutions, which have helped make it the leading industrial power in the world. During the first 200 years of the existence of America, industry has always been an important activity to promote economic growth and development, which, in turn, brought unconceivable material wealth and abundance, high standard of living — the key to realize American Dream.

3. Service Industry

Service industry (alternatively called tertiary industry) is one of the three economic sectors and often defined by exclusion of the two previous sectors. As is indicated by the term, service industry does not produce any form of tangible goods, such as corns or automobiles. Instead, it provide services like transportation, distribution and sale of goods from producer to a consumer, tourism, entertainments, insurance, accounting, etc.. Goods may be transformed in the process of providing a service, as happens in the retailing or restaurant; however, the focus is on people interacting with people and serving the customer rather than transforming physical goods.

Over time, the service industry has gradually developed in the rapid expansion of primary and second industries; particularly since 1950s, the US economy has become increasingly involved in the provision of intangible services; the next five decades have witnessed the service industries growing much faster than other sectors; and up till 2008, when they has taken up 70.2% of the US GDP, the service industry could and should be considered as the indisputable pillar of the US economy.

Service industries vary in size from small firms to large corporations. Some, particularly in Northeast regions, have developed into nationwide chains. Presently, the service sector absorbs over 75% of the labor forces for America, a good many of which are freed or laid-off by rising productivity in agriculture and second sector, notably manufacturing. The significant role service industries are playing in the US economy can be shown by the following statistics: in the 1980s alone, the service-providing sector had a net increase of 20 million jobs, which exceeded the net 19 million increases in the holistic economy; the two industries adding the most jobs were business service and health care, and 27% of the net employment gain in 1980s was in these two sectors.

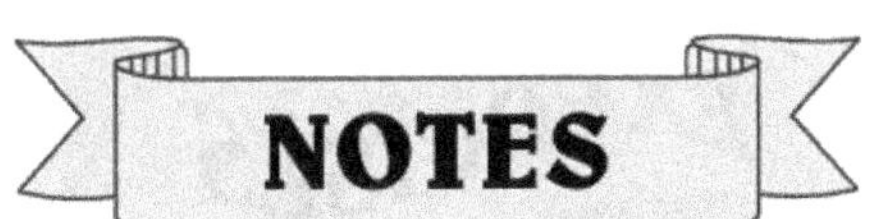

1. **result from**：由……产生。
2. **except for**：除……以外。
3. **debut**：初次登场，开张。

   debut 可作为动词广泛使用，例如：

   Her new series will debut next March on network television.

   此用法在与娱乐和表演艺术相关时，已被认可；但被用作其他种类的介绍时没有被完全接受，如对产品、出版物的介绍。又可用作名词，表示首次在公众面前露面、一件事的开端之意，例如：the debut of a new foreign policy。
4. **When the conflicts between the industrialized North and slavery-protective South had been upgraded to civil warfare…**

   此句中修饰北方、南方的定语形容词 industrialized 和 slavery-protective 分别表示当时二者的经济发展状况，可理解为：

   (At that time) the North was more developed in industry while the South still protected slavery; and when the conflicts between them had been upgraded to civil warfare…
5. **GDP**：Gross Domestic Product 国内生产总值。
6. **GNP**：Gross National Product 国民生产总值。
7. **New Deal**：新政，指 20 世纪 30 年代美国总统富兰克林·罗斯福颁布实行的一系列旨在挽救美国经济、改革社会的政策纲领的名称。
8. **stagflation**：滞胀，指同时存在高通货膨胀率、高失业率和经济停滞的萧条经济形势。

I. True or False

1. The main characteristic of colonial economy is the trapping and trading in furs.
2. The first bank was built up in 1791 to facilitate the flow of currency and to assume the public debts that the colonies had incurred during the Revolutionary War.
3. The United States had not achieved its top economic position in the world until the 20th century.
4. Monopoly was the idealized economic situation in America in the 20th century to guarantee the businessmen's utmost benefits.
5. The region between Appalachians and the Rockies ranks as the most important crop-growing areas in America.
6. As farm population has decreased in recent years, the agricultural efficiency is sharply reduced.
7. The Northeast region of America is the only industrial region, with New York, Philadelphia, Boston, and Detroit as the examples.
8. Most people in America now are working in the service industry.

II. Short Answer Questions

1. Why is Alexander Hamilton assumed as one of the nation's founding fathers?

____

____

2. What was Jeffersonian democracy?

____

____

3. What was the function of the internal system of transportation?

____

____

4. What does GNP stand for?

____

____

5. What made the economic recession of America in the 1970s?

____

____

6. Why has the farm population decreased over the years?

____

____

7. What does "secondary sector of the economy" refer to?

____

____

SUMMARY

In 232 years of development after the War of Independence, the United States has grown into a huge, integrated, industrialized and the world's largest national economic power. Despite the unavoidable cycles of upturns and downturns, the US economy has shown signs of steady and sometimes vigorous growth. After a marginally successful colonial economy characterized by traditional agriculture, farming and home handicraft, the 13 independent states in the north established their nation as a unified "common" market and sought a series of measures and government policies to develop farming economy and nurture infant industries. Throughout the 19th century, the United States grew and expanded drastically in all aspects conceivable for the development of a country with several historic events such as Westward Movements, Industrial Revolution and Civil War. The industrial advantages of the North helped secure a Northern victory, which laid the groundwork for the modern US industrial economy. By 1900s, the United States had overtaken Britain as the world's greatest industry-dominated nation with the most powerful economy.

The 20th century has witnessed great fluctuations in the US economic development; with increasing industrialization and urbanization, and the emergence of trust corporations in the first two decades, the United States has entered the last stage in the development of capitalism — imperialism; the post-war prosperity has boosted every economic indicator to jump and thus has become a golden era of American capitalism; having recovered from the terrible stagflation of 1970s, Americans ended the 1990s with the longest peacetime economic expansion in history and a restored sense of confidence. Nowadays, the United States find itself more closely intertwined with and integrated into the global economy than ever before and American policy-makers had to weigh global economic conditions for their economy to excel. The US economy, as calculated by sector, is highly diversified in the sense that it owns the most successful traditional industries of efficient agriculture and advanced manufacturing, and the most developed service industries unparalleled by any other country in the world. Though there will continue to be cycles of rises and setbacks in capitalism, the United States still remains and will remain one leading economic power in the world.

Chapter 6

Education

HIGHLIGHTS

compulsory education — post-secondary education — public school system — private school system — charter schools — school vouchers

From the beginning, when Americans established their basic system of public schools in 1825, they have shown most attention and concern for education. Over the next one century and three quarters, either through federal or state **legislations** (立法), education in the United States developed considerably both in size and kind, which has helped make it among the nations with the world's most advanced and prestigious education. According to *The World Factbook*, in the year 2000, there are more than 54 million students attending compulsory education and about 17 million are enrolled in over 5,000 higher institutions. Nowadays, the country has a basic reading **literacy** (读写能力) rate at approximately 99%.

The current educational systems in the United States are based upon one ideal **premise** (前提) of equality of opportunity. At any rate, from elementary through college, Americans hold the belief that everyone deserves an equal and fair opportunity to obtain a good education.

I. Primary and Secondary Education

1. The Educational Ladder

American public school system can be viewed as an educational ladder, ranging from primary (often known inside the United States as the elementary schools) to secondary (high schools) and finally higher levels (college undergraduate and graduate programs) of educations.

School participation is **mandatory** (必要的，必须履行的) and almost universal at primary and secondary levels, which are thus often referred to as "compulsory education". The requirements of primary and secondary levels can generally be satisfied by attending public schools, state certified private schools, or an approved home school program. *United States Census* (2000) has shown that approximately 1.7% of parents chose to educate their own children at home.

For the educational ladder, the starting age is, generally speaking, five years old and ending at 16 to 18, but can vary slightly from state to state. Most American children begin school by kindergartens today, though kindergartens did not become common until after the 20th century. Then usually there are six years of elementary school, two years of junior high school (alternatively called junior middle school) and four years of senior high school. School systems may divide these twelve years up differently, like variants of 6-3-3 or 5-3-4, but all do guarantee twelve years of compulsory education.

2. Primary Education

Children in the proper age range are supposed, or obligated by law, to participate in elementary schools to receive primary level of education. The elementary school generally covers kindergarten through fifth grade, and sometimes, the first eight grades or up to fourth grade or sixth grade, where basic subjects are taught. The whole set of curricula, as a unique practice in the United States, is determined by individual school districts at the local instead of state or federal level (as will be explained in the later part of this chapter). Local school districts have the law-endowed responsibilities to select curriculum guides, textbooks, content of study and whatever they consider as best for their students for a given grade. It then has become an unavoidable fact that school systems vary widely not only in the way curricular decisions are made but also in how teaching and learning take place. In general, elementary students learn basic arithmetic, and sometimes rudimentary algebra in mathematics, English proficiency, such as basic grammar, spelling, and vocabulary, and fundamentals of other subjects. A typical classroom usually includes 20 to 30 students in public schools and teachers typically instruct according to students' diverse learning needs. Overall, the developments of students' social studies, science and other content areas have received prior attention.

Former President Bush Signing the *No Child Left Behind Act* at Hamilton H. S.

In view of various curricula, teaching and learning provisions required by individual school boards and different school districts, the Congress passed a new federal legislation of *No Child Left Behind Act* (NCLB) to **mandate** (命令，要求) *Adequate Yearly Progress* (AYP), which helped, to some extent, set some national learning standards. Having enacted the theories of standards-based education reform, NCLB was proposed by former President George W. Bush's on January 23, 2001, immediately after taking office. The law promoted an annual state-wide standardized test to all students, an *Adequate Yearly Progress* (AYP) made by schools to monitor students' academic achievements, and additionally an increased focus on reading and reauthorized the *Elementary and Secondary Education Act* (ESEA) of 1965, aiming to improve the performance of US primary and secondary schools by increasing the standards of accountability for states, school districts and schools, as well as providing parents more flexibility in choosing which schools their children will attend. Essentially, NCLB does not assert a national achievement standard, but requires individual states to develop assessments in basic skills to be given to all students in certain grades, if those states are to receive federal funding for schools. Over the time of this law, Congress increased federal funding of education, of which NCLB received a 40.4% increase from \$17.4 billion in 2001 to \$24.4 billion in 2007, especially the funding for reading which quadrupled from \$286 million to \$1.2 billion.

3. Secondary Education

Junior high school is an intermediate for primary level students to adjust to the environment of the secondary or high school level. Usually, the junior grades range from seventh to eighth, and sometimes from sixth or ninth, and even ninth grade only in some school districts. Starting from the ninth grade, grades become part of a student's official **transcript** (成绩单), basically reflective of his educational development including several factors such as academic studies and attendance records. So those who plan to apply for college or employment in the future are supposed to take responsibility for their own education ever since.

Generally, at the high school level, American students are allowed more independence as choosing their own classes from a broad variety of courses without special emphasis on any particular subject. Though varying widely among school districts or even individual schools for different financial, environmental and instructional capacities, the curricula are basically **two-fold** (两部分的, 双重的): one being compulsory programs of sciences (normally biology, chemistry and physics), maths, English, social sciences (various courses of history, government, economics, etc.), and probably a "health" course in which students learn about anatomy, nutrition, first aid, sexuality, birth control, anti-drug use and so on; the other being a wide variety of electives commonly as:

- Visual (drawing, sculpture, painting, photography, film)
- Performing arts (drama, band, chorus, orchestra, dance)
- Technology education (woodworking, metalworking, automobile repair, robotics)
- Computers (word processing, programming, graphic design)
- Athletics (football, baseball, basketball, soccer, track and field, cross country running,

swimming, tennis, gymnastics, water polo, wrestling, cheerleading, volleyball, lacrosse, ice hockey, field hockey, boxing, skiing, snowboarding)

- Publishing (journalism, student newspaper, yearbook, literary magazine)
- Foreign Languages (Spanish, French are common; Latin, Greek, German, Italian, Arabic, Chinese, and Japanese are less common)
- Junior Reserve Officers' Training Corps

What is likely to differentiate American secondary school system from the rest of the world is that many high schools provide Advanced Placement (AP) or International Baccalaureate (IB) courses. Generally speaking, these advanced courses, often intended for the 11th or 12th graders, are special forms of honor classes where the curriculum is more challenging and lessons more aggressively paced than standard courses, even to the degree equivalent of the first year of college courses. Most post-secondary institutions take AP or IB exam results into consideration in the admissions process, or may grant unit credit which enables students to graduate early. Here we will take the AP program as an instance to elaborate. The AP program is one that offers college level courses at high schools across the United States. The history of AP program goes back to 1952 when three prep schools — the Lawrenceville School, Phillips Academy and Phillips Exeter Academy — and three universities — Harvard University, Princeton University and Yale University, under the Ford Foundation, together issued the report *General Education in School and College: A Committee Report* to recommend allowing high school seniors to study college level material and to take achievement exams that allowed them to attain college credit for this work. The College Board, a non-profit organization based in New York City, has run the AP program since 1955, whose functions have been to develop and maintain guidelines for the teaching of Sparta level courses in various subject areas, to run AP examinations, and to support teachers of AP courses. In 2006, over one million students took over two million AP tests, and the scores are used by some colleges to exempt students from introductory coursework if they demonstrate mastery through an AP test. In some high schools with an exam exemption policy, an AP exam can also be taken in place of the school's final exam, in which case student was given the final quarter or semester grade without participating the school's exam.

II. Post-secondary Education

After high school, the majority of students go on to get post-secondary education, better known as college or university education in the United States, which refers to a variety of institutions of higher education, including public universities, private universities, liberal arts colleges, and **community colleges** (社区学院). According to the United Nations Educational,

Scientific, and Cultural Organization (UNESCO) statistics, the United States now has the second largest number of higher education institutions in the world, with a total of 5,758, an average of more than 115 per state. In spite of the sky-rocketing costs in recent years, the percentage of Americans seeking a college education never stops to grow. In 1900, about less than 10% of college-age Americans entered post-secondary institutions; while the 2006 American Community Survey conducted by the United States Census Bureau (USCB) found that 52.6% of the population had attended some college, among which 27.2% earned a bachelor's degree, and 9.9% earned a graduate or professional degree. Altogether, there are more than 17 million students attending or having attended college.

1. Post-secondary Educational System

The American university system is similar to the primary and secondary levels in the sense that it possesses a high degree of autonomy as is often called "decentralized", in large part because the *Tenth Amendment to the United States Constitution* reserves all powers not granted to the federal government or explicitly denied to the US states "for the States respectively, or to the people." What differentiates is that all American tertiary institutions, even public schools, charge **tuitions** (学费) and fees, and are characterized by high competitiveness and selectiveness. Such system, under which academic excellence is promoted by strong funding and volumes of researches, has been imitated internationally and most sought after by overseas students. According to Webometrics Ranking of World Universities, as measured by awards and research output, 103 of the world top 200 institutions are in the United States.

Community colleges are often open admissions, with low tuition. Two years of study at community colleges usually offers students with an associate degree, and some of these associate degrees are in **vocational** (职业的，行业的) or technical fields. Four-year colleges, or undergraduate studies, usually offer a greater range of studies and have a larger number of students who will afterwards receive a bachelor's degree, such as the B.A. (Bachelor of Arts) or B.S. (Bachelor of Science). This is generally what it means when Americans refer to a "college diploma". Like high school, the four undergraduate grades are commonly called freshman, sophomore, junior, and senior years. There is also the possibility for students to transfer to a 4-year institution for a bachelor's degree after having earned an associate's degree at a 2-year college.

The bachelor's degree can be followed by graduate studies which lead to master's and doctoral degrees in universities. Generally, people in the United States use the word "college" to refer to a small school that does not offer graduate degrees or to a 2-year community college; while universities, in the strict sense, are research-oriented institutions providing both undergraduate and graduate education. The Carnegie Classification of Institutions of Higher Education distinguishes among institutions on the basis of the prevalence of degrees they grant and considers the granting of master's degrees necessary, though not sufficient, for an institution to be classified as a university. A variety of graduate programs grant diversified master's degrees, such as the M.A. (Master of Arts), M.S. (Master of Science), M.B.A. (Master of Business Administration), or M.F.A. (Master of Fine Arts), while the doctorate is often the Ph.D. (Doctor of Philosophy). In addition, some universities provide professional studies for those who have earned a bachelor's degree or at least three years of undergraduate schooling depending on the program. Degrees will be awarded in such professions as law, medicine, dentistry, journalism and business, and graduates with this kind of degrees are to be practitioners instead of academic scholars or researchers.

2. Admission Policies

Though admission policies vary from one university to the next, most determine admission based on several factors such as the rigor and grades earned in high school courses taken, class ranking, student's GPA and SAT scores. Most colleges also consider more subjective factors such as a commitment to extracurricular activities, a personal essay, and possibly an interview. GPA is Grade Point Average, a quantitative figure representing a student's accumulated grades, which assign points to each letter grades: A = 4 points, B = 3 points, C = 2 points, D = 1 point, and E = 0 point. Scholastic Aptitude Test (SAT) is one standardized examination taken by high school students throughout the nation and each university decides the minimum SAT score to accept. While numerical factors rarely ever are absolute required values, each college usually has a rough threshold below which admission is unlikely. Some students, rather than being rejected, will be "wait-listed" for a particular college or university and may be admitted if another student who was previously admitted decides to give up the opportunity.

Ivy Covering West College, Princeton University

3. The Ivy League

Ivy League is usually used to refer to a group of eight private institutions (Brown, Columbia, Cornell, Dartmouth, Harvard, Pennsylvania, Princeton, and Yale) of higher education in the Northeastern United States with connotations of academic excellence, selectivity in admissions, and social elitism. The name is derived from the ivy plants, symbolic of their ages, which cover many of these institutions' historic buildings. Over the years these eight universities have had common interests in scholarship as well as in athletics.

The coinage of the phrase was traced back to the early 1930s when undergraduate newspapers of these universities simultaneously ran an editorial advocating the formation of an "Ivy League". The first move toward this end, however, was not taken until 1945; and in that year, the eight presidents entered into the first *Ivy Group Agreement* "for the purpose of reaffirming their intention of continuing intercollegiate football in such a way as to maintain the values of the game, while keeping it in fitting proportion to the main purposes of academic life". To achieve this objective two inter-university committees were appointed: one, made up primarily of the college deans, was to administer rules of eligibility; the other, composed of the athletic directors, was to establish policies on the length of the playing season and of preseason practice, operating budgets, and related matters. The term became official, especially in sports terminology, after the formation of the National Collegiate Athletic Association (NCAA) Division I athletic conference in 1954, where the presidents extended the Ivy Group Agreement to all intercollegiate sports; and much of the nation polarized around favorite college teams since then. Nowadays, the use of the phrase is no longer limited to athletics, and now represents an educational philosophy inherent to the nation's oldest schools.

Institution	Year Founded	Location	Athletic Nickname	Motto
Harvard University	1636 as New College	Cambridge, Massachusetts	Crimson	Veritas (Truth)
Yale University	1701 as Collegiate School	New Haven, Connecticut	Bulldogs	Lux et veritas (Light and truth)
University of Pennsylvania	1740	Philadelphia, Pennsylvania	Quakers	Leges sine moribus vanae (Laws without morals are useless.)
Princeton University	1746 as College of New Jersey	Princeton, New Jersey	Tigers	Dei sub numine viget (Under God's power she flourishes.)
Columbia University	1754 as King's College	New York City, New York	Lions	In lumine Tuo videbimus lumen (In thy light shall we see the light.)
Brown University	1764 as College of Rhode Island	Providence, Rhode Island	Bears	In Deo speramus (In God we hope.)
Cornell University	1865	Ithaca, New York	Big Red	I would found an institution where any person can find instruction in any study.
Dartmouth College	1769	Hanover, New Hampshire	Big Green	Vox clamantis in deserto (A voice crying in the wilderness.)

Seven of the eight Ivy League schools were founded during America's colonial period, thus even older than the American Revolution; the exception is Cornell, which was founded in 1865 just after the American Civil War. Ivy League institutions, therefore, account for seven of the nine "colonial colleges" chartered before the American Revolution, and it was these seven that provided the overwhelming majority of the higher education in the Northern and Middle Colonies. Ivy League colleges have always been holding an outstanding and iconic status which is related to their stellar academic reputations, and they all place near the top in the *US News & World Report College and University Rankings*. Moreover, "Harvard-Yale-Princeton" (or sometimes the initialism *HYP*) are, regardless whichever ranking system is used, considered to be the Big Three, as American sociologist E. Digby Baltzell writes, "the three major upper-class institutions in America have been Harvard, Yale, and Princeton."

The Ivy League institutions are privately owned and controlled, though some of them, like Cornell University, receive funding in the form of research grants from federal and state governments. In terms of financial endowment, Ivy League universities rank within the top one percent of the world's academic institutions, with Harvard's US$ 28.8 billion being the largest financial endowment of any academic institution in the world. The Ivy League schools are also highly selective, with acceptance rates ranging from about 7% to 20% from an application pool that consists of the top high school students in the country. Undergraduate enrollments among the Ivy League schools range from about 4,000 to 14,000, making them larger than those of a typical private liberal arts college and smaller than a typical public state university. Take Yale as an example, for the Class of 2012, Yale accepted 1,892 students out of the 22,813 total early and regular applicants, hitting a University record — low acceptance rate at 8.3%; for the Class of 2013, Yale has reported receiving 25,925 applications, and anticipates — an overall acceptance rate between 7.3% and 7.7%.

The phrase Ivy League historically has been perceived as connected not only with academic reputation and selective admission, but also with social elitism. Since establishment, Ivy League has or had an identifiable "protestant tone" in terms of religious affiliation, and was specifically associated with the WASP (White Anglo-Saxon Protestant). One is considered a WASP by virtue of being upper-class descendants of early Catholic settlers, overwhelming Anglican English aristocrats, high ranking peers with histories in the upper class Northeastern establishment, or people with powerful and respected social status for hereditary wealth or political influence. Some writers in the 20th century actually warned about "Ivy League Snobbery" and class discrimination, such as "We Ivy Leaguers (read: mostly white and Anglo) know that an Ivy League degree is a mark of the kind of person who is likely to succeed..."

We drew recruits from Harvard, Yale, Princeton, and many another college; from clubs like the Somerset, of Boston, and Knickerbocker, of New York; and from among the men who belonged neither to club nor to college, but in whose veins the blood stirred with the same impulse which once sent the Vikings over sea.

—Theodore Roosevelt (1899)

Ivy League institutions are widely regarded as the leading and most prestigious universities in the world also in the sense that they have produced many renowned alumni and faculty. Political leaders John Adams, Theodore Roosevelt, Franklin Roosevelt, John F. Kennedy, and Barack Obama; philosopher Henry D. Thoreau and author Ralph W. Emerson; poets T. S. Eliot and E. E. Cummings; computer tycoon but college dropout Bill Gates are among the best-known figures in Harvard, and 75 Nobel Prize winners are affiliated with the university. All the US presidents between 1989 and 2008 were Yale graduates, namely George H. W. Bush, Bill Clinton (who attended Yale Law School along with his wife, Hillary Clinton, United States Secretary of State in the present administration), and George W. Bush; there is also a long list of Yale University people, including Nobel Laureates, Pulitzer Prize winners, statesmen, Supreme Court justices, senators and governors, artists, athletes, activists, and numerous others. Princeton University has been and is home to a renowned group of scholars, scientists, writers, chief justices, and statesmen, including two presidents, James Madison and Woodrow Wilson, Chief Justice Oliver Ellsworth, and additionally, the First Lady Michelle Obama.

Ⅲ. Public and Private School Systems

Different from most other industrialized countries, there is no centralized educational system or uniform curriculum requirement on the national scale in the United States, which has left K-12 students in most areas with the choices between free tax-funded public schools and privately-financed private schools.

1. Public School System

Public education is provided by government, with control and funding coming from three levels: federal, state and local. The federal government does not operate public schools, but is playing three major roles: (1) legislating compulsory schooling, (2) financing schooling, (3) administering schools. Individual state governments usually hold the responsibility to make educational standards, materials and standardized testing decisions, while local communities form school districts, usually with independent officials and **budgets** (预算) separate from other local **jurisdiction** (权限), to meet the state's dictates. In this case, school boards of education are locally elected, whose functions are to select school guidelines, curricula, funding and other school policies that are reflective of the state's learning standards and benchmarks in primary and secondary levels.

All public school systems are required to provide an education free of charge to everyone of school age in their districts. Admission to individual public schools is usually based on residency. Since local property taxes have been a primary and major means to finance public schools, they vary significantly from one district to another in the quality, resources, class size and other conditions they have available for students. Geography is one crucial factor and schools in more affluent districts with middle class or wealthier families which have more tax money to spend on education, generally speaking, are more highly regarded. The largest public school system in the United States is in New York City, where more than one million students are taught in 1,200 separate public schools. Such immense size makes New York City public school system nationally influential in determining standards and materials, such as textbooks.

Ever since the creation of public school systems, those who are in favor of public schools believe that they reaffirm the value of equality by being open to all classes and by financing with tax money collected from all citizens. Public institutions fulfill the fundamental human right to be educated in the same "common school" regardless of race, ethnics, class and gender differences, which would in turn help reduce socio-cultural and class distinctions in the United States. However, public schools are by no means immune from criticism. Many claim that current system leads to quality differences based on geography, which is not fair to all students; and problems, such as lack of social mobility, poor academic achievements, ineffective teaching methodology, financial mismanagement and inability to meet the changing demands of students and parents, need to be responded and reformed.

2. Private School System

However, while the great majority of children choose public schools, several others select to attend private schools. In the year 2000, 5.2 million (about 10.4%) of those enrolled in compulsory education were participating **parochial** (教区的) or **nonsectarian** (无宗派的) private schools. As opposed to public school systems, the term "private school" in the United States can be applied to any school for which the facilities and funding are not provided by the federal, state, or local government.

A vast number of private schools, for historical reasons, are parochial schools that are affiliated with religious denominations and receive financial support from them, though parents must also pay tuition, and their major function is to provide religious instructions which public school programs never do. There are also a small minority for-profit prestigious independent institutions, or elite private schools as is often called, to serve mainly children from upper class. Despite the enormous tuition costs, the wealthy parents would like to choose elite private schools for their children so that they will, on one hand, get excellent education, while more importantly to associate with other upper-class children and maintain their upper-class position as held by their parents.

Unlike public school systems, private schools are generally funded through student tuitions, **endowments** (捐赠, 捐款), donations and grants from religious organizations or private individuals. Thus admission to these private schools is highly selective, and they have no legal obligation to accept any interested student. School guides, curricular decisions, content of study programs and other school policies within private schools are made differently than in public schools either, so long as they follow the state's educational standards and regulations. As a matter of fact, private schools offer the advantages of high quality programs, smaller class sizes, a higher teacher-student ratio across the school day, greater individualized attention and in the more competitive schools, expert college placement services, in an attempt to provide a level of education equal to or better than that available in public schools.

Private schooling in the United States has been debated by educators, lawmakers, and parents all through the history of education. Despite the fact that there are potential conflicts between the **elites'** (精英) concept and American ideal of equality of opportunity, United States Supreme Court precedent appears to allow educational choice with some of the most relevant Supreme Court case law on private schools' issues such as Runyon v. McCrary, 427 US 160 (1976); Wisconsin v. Yoder, 406 US 205 (1972); Pierce v. Society of Sisters, 268 US 510 (1925); Meyer v. Nebraska, 262 US 390 (1923). What is most important is the fact that public institutions as mainstream education systems do not and will not be replaced.

3. School Movements and Reforms

In response to the criticism toward the current school systems and educational legislations, efforts have been made by all sources, federal and state governments, school districts and parents, to improve public schools, which aroused a series of movements and reforms. Two of these movements, charter schools and school vouchers, stand out so far as effective and wide-spread common practice.

By definition, charter schools in the United States are elementary or secondary schools that receive public money but have been freed from some of the rules, regulations, and statutes that apply to other public schools in exchange for some type of accountability for producing certain results, which are set forth in each school's charter. Charter schools, technically speaking, are independent public schools free from tuition, but in many respects operate similarly to non-religious private schools. Considerable autonomy can be guaranteed for charter schools, which enable them to provide a curriculum that specializes in a certain field or simply to seek a better and more efficient general education than traditional public schools. Charter schools can be founded by teachers, parents, community members, or activists who feel restricted by traditional public schools. Current laws allow charter schools to be authorized by multiple charter-granting agencies, and then allocate a level of funding consistent with the statewide per pupil average. There are both non-profit charter schools, as is often established by non-profit groups, universities, and some government entities (but not affiliated with local school districts), and for-profit ones. Three basic values of charter schools, namely opportunity, choice, and responsibility for results, have promoted great popularity across the United States in the past decade. With more than 40 states participating in this reform effort and a significant number of schools established, charter schools have become one of the fastest growing innovations in American educational policy.

Currently, at least in most of the states, parents who pay for private schooling are still charged taxes used to fund public schools. Some have argued that since their child attends a private school, they should be able to take that part of tax the public school no longer needs and apply the money to private school tuition in the form of vouchers; this is the basis of the school choice movement. School vouchers, or education vouchers, are a certificate issued by the government by which parents can pay for the education of their children at a school of their choice, rather than the public school to which they are assigned. By nature, this voucher program redirects the flow of education funding by channeling it directly to individuals rather than to local school districts. Ever since the Nobel Prize winning economist Milton Friedman proposed a voucher system to improve American government educational system, the city of Washington D.C. and three of the 50 states — Florida, Ohio and Wisconsin are experimenting voucher systems at a state level, and private voucher programs are, on a comparatively larger scale, commonly seen. Of course, the voucher system has its advocates on the ground that parental choice for a better education for their children in the middle-class and wealthy families can be fulfilled, and that voucher systems will promote free market competition among schools of all types and, in turn, will promote high quality education for all children. However, strong criticisms arise extensively from low-income minority families to public school teacher unions, from school boards to economist critics. School vouchers have since been introduced but are controversial as they reflect political and ideological splits as well as the role of unions in education. It remains to be seen how far this voucher system can go and whatever new direction the US education reform is going to take. What is for sure, however, is that these measures, however extensive or bold, have had, as is widely agreed, negligible effects on the quality of the US school systems.

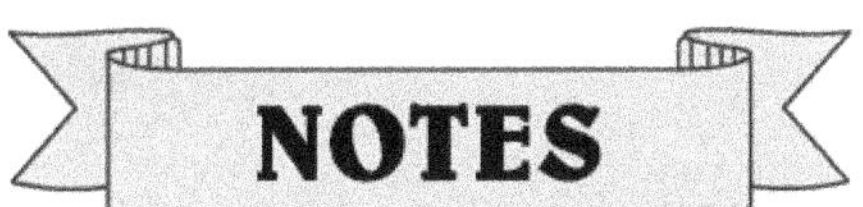

1. **be enrolled in**：入学；入伍。
2. **be affiliated with**：与……有关系；隶属。
3. **school district**：学区。
4. **school board**：学校董事会。
5. **Junior Reserve Officers' Training Corps (JROTC)**：初级预备役军官训练团，是一个由美国武装部队资助、在全美中学开展的青少年军事培训计划。该计划是美国国会于 1916 年通过的《国防法》的一部分，授权军队在公立学校中培养预备役人才。《美国法典》阐释该计划的目的是向美国中学生灌输"公民权、为国家服役、个人的责任感和成就感"等价值观念。
6. **K-12 students**：读作"kay twelve"或者"kay through twelve"。这一表达方法是从幼儿园（Kindergarten）到第 12 年级（12th grade）的缩写，一般认为是美国、加拿大等国教育系统中义务教育的第一年和最后一年，因此该句使用这一表达方法指代初等教育和中等教育的总称。
7. **Charter Schools**：政府特许学校。
8. **School Vouchers**：美国教育学券制，又称持券择校制度。

I. True or False

1. It is the National Education Ministry who has the law-endowed responsibilities to select curriculum guides, textbooks, content of study and whatever they consider as best for their students for a given grade.
2. Attendance means nothing in American education.
3. American high school students have both compulsory courses and elective courses as well.
4. A college simply means a small school that does not offer graduate degrees or a 2-year community college.
5. The federal government provides funding not only for public schools, but for private schools as well.
6. School guides, curricular decisions, content of study programs and other policies are the same in public schools and private schools.
7. Federal government is said to provide funds for public schools, but in fact that is from the taxes people in the state pay.

II. Short Answer Questions

1. What is *No Child Left Behind Act* for?

____

____

2. Why do the junior grades differ from state to state?

____

____

3. How do American universities select their students?

____

____

4. What do “GPA” and “SAT” stand for respectively?

____

____

5. What is the difference between charter schools and school vouchers?

____

____

SUMMARY

The United States, in terms of education and development, is among the world's most advanced and prestigious nations, with a basic reading literacy rate at approximately 99%. The US educational systems are based upon one ideal premise of an equal and fair opportunity open to all classes and races. There is no centralized educational system or uniform curriculum requirement on the national scale in the United States; rather, it is one highly "decentralized" and characteristic of considerable autonomy at state and local level.

Americans view their public school system as an educational ladder, ranging from primary to secondary (compulsory at these stages) and finally higher levels of educations; they are free to choose between free tax-funded public schools and privately-financed private schools. The federal government plays major roles in legislating compulsory schooling, financing schooling and administering public school system. Individual states generally hold the responsibility to operate public schools and set educational standards; while local school districts and school boards function to select curricular, teaching and learning styles and other school policies.

Private schools refer to any school for which the facilities and funding are not provided by the federal, state, or local government, but through student tuition, endowments, donations and grants from religious organizations or private individuals. Private schools are either parochial with major functions to provide religious instructions or elite private schools to serve mainly the children from upper class. Offering advantages like high quality programs, smaller class sizes and greater individualized attention, private schools provide a level of education equal to or better than that available in public schools. In recent years, charter schools and school vouchers are reformational efforts made by all sources concerned to improve public schools, increase school choices and availability, and innovate American educational policies.

Chapter 7

Social Life and Customs

HIGHLIGHTS

family life — food and dining customs — tourism — recreation — social manners — holidays

I. American Family

Families exist in virtually all societies of which we have record, in the past as well as at present. And families, like all other human institutions, are changing over time. The American family is no exception.

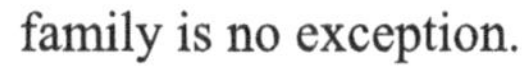

America is a country that has more immigrants than any other country in the world. Different peoples came to America from different nations and places at different times. It is estimated that of the 300 million people, more than 16% were born in other countries or are the children of at least one foreign-born parent. They have different social customs and personal habits.

1. Family Structures

What is the typical American family like? If Americans are asked to name the members of their families, family structure becomes clear. Married American adults will name their husband or wife and their children, if they have any, as their immediate family. If they mention their father, mother, sisters, or brothers, they will define them as separate units, usually living in separate households. Aunts, uncles, cousins, and grandparents are considered extended family.

Traditionally, the American family has been a nuclear family, consisting of a husband, a wife, and their children, living in a house or an apartment. Grandparents rarely live in the same home with their married sons and daughters, and uncles and aunts almost never do. In the 1950s, the majority of American households were the classic traditional American family — a husband, a wife, and two children. The father was a full-time worker who earned enough money to allow the mother to be a full-time housewife (at least until the children are in school). While this family pattern is still very much cherished by many Americans, particularly those with strong conservative ideas, it is fading out fast as a typical family model in the United States. At present, only about 10% of households in America are composed of a father who is in the labour force, a mother who is a housewife, and children under the age of 18. They still have close relationships among their relatives or the whole family group, the "nuclear family" is economically independent of the rest of the family. Parents and children often visit each other and the same applies to the married brothers and sisters when they live quite near. Loneliness usually comes to the aged men and women who really suffer greatly for they cannot be well-looked after or usually do not have enough retirement incomes.

The new family pattern that emerges or become more prominent in contemporary American society is single-parent family. This type of family, as indicated by its name, has only one parent, who can be an unmarried woman with adopted or her own children. This single parent can also be a divorced or separated man/woman with his/her own child/children, or a widowed man/woman with his/her child/children. With a growing number of people never married, plus an ever increasing divorce rate, America has seen an explosion in the number of single-parent families over the last 25 years.

The next popular family structure — "DINK", which means "Double Income, No Kids", has become a new lifestyle for young couples in big cities. DINK families have been growing steadily in number since the 1980s. This was once a rare species and given that it does not breed, you would assume that its present **aberration** (异常) would quickly die out, but not so. It is a growing phenomenon — millions of couples in America who are married not to have children. The truth is that a single income family is the dying breed. When both partners in a marriage have to work to survive, then the raising of children is something which does not come easily. If you have them, you have them late and you can only have one or two, as the financial burden is becoming too much to bear. Loss of the second income can easily bankrupt many a family. So, to become a "DINK" is the only easy solution.

2. Marriage and Divorce

(1) Marriage

The survey in the United States shows that a good marriage ranks at the top of most people's sources of satisfaction — above wealth, fame, and status, above good health and good jobs, and above other friendships and relationship. Again and again, however, statistics seem to indicate that marriage rate of America in 20th century has been on the decline over the past 30 years.

Over the years the value placed on marriage itself is determined largely by how happy the husband and wife make each other. Happiness is based primarily on companionship. The majority of American women value companionship as the most important part of marriage. Other values, such as having economic support and the opportunity to have children, although important, are seen by many as less important.

Today, Americans are again reviewing their values and taking a hard look at marriage. Since the experiments of the 60s and 70s did not work for many, American couples are striving to build relationships that embody more conventional values of the past — loyalty, trust, commitment, and permanence. Couples are deliberately choosing marriage as a lifestyle, knowing that it is riskier and more challenging today than that in the past. They try to convince each other that a good marriage is a relationship in which two people respect and like each other, become friends, and agree on mutual values and goals. They learn that a crisis is an important element within marriage, for a crisis can be an opportunity for growth as well. Anyway, with divorce rate going high and marriage rate going down, they are still willing to work together for a successful relationship that combines quality and stability.

(2) Divorce

Ironically, the rate of divorce in America ranks first in the world. Indeed, divorce is so common in the contemporary United States that everyone knows someone who has divorced and many Americans have lived through a divorce of their own or their parents. A divorce is almost free if a marriage is found to be a mistake by the couple. The divorce rate has almost doubled in the past 50 years, and it is calculated that in the early 1990s about two-thirds of all first marriages in the United States ended in divorce. Divorce brings about a series of social problems, such as the increase of criminals and orphans.

If the couple are not happy, the individuals may choose to get a divorce. A divorce is relatively easy to obtain in most parts of the United States. Most states have "no-fault" divorce. To obtain a no-fault divorce, a couple states that they can no longer live happily together, that they have irreconcilable differences, and that it is neither partner's fault. Divorce is now so common that it is no longer socially unacceptable, and children are not embarrassed to say that their parents are divorced.

Why do so many marriages end in divorce? The likelihood of divorce is influenced by several factors, including age of the couple, the couple's race, region of residence, education, and social class. Several sociologists in the United States, most notably Gerald Leslie, Sheila Korman, Graham Spanier, and Paul Glick, have conducted surveys on the effects of the above factors on divorce, and have found certain patterns among them, indicating that particular factors make a couple more or less likely to seek a divorce.

Nevertheless, many Americans believe that personal fulfillment is possible in marriage. So when their marriage "fails" to deliver what they hope to get, they find it difficult to justify remaining in an unsatisfactory marriage, resulting in a fresh effort to seek a more satisfactory marriage. Generally speaking, young people who divorce quickly remarry; older people are much less likely to remarry. In terms of gender, American men are more likely to remarry than American women, and they tend to remarry more quickly, too. Among divorced women, however, those without children are more likely to get remarried than those with children. As for differences in race/ethnicity, statistics seem to indicate that more divorced white women remarry than those **Hispanic** (拉丁美洲的) and black women who get divorced. Whatever the case, in marriage, divorce, and remarriage, Americans all have high rates.

3. The Role of the Child

The American emphasis on the individual, rather than the group, affects children in a contradictory way. On the one hand, it may cause them to get more attention and even have more power than they should. On the other hand, because most children have mothers who are working outside the home, they may not get enough attention from either parent. Worst yet, parents who feel guilty for not having enough time with their children may give them more material things to compensate for the lack of attention. Working parents constantly struggle to find enough time to spend with their children.

Some American families tend to place more emphasis on the needs and desires of their children than on the children's social and family responsibilities. In the years after World War II, much stress was placed on the psychological needs of children and the number of experts in this field increased enormously. Child psychologists, counselors, and social workers were employed to help children with problems at school or in the family. Many books on how to raise children became best-sellers. Sometimes these books offered conflicting advice, but almost all of them shared the American emphasis on the development of the individual as their primary goal.

The current generation of parents seems more concerned about teaching their children responsibility. Although Americans may not agree on how to best nurture and discipline their children, most still hold the basic belief that the major purpose of the family is the development and welfare of each of its members as individuals.

II. Food and Drinks

"You are what you eat." Nutrition experts often use this saying to promote better eating habits. What we put in our mouths does become a part of us. But we can look at this statement another way. What we eat reflects who we are — as people and as a culture. Do you want to understand another culture? Then you ought to find out about its food. Learning about American food can give us a real taste of American culture.

1. Food

What is "American food"? At first you might think the answer is easy as a pie. To many people, American food means hamburgers, hot dogs, fried chicken and pizza. If you have a "sweet tooth", you might think of apple pie or chocolate chip cookies. It is true that Americans do eat those things. But are those the only kind of **vittles** (食物) you can find in America?

Except for Thanksgiving turkey, it is hard to find a typically "American" food. The United States is a land of immigrants. So Americans eat food from many different countries. When people moved to America, they bring their cooking styles with them. That is why you can find almost every kind of ethnic food in America. In some cases, Americans have adopted foods from other countries as favorites. Americans love Italian pizza, **Mexican tacos** (墨西哥玉米饼) and **Chinese egg rolls** (中国炸春卷). But the American version does not taste quite like the original.

Americans living at a fast pace often just "grab a quick bite". Fast-food restaurants offer people on the run everything from fried chicken to **fried rice** (炒饭). Microwave dinners and instant foods make cooking at home a snap. Of course, one of the most common quick American meals is a sandwich. If it can fit between two slices of bread, Americans probably make a sandwich out of it. Peanut butter and jelly is an all-time American favorite.

Americans on the run also tend to eat a lot of "junk food". Potato chips, candy bars, soft drinks are popular treats. Many people eat too many of these unhealthy snacks. But others opt for more healthy eating habits. Some even go "all natural". They refuse to eat any food prepared with chemicals or additives.

American culture is a good illustration of the saying "You are what you eat." Americans represent a wide range of backgrounds and ways of thinking. The variety of foods enjoyed in the United States reflects the diversity of personal tastes. The food may be international or regional. Sometimes it is fast, and sometimes it is not so fast. It might be junk food, or maybe natural food. In any case, the style is all-American.

2. Drinks

(1) Coffee and Tea

Coffee and tea are two of the most popular hot drinks in the United States. Coffee is ordered almost at all hours of the day. In the light of statistics, Americans drink 500 million cups of coffee each day. Sometimes "coffee break" is taken among the workers in the middle of the morning or afternoon.

However, tea is not as popular to the Americans as it is to other nationalities. Accordingly, the quality of American tea is not as satisfactory as that of other countries. But in public restaurants, one may be served by being given a cup or a pot of hot water together with a tea bag; thus if he likes to have strong tea, he can make it himself. During warm weather, iced tea is perhaps the most popular drink of all, but iced coffee is also drunk.

(2) Beer

Beer is the most popular alcoholic beverage in the United States and it accounts for about 85% of all American alcoholic beverage consumption. Within the United States beer is manufactured by over 1,400 breweries which range in size from beverage industry giants to small brew pubs that sell their beer only on premises. Many people in the United States also enjoy the hobby of home brewing. The United States produces about 230 million hectoliters of beer annually and leads the world in beer production with regards to volume. The number of breweries in the United States ranks first in the world. Beer consumption by Americans is about 85 liters annually, which in 2002 ranked eighth in the world.

America produces beers in many styles. The most common style of beer in America is pale lager, which is historically related to **pilsner** (比尔森啤酒). The English styles of **pale ale** (麦

酒), **IPA** (印度麦酒), brown ale, **porter** (黑啤酒) and **stout** (浓烈黑啤酒) are widely brewed in America. Because of the distinctive flavors of American hops, **American Pale Ale** (美国麦酒) and IPA are considered a style of their own, and many recognize American stout and brown ale as their own style as well. American breweries also produce ales inspired by **Belgian beers** (比利时啤酒). **Steam beer** (鲜啤酒) is the first style of beer to originate in the United States.

(3) Soft Drinks

Soft drink is a beverage that does not contain alcohol. Carbonated soft drinks are commonly known as soda, **soda pop** (汽水), pop, coke or tonic in the United States. The name "soft drink" specifies a lack of alcohol by way of contrast to the term "**hard drink** (烈性酒)". Beverages like colas, flavored water, sparkling water, iced tea, lemonade, squash, and fruit punch are among the most common types of soft drinks, while hot chocolate, hot tea, coffee, milk, tap water, juice and milkshakes do not fall into this classification. Many carbonated soft drinks are optionally available in versions sweetened with sugars or with non-caloric sweeteners.

3. Dining Out

Dining out is also an important part of American social life. For single men and women, dates often begin with dinner at a nice restaurant. Married couples often get together in groups to eat out, especially on weekends. In their desire to use time efficiently, Americans may rush through breakfast and lunch, but dinner is usually a more leisurely meal at which enjoyment of food is enhanced by pleasant conversation.

Since America is a "melting-pot", consisting of so many different nationalities, almost any kind of restaurant can be found in most of the large cities in America. Some restaurants serve hamburgers, French fries and milkshakes. They also serve cheese with their hamburger called a cheeseburger. They have a chicken sandwich and a fish sandwich which includes butter and a green vegetable called **lettuce** (生菜). Drinks are milk, coffee, tea, colas, or fruit juice.

Some fast-food restaurants also have a window where cars can drive to pick up food. This means that people can eat in the car as they drive to another city. The reason they call it fast-food is that it can be picked up fast without waiting.

At fast-food restaurants, it is possible that you will not understand the kind of special language spoken there while ordering food. For example, "draw one" or "shoot one" means "pour a cup of coffee"; "BLT" means "bacon, lettuce and tomato sandwich". You may be asked if your order is "for here" or "to go". They say, "A burger, fries and a coke!" Though it is not polite, it is efficient. So when you are in America, try to order this way. After all, in America do as the Americans do.

III. Leisure Time in America

Do Americans enjoy more or less leisure time in the 21st century than they did in the decades before? Has the long-term rise of women employment come at the expense of time spent with family, friends, and in recreation? Do more educated persons enjoy more leisure time? What happened to leisure time differences between more and less educated persons in recent decades as their wage differences expanded?

1. Tourism

Since the 1940s, almost every American employee has received an annual vacation with pay, and it has become customary to use this time off for travel. Vacations are usually family affairs. Some families stay home to enjoy the local recreational facilities. But most vacationers prefer to travel, either within the United States or to other countries.

The nation's major cities are among its most popular tourist attractions. All year round, tourists jam the streets and hotels of Manhattan. They come to see the skyscrapers, visit museums, art galleries, opera houses, theaters, and famous specialty shops, and eat in the elegant and exotic restaurants. Besides New York, people are also attracted by cities like Los Angeles, San Francisco, New Orleans, and Philadelphia. With Hollywood as the home of the American movie industry, and Disneyland, the nation's most fabulous amusement park, Los Angeles becomes a fascinating place for people of all ages. As for San Francisco, it is the leading seaport of the Pacific Coast. It is famous for its bridges, cable cars, breathtaking scenery and seafood. To the visitors, New Orleans has its especial attraction. With many remainders of Old Europe and the Old South, this birthplace of jazz gives people a feeling of continental flavor. Compared with other cities, Philadelphia stands as a historical place. People come there to see the Liberty Bell which had announced the signing of the *Declaration of Independence*, and visit the building where the nation's *Constitution* had been signed.

For travelers interested in beautiful scenery, natural wonders, and wildlife, the United States has 38 national parks. These parks include **Yellowstone** (黄石国家公园), **Grand Canyon** (大峡谷), **Glacier National Park** (国家冰川公园), and **Yosemite** (约塞米蒂国家公园)in the West. In the East, there is the Florida Everglades, which makes up one of the largest swamplands in the world. It is rich in birds and animal lives.

Most Americans have a desire to visit other countries. And they are free to go almost anywhere in the world. Obtaining passport is a routine matter. So millions of Americans travel to Canada and Mexico every year. The islands of the Caribbean — Jamaica, Haiti, the Dominican

Republic, and Puerto Rico — are also big tourist attractions. And about three million Americans visit Europe every year.

Whether traveling within the United States or abroad, for most Americans a vacation stands as an attractive opportunity for fun, relaxation, and a change of scene. It is a chance for family members to spend leisure time together and get to know each other better. It is one of the happiest American traditions.

2. Sporting Activities

In many parts of the world there are four seasons: spring, summer, autumn and winter. In America, there are only three: football, basketball and baseball. That is not completely true, but almost. In every season, Americans have a ball. Americans watch football on television in autumn, basketball in winter, and baseball in spring. If you want to know what season it is, just look at what people are playing. For many Americans, sport does not just occupy the sidelines; however, it takes the center court.

(1) American Football

Today's preeminent spectator game in America is football, which was derived from the British game of rugby. Americans have been playing football since the earliest colonies were established more than 300 years ago. Settlers brought the game with them from England. In those days the game of football had few rules. A team could have as many as 100 players. The size of the field was never the same. Players wore no protective clothing. So they often got hurt. Today certain rules are fixed, for example, the field is always the same size, and players wear protective equipment, but they still get hurt.

A Quarterback Passing

The American football is played in almost every college and university in the country. In American football there are 11 players on each side, and they are dressed in padded uniforms and helmets because the game is rough and injuries are commonly to occur. However, anyone who has not attended a large college football game has missed one of the most colourful aspects of American college life. The student spectators are led in cheering for their teams by trained, uniformed student cheerleaders, many of whom are pretty girls. Outstanding high school football players are usually encouraged to come to a college or university by offers of scholarships. The urge to win is so keen, that many colleges actively seek outstanding players for their student body. Apart from the university football teams, there are many professional teams, and they play in large stadiums on Saturday afternoons. Televised professional football is arguably the most exciting sporting event of any kind in today's American culture. There are professional football teams in nearly all of the major cities of the United States.

There are 28 teams in the National Football League. The league is divided into two conferences. Each conference has three divisions. The teams that win most of the games in their division along with three other teams with good records compete for the conference championship. These games are called **playoff games** (季后赛). The first will begin on Saturday before the New Year. The playoff games continue for three weeks. The two conference champions then meet in the Super Bowl to decide the league championship.

(2) Basketball

Basketball was born in 1891 in Springfield, Massachusetts, when YMCA (Young Men's Christian Association) physical education instructor James Naismith (1861－1939) hung up a couple of peach baskets on poles at opposite ends of the gymnasium and used a soccer ball to create an "indoor" sport for students during the winter.

NBA (the National Basketball Association) is the most famous league in America. And it is also the major professional basketball league in the world, with teams from the United States and Canada. With the addition of the **Toronto Raptors** (多伦多猛龙队) and the **Vancouver Grizzlies** (温哥华灰熊队) prior to the 1995–1996 season, the NBA expanded to 29 teams competing in two conferences, the Eastern and Western, in four separate divisions. Each team conducts a training camp in October to determine its 12-player **roster** (运动员名单). Training camp allows each team to evaluate players, especially **rookies** (新手), to assess the team's strengths and weaknesses, and to prepare players for the upcoming season through a series of on-court drills and practice of offensive and defensive strategy. After a series of exhibition games, the NBA begins its 82-game regular season in the first week of November. In the second week of February, the NBA interrupts its season to celebrate the annual NBA All-Star game, featuring the game's best players as selected by the general balloting of fans throughout the United States and Canada. After the NBA season concludes in the third week in April, a total of 16 teams qualify for the playoffs (eight teams from each conference). In each conference the two division winners are guaranteed a playoff spot. The remaining playoff spots in each conference are awarded on the basis of win-loss records to the six next-best teams, regardless of division. The playoffs start with the teams with better records playing the teams with worse records in a best-of-five series, in which the winner is the first team to win three games. In subsequent rounds best-of-seven series

are played, with the first team to earn four victories winning the round. The playoffs continue in this **elimination scheme** (淘汰赛) until a conference champion is crowned. The champions from the Eastern and Western conferences then meet in a best-of-seven series to determine the NBA champion.

Today, professional basketball has become a billion-dollar sport. Thanks to the media, and a number of rule changes in the last 20 years including the 30 second shot clock, 3-point shots and the intensity of slam dunks, basketball has become a fast-paced game of non-stop action that many now believe it has replaced baseball as the national sport. The 1997 NBA Finals were broadcasted to 175 countries. 93 telecasters speaking 41 languages showed the games to more than 600 million households on six continents.

(3) Baseball

Long known as America's "favorite national pastime", baseball was actually derived from the English game of cricket. The original rules were invented by Alexander Cartwright. In 1845, he diagrammed a ball field with 90-foot baselines and a home plate batter's box. Today's game is an extensive modification of his scheme. Cartwright's baseball was called the "New York Game". The sport was called the "National Pastime" in the 1920s.

In 1967, when the two major professional leagues — American League and the National League, played baseball, more than 24 million people went to watch. In baseball there are nine people on each side. The two teams alternate at the bat (the offense) and in the field (the defense). Each pair of turns at bat is called an **inning** (局). There are nine innings in a game. Like football, baseball enjoys immense popularity among Americans, particularly among men. Professional baseball teams have enthusiastic followings, and important baseball games arouse great interest among American sports fans, being followed on television all across the nation. Like football, baseball is also a large-scale commercial enterprise in the United States, bringing huge financial rewards to players and management. More than any other American sport, baseball lends itself to legend. The statistical records give each game a mythic dimension as the hits, runs, errors, and strikeouts are carved into money and the record books.

3. Music

James Fenimore Cooper, an early American writer, once said, "The Americans are almost ignorant of the art of music." If that was once true, you would never know it today. Most Americans, even those without a musical bone in their bodies, have a favorite style of music.

Many people enjoy classical and folk music from around the world. But other popular music styles in America were "made in the U.S.A.".

Jazz music, developed by African-Americans in the late 1800s, allows performers to freely express their emotions and musical skill. Instead of just playing the melody, jazz musicians improvise different tunes using the same chords. The peak of jazz music came in the 1920s, known as "The Jazz Era". This period produced musicians like Louis Armstrong, Benny Goodman and Duke Ellington. These musicians later created the "Big Band" sounds of the 1930s. Different styles of jazz developed in different cities, such as New Orleans, Chicago, New York and Kansas City. Composer George Gershwin brought jazz into the world of classical music with pieces like "**Rhapsody in Blue** (蓝色狂想曲)".

The 1950s saw the development of an explosive new music style: Rock and roll. Performers like **Elvis Presley** (猫王) and songs like Bill Haley's *Rock Around the Clock* made rock music widely popular. This powerful music style addresses issues like love, sex, drugs, politics and death. Often it rebels against the accepted values of society. Rock concerts, featuring loud music and sometimes weird stage acts, have become a major part of American youth culture. Music videos on television have spread the message of rock to the far corners of the globe.

And the beat goes on. Pop music represents popular styles, like the music of **The Carpenters** (卡朋特乐队), that have wide appeal. "Golden oldies" from the past bring back pleasant memories for many. Rap music, which burst onto the music scene in the 1970s, is actually more like a rhyming chant. Rappers give a strong, sometimes vulgar, message about life in the streets.

In America, music is a shared experience. People grow up with piano lessons, chorus classes and marching band practices. They can talk about their tastes in music when there is not anything else to talk about. If James Fenimore Cooper were here today, he would surely have to change his tune.

4. Movie

The United States was the first country to turn film into a popular form of entertainment and important industry. There are many film-making companies, such as MGM (Metro Goldwyn Mayer), Paramount, Warner Brothers, Radio Keith, United Artists, 20th Century Fox, Universal and Columbia Pictures, etc. There are also many film studios in America today, among which Hollywood is the earliest and the best.

(1) Hollywood

Hollywood, situated northwest of Downtown, is a district in the city of Los Angeles, California. Due to its fame and cultural identity as the historical center of movie studios and

movie stars, the word "Hollywood" is often used as a metonym for the American film and television industry. Today much of the movie industry has dispersed into surrounding areas such as Burbank and the Westside, but significant **ancillary industries** (附属产业) such as editing, effects, props, post-production, and lighting companies remain in Hollywood.

Banks, restaurants, clubs and movie palaces sprang up, catering to the demands of the burgeoning film industry. The needs of this thriving new industry created radical changes in the community causing a clash between older and newer residents. Acres of agricultural land south of what-is-now **Hollywood Boulevard** (好莱坞大道) were subdivided and developed as housing for the enormous numbers of workers that movie-making required.

Hollywood has been anything but static, however, and after a few decades as the capital of film glamour, the neighborhood changed again. Although much of the studio work remained in Hollywood, many stars moved to Beverly Hills, and the elegant shops and restaurants left with them. In the 1960s, music recording studios and offices began moving to Hollywood an offshoot of the nightclubs further west on **Sunset Boulevard** (日落大道). Other businesses, however, continued to migrate to different parts of the city. Hollywood today is a diverse, vital, and active community striving to preserve the elegant buildings from its past. Most of the movie industry remains in the area, although the neighborhood's outward appearance has changed.

In 1985, the Hollywood Boulevard commercial and entertainment district was officially listed in the National Register of Historic Places protecting the neighborhood's important buildings and **seeing to** (留心，注意) it that the significance of Hollywood's past would always be a part of its future.

(2) Oscar

The Academy Awards, widely known as the Oscar, are awards of merit presented annually by the Academy of Motion Picture Arts and Sciences (AMPAS) to recognize excellence of professionals in the film industry, including directors, actors, and writers. The formal ceremony at which

Image of the Academy Award

the awards are presented is one of the most prominent film award ceremonies in the world. The Oscars, and the Academy of Motion Picture Arts and Sciences itself, were conceived by Metro Goldwyn Mayer studio boss, Louis B. Mayer.

The first Academy Awards ceremony was held on Thursday, May 16, 1929, at the Hotel Roosevelt in Hollywood to honor outstanding film achievements of 1927 and 1928. It was hosted by actor Douglas Fairbanks and director William C. DeMille.

The official name of the Oscar statuette is the Academy Award of Merit. The name is said to have been born when Margaret Herrick saw the statuette on a table and said: "It looks just like my uncle Oscar!" Made of gold-plated Britannia on a black metal base, it is 13.5 inch high, weighs 11 pound and depicts a knight rendered in Art Deco style holding a crusader's sword standing on a reel of film with five spokes. The five spokes each represent the original branches of the Academy: Actors, Writers, Directors, Producers, and Technicians.

The major awards are presented at a live televised ceremony, most commonly in February or March following the relevant calendar year, and six weeks after the announcement of the nominees. This is an elaborate **extravaganza** (铺张华丽的娱乐表演), with the invited guests walking up the red carpet in the creations of the most prominent fashion designers of the day. The Academy Awards is televised live across the United States (excluding Alaska and Hawaii) and gathers millions of viewers worldwide. The 2008 ceremony was watched by more than 32 million Americans.

5. Broadway

Broadway theatre, commonly called Broadway for simple, refers to theatrical performances presented in one of the 39 large professional theaters with 500 seats or more located in the Theatre District in Manhattan, New York City. Along with London's West End theatre, Broadway theatre is usually considered to represent the highest level of commercial theatre in the English-speaking world.

Broadway Street

The modern musical was born in 1943 with Rodgers and Hammerstein's Oklahoma, which revolutionized the way dance, music and dialogue were used to develop the plot and characters. Other songwriters of the 1940s, 50s and 60s capitalized on that winning formula to write so many hit musicals, that the era is now referred to as "Broadway's Golden Age". Since then, American musicals have been translated and produced on stages all over the world. The music has become a mainstay among vocalists and jazz musicians, making clear the expression that the music of Broadway is truly "America's Classic Music".

Today, watching a Broadway show is a common tourist activity in New York, and Broadway shows sell about a billion dollars worth of tickets annually, helping the tourist industry to generate billions more in restaurant and hotel revenues. The TKTS booths sell same-day tickets for many Broadway and Off-Broadway shows at a discount of 25%, 35%, or 50%. This service helps sell seats that would otherwise go empty and makes seeing a show in New York more affordable. Many Broadway theatres also offer special student rates, same-day "rush" or "lottery" tickets, or standing-room tickets to help ensure that their theatres are as full, and their "**grosses** (总利润)" are as high as possible. Total Broadway attendance in the 2007–2008 season was 12.27 million, which was approximately the same as the 2006–2007 season.

6. Internet

The popularity of home computers and "surfing the Net" has brought a whole new world of leisure time activities to Americans. Estimates are that more than a third of adults spend some of their leisure time on the Internet. Some value the enormous educational opportunities it brings, while others prefer spending their time in "chat rooms", having discussions with others online, communicating with friends or family via e-mail and instant messaging, or playing the latest computer games. Computers are also extremely popular with children and teenagers, and this of course raises questions of where they are traveling on the Internet and what they are seeing. Now parents have to worry about monitoring the computer, in addition to monitoring the TV.

There is a debate about whether the Internet should be regulated by the federal government. On the one hand, there have been instances where adults have met children or teenagers over the Internet and have persuaded them to meet in person. In several instances teenagers have been **kidnapped** (绑架). Parents have great fear about their children meeting strangers on the Internet and about their possible exposure to pornography. It is against the law to send pornography through the mail, and many believe it should be outlawed on the Internet as well.

On the other hand, many Internet users believe that government regulation could threaten the growth and vitality of the Internet. Some would argue that the lack of regulation has permitted the Internet's explosive growth and the development of new technologies to deliver it. Wireless technology now allows Americans to access the Internet just about anywhere. For example, they can use their laptop computers to connect to a wireless network and access the Internet while having coffee in a **Starbucks** (星巴克). But this access is not limited to laptops. Technological convergence has brought the Internet to Personal Communication Systems (PCS).

Now many Americans have cell phones and handheld devices that have multiple functions: talking on the phone, taking and exchanging pictures, instant messaging, sending and receiving e-mail, surfing the Internet, playing games, voice recording, paging, and communicating by coast-to-coast walkie-talkies. Many people are happy that technology has made it possible for them to communicate with just about anyone anywhere. However, this 24/7 access (24 hours a day, 7 days a week) has a huge impact on leisure time and Americans' ability to relax.

IV. Social Manners and Etiquettes

Each type of society has its own set of manners and etiquettes. We propose to discuss manners and etiquettes universally followed in America. Needless to say that manners and etiquettes are ingredients of social behaviour, an integral part of one's persona and not a vehicle to create an impact or impress others. Therefore, every individual should try to **imbibe** (吸取) manners and etiquettes for day to day conduct of life both at home and outside.

1. Table Manners

Similar to other countries, the United States has its own peculiar dining custom. Many table manners evolved out of practicality. For example, it is generally impolite to put elbows on tables, since doing so creates a risk of tipping over bowls and cups. Each family or group sets its own standards for how strictly these rules are to be enforced.

(1) Table Setting

Bread or salad plates are to the left of the main plate, beverage glasses are to the right. If small bread knives are present, lay them across the bread plate with the handle pointing to the right. Modern etiquette provides the smallest numbers and types of **utensils** (器具) necessary for dining. Only utensils which are to be used for the planned meal should be set. Even if needed, hosts should not have more than three utensils on either side of the plate before a meal. If extra utensils are needed, they may be brought to the table along with later courses. If a wine glass and a water glass are set, the wine glass is on the right directly above the knife. The water glass is

A Formal Table Setting

to the left of the wine glass at a 45 degree angle, closer to the diner. Glasses designed for certain types of wine may be set if available. If only one type of glass is available, it is considered correct regardless of the type of wine provided. Hosts should always provide cloth napkins to guests. When paper napkins are provided, they should be treated the same as cloth napkins, and therefore should not be balled up or torn. Coffee or tea cups are placed to the right of the table setting, or above the setting to the right if space is limited. The cup's handle should be pointing right.

(2) Before Dining

Men should not wear a hat at the dinner table. Women should not wear hats inside their own homes. The gentlemen stand behind their chairs until the women are all seated before sitting down to a formal meal. A prayer may be customary in some households, and the guests may join in or be respectfully silent. Most prayers are made by the host before the meal is eaten. Hosts should not practice an extended religious **ritual** (仪式) in front of the invited guests who have different beliefs. Do not start eating until every person is served request that you begin without waiting. At more formal occasions all diners should be served at the same time and will wait until the hostess or host lifts a fork or spoon before beginning. Keep your napkin on your lap. At more formal occasions all diners will wait to place their napkins on their laps until the host or hostess places his or her napkin on his or her lap. Wait until your hostess picks up her fork or spoon before starting to eat.

(3) General Manners while Dining

When a dish is offered from a serving dish, as the traditional manner, the food may be passed around or served by a host or staff. If passed, you should pass on the serving dish to the next person in the same direction as the other dishes are being passed. Place the serving dish on your left, take some, and pass to the person next to you. You should consider how much is on the serving dish and not take more than a proportional amount so that everyone may have some. If you do not care for any of the dish, pass it to the next person without comment. If being served by a single person, the server should request if the guest would like any of the dish. The guest may say "Yes, please." or "No, thank you." Dip your soup spoon away from you into the soup. Eat soup noiselessly, from the side of the spoon. When there is a small amount left, you may lift the front end of the dish slightly with your free hand to enable collection of more soup with your spoon. Taste food before adding **seasoning** (调味品), such as salt or pepper. If you are having difficulty getting food onto your fork, use a small piece of bread or your knife to assist. Never use your fingers or thumb. You may thank or converse with the staff, but it is not necessary, especially if engaged in conversation with others. It is acceptable in the United States not to accept all offerings, and not to finish all the food on your plate. No one should ask why another does not want any of a dish or why he has not finished a serving. Chew with your mouth closed. Do not **slurp** (出声的吃), talk with food in your mouth, or make loud or unusual noises while eating. Say "Excuse me," or "Excuse me. I'll be right back," before leaving the table. Do not talk excessively loud. Give others equal opportunities for conversation. **Burping** (打嗝), coughing, yawning, or sneezing at the table should be avoided. If you do so, say, "Excuse me." Do not "play with" your food or utensils. Never talk on your phone at the table. If an urgent matter arises, apologize, excuse yourself, and step away from the table so your conversation does not disturb the others. If food must be removed from the mouth for some reason, it should be done with the aid of a napkin to cover the mouth if possible, using the same method which was used to bring the food to the mouth. Gentlemen should stand when a lady leaves or rejoins the table in formal social settings.

(4) At the End of the Meal

When you have finished your meal, place all used utensils onto your plate together, on the right side, pointed down, so the waiter knows you have finished. Do not place used utensils on the table. Except in a public restaurant, do not ask to take some uneaten food or leftovers home, and never do so when attending a formal dinner. A host may suggest that extra food be taken by the guests, but should not insist. When you have finished your meal, do not place the used napkin directly on your dinner plate. Leave it on the table to the left of your plate when you leave at the end of or during a meal. Do not leave it on the chair as it may soil the **upholstery** (椅子套). Wait for your host or hostess to rise before getting up from a dinner party table. Thank your host when leaving a dinner party. Once dessert or after-dinner coffee is served, be wary not to overstay your welcome. The party who first wishes to end the event should rise and say something like, "This has been such a nice evening. We hope we can see you again soon."

2. Wedding Ceremony

Weddings in the United States vary as much as the people do. There are church weddings with a great deal of fanfare; there are civil weddings with little ceremony; there are weddings on mountain-tops with guests in bare feet; and there are weddings on the ocean floor with oxygen tanks for the guests. But many weddings, no matter where or how they are performed, include certain traditional customs.

For instance, the bride and groom often exchange rings. The rings are usually worn on the fourth finger of the left hand, and are exchanged during the ceremony. The rings symbolize the couple's commitment to one another. After the ceremony there is often a party, called a "reception". There the food is so plentiful that it almost takes the spotlight away from the couple. The kind of food varies, depending on the cultural heritage of the couple, and on the finances and preferences of the bride's family. It is the family of the bride which more often **foots the bill** (付账) for the reception. And a wedding cake, layered and decorated, sits in a corner — waiting to be cut. Tradition has it that the bride and groom cut the cake, holding the knife together. The bride and groom often feed each other a piece of cake before serving the guests. Soon thereafter, the bride stands in the center of the room, often on a chair, and throws her bouquet of flowers to the assembled unmarried women at the reception. Tradition says that whoever catches the flowers will be the next bride. Some women eagerly attempt to catch the bouquet; others shy away.

And then it is time for the bride and groom to set off. The honeymoon nowadays varies considerably — dictated by wealth, time and preference. Sometimes the couple will spend a single night at a nearby hotel; sometimes they will spend two weeks at a remote vacation spot. The expense of the trip is assumed by the groom.

Though it is common to get married with a large group of relatives and friends present, it is by no means essential. Some couples simply go to City Hall and have a local judge perform the ceremony. To be legally wed, a couple need only fulfill the requirements set by the state in which the ceremony is performed. Once given a license, the couple then appears before someone authorized to perform marriages (usually a judge or religious leader), and within a few minutes, they have "**tied the knot** (结婚)". Some couples elope to get married without fanfare or to escape parental disapproval. People marrying for the second time often do so in a quiet way, without a large party.

A Wedding Cake

3. Others

When you receive an invitation, Americans feel that the first rule of being a polite guest is to be on time. If a person is invited to dinner at 6:30, the hostess expects him to be there at 6:30 or not more than a few minutes after. Because she usually does the cooking, she times the meal so that the hot rolls and the coffee and meat will be at their best at the time the guests come. If they are late, the food will not be so good, and the hostess will be disappointed. When the guest cannot come on time, he calls his host or hostess on the telephone, gives the reason, and tells at what time he can come.

Send flowers to your hostess beforehand when you are invited. Otherwise, flowers sent later as a thank-you for a very special evening are always appreciated. Ordinarily, however, neither a gift sent later nor a note is necessary, and your verbal thanks when you leave are sufficient. A phone call the next day to say how much you enjoyed the evening is always welcome. The custom of taking wine as gift to a small dinner party is becoming customary.

A caller should give his or her name as soon as the phone is answered. Not only is it courteous, but it is helpful as well since it gives the person being called the chance to gather papers or whatever may be required by the caller, or to get to a more convenient telephone.

The calls of **condolence** (吊唁) should be made as soon as possible after hearing the death. If the friends are very close, you will probably be admitted to speak to them. If you are, you should offer your services to help in any way you can. There are countless ways to be helpful, from assisting with such needs as food and child care, to sending telegrams, making phone calls, and answering the door. If they do not need anything, you offer your sympathy and leave without delay.

V. Holidays and Festivals

Americans celebrate a variety of holidays throughout the year. American holidays can be secular, religious, international or uniquely American. With the wide variety of holidays and many levels of American government it can be confusing to determine what public and private facilities are open on a given holiday. You can usually find out in the daily newspaper or by calling the office you wish to visit.

1. New Year's Day

New Year's Day is the first day of the New Year. On the modern **Gregorian calendar** (阳历), it is celebrated on January 1, as it was also in ancient Rome. In all countries using the Gregorian calendar as their main calendar, except for Israel, it is a public holiday, often celebrated with fireworks at the stroke of midnight as the new year starts. The celebration of this holiday begins the night before, when Americans gather to wish each other a happy and prosperous coming year.

2. Lincoln's Birthday

Lincoln's Birthday is a legal holiday in some states including Illinois, Connecticut, California, Missouri, New York, New Jersey and Indiana. It is observed on the anniversary of Abraham Lincoln's birth on February 12, 1809.

The day is marked by traditional wreath-laying ceremonies at Abraham Lincoln Birthplace National Historic Site in Hodgenville, Kentucky, and at the Lincoln Memorial in Washington, D.C. The latter has been the site of a ceremony ever since the Memorial was dedicated. Since that event in 1922, observances continue to be organized by the Lincoln Birthday National Commemorative Committee and by the Military Order of the Loyal Legion of the United States. A wreath is laid on behalf of the President of the United States, a custom also carried out at the gravesites of all the United States presidents on their birthdays. Lincoln's tomb is in Springfield, Illinois.

Many states that had formerly observed Lincoln's birthday have created a joint holiday to honor both Lincoln and George Washington, sometimes calling it "Presidents'Day". It coincides with the Federal holiday officially designated "Washington's Birthday", observed on the third Monday of February. There has never been an annual Federal holiday honouring Lincoln.

3. Valentine's Day

February 14, Valentine's Day, is sweethearts' day, on which people in love with each other express their tender emotions.

Originally, Valentine's Day is a Western European Christian holiday. It was the feast of Lupercalia and was Christianized in memory of the martyrdom of Saint Valentine in A.D. 270. St. Valentine came to be associated, in medieval times, with the union of lovers under conditions of **duress** (威逼). The holiday is celebrated on February 14 by the exchange of romantic or comic verse messages called "valentines". The first commercial valentine greeting cards produced in the United States of America were created in the 1840s by Esther A. Howland. Today million of such cards are sold annually.

Valentine's Day 2008 Poster

Today, people sometimes put their love message in a heart-shaped box of chocolates, or a bunch of flowers tied with red ribbons. Words or letters may be written on the flower covered card, or something else. Whatever the form may be, the message is almost the same — "Will you be my valentine?".

The symbol of valentine is a picture with a Heart and Cupid armed with bow and arrow.

Many universities, high or elementary schools hold a sweethearts' ball for the young students to celebrate Valentine's Day.

4. Washington's Birthday

Washington's Birthday is a United States federal holiday celebrated on the third Monday of February. It is one of permanent holidays established by Congress. As Washington's Birthday or Presidents' Day, it is also the official name of a concurrent state holiday celebrated on the same day in a number of states.

Titled Washington's Birthday, the federal holiday was originally implemented by the United States of America federal government in 1880 for government offices in the District of Columbia and expanded in 1885 to include all federal offices. As the first federal holiday to honor an American citizen, the holiday was celebrated on Washington's actual birthday, February 22. On January 1, 1971 the federal holiday was shifted to the third Monday in February by the ***Uniform Monday Holiday Act*** (美国统一假期法案). A draft of the *Uniform Holidays Bill* of 1968 would have renamed the holiday to Presidents' Day to honor both Washington and Lincoln, but this proposal failed in committee and the bill as voted on and signed into law on June 28, 1968 kept the name Washington's Birthday.

5. April Fools' Day

April Fools' Day or All Fools' Day, although not a holiday in its own right, is a notable day celebrated in many countries on April 1. The day is marked by the commission of hoaxes and other practical jokes of varying sophistication on friends, family members, enemies, and neighbours, or sending them on fool's errand, the aim of which is to embarrass the gullible. Traditionally, in America it is the custom to play tricks on people on that day. Children are allowed to play harmless jokes until 12 o'clock. If you play a trick on someone after this time you are the April Fool.

6. Easter

Colored Easter Eggs

Easter falls on the first Sunday after the full moon that occurs on or after March 21. It is the most important religious feast in the Christian liturgical year. Christians believe that Jesus was resurrected from the dead two days after his **crucifixion** (钉死在十字架上), and celebrate this resurrection on Easter Day, or Easter Sunday, two days after **Good Friday** (耶稣受难日). The year of his death and resurrection is variously estimated between the years A.D. 26 and 36.

Easter also refers to the season of the church year called **Eastertide** (复活节) or the Easter Season. Traditionally the Easter Season lasted for the 40 days from Easter Day until **Ascension Day** (耶稣升天节) but now officially lasts for the 50 days until **Pentecost** (圣灵降临节). The first week of the Easter Season is known as Easter Week or the **Octave** (节日的第八天) of Easter. Easter also marks the end of **Lent** (四旬斋), a season of prayer and **penance** (苦修).

Many cultural elements, such as the Easter Bunny, Easter Eggs, have become part of the holiday's modern celebrations, and those aspects are often celebrated by many Christians and non-Christians alike.

7. Mother's Day

Mother's Day holiday in the United States celebrates motherhood generally and the positive contributions of mothers to society. It falls on the second Sunday of each May. American children of all ages treat their mothers to something special. It is the one day out of the year when children, young and old, try to show in a tangible way how much they appreciate their mothers. In the United States, Mother's Day did not become an official holiday until 1915. It is the result of a campaign by Anna Marie Jarvis, who, following the death of her mother on May 9, 1905, devoted her life to establishing Mother's Day as a national holiday.

On Mother's Day morning some American children follow the tradition of serving their mothers breakfast in bed. Other children will give their mothers gifts which they have made themselves or bought in stores. Adults give their mothers red carnations, the official Mother's Day flower. If their mothers are deceased they may bring white carnations to their grave sites. All children have the same purpose, to express the love, gratitude and reverence one feels for his or her mother.

8. Memorial Day

Memorial Day is a United States federal holiday observed on the last Monday of May. Formerly known as Decoration Day, it commemorates American men and women who died while in military service to their country. This is a national holiday in the United States. On Memorial Day the war dead are remembered as the nation's heroes at solemn pubic services, at burial grounds, at places of worship, and in the hearts of the American people. Flowers and flags are placed on their graves as symbols of human affection and patriotic duty; moving speeches recall their heroic deeds; and fervent prayers are offered for peace among mankind.

The day which originally commemorated those who died in Civil War has now become a day to remember the deeds and sacrifices of all war dead. Throughout the world, wherever American soldiers are buried, Memorial Day is observed. At the **Tomb of the Unknown Soldier** (无名冢) in **Arlington National Cemetery** (阿林顿国家公墓) near Washington, D.C., the war dead are remembered every year in an august gathering. There, before the gathering, the President of the United States, or his representative, lays a wreath at the foot of the tomb to the memory of all who have died in battle. There, too, prayers for peace combine with praise for valour.

The gravestones at Arlington National Cemetery are graced by US flags on Memorial Day.

9. Flag Day

In the United States, Flag Day is celebrated on June 14. It commemorates the adoption of the flag of the United States, which happened that day by a resolution of the Second Continental Congress in 1777. In 1916, President Woodrow Wilson issued a proclamation that officially established June 14 as Flag Day; in August 1949, National Flag Day was established by an act of Congress. Flag Day is not an official federal holiday, though on June 14, 1937, Pennsylvania became the first US state to celebrate Flag Day as a state holiday.

Children are part of the honor guard for the Flag Day parade at Tecumseh Elementary School.

The week of June 14 is designated as "National Flag Week". During National Flag Week, the president will issue a proclamation urging US citizens to fly the American flag for the duration of that week. The flag should also be displayed on all Government buildings. Some organizations hold parades and events in celebration of America's national flag and everything it represents.

The National Flag Day Foundation holds an annual observance for Flag Day on the second Sunday in June. The program includes a ceremonial raising of the flag, recitation of the **Pledge of Allegiance** (对美国的效忠宣誓), singing of the National Anthem, a parade and more.

10. Father's Day

The idea of a special day to honour mothers was first put forward in America in 1907. Two years later a woman, Mrs. John Bruce Dodd, in the state of Washington proposed a day to honour the head of the family — the father. Her mother died when she was very young, and she was brought up by her father. She loved her father very much.

In response to Mrs. Dodd's idea that same year — 1909, the state governor of Washington official proclaimed the third Sunday in June Father's Day. The idea was officially approved by President Woodrow Wilson in 1916. In 1924, President Calvin Coolidge recommended national observance of the occasion, "to establish more intimate relations between fathers and their children, and to impress upon fathers the full measure of their obligations". The red or white rose is recognized as the official Father's Day flower.

Father's Day celebrations in the United States take place with lot of gaiety and enthusiasm. The day is observed as a time for family reunion in families, as children who are staying away from families take time out to celebrate the day with their father. Indulging daddy with breakfast in bed and gifts like cards, flowers, chocolates and neckties is the traditional way of celebrating Father's Day.

When children cannot visit their fathers or take them out to dinner, they send a greeting card. Traditionally, fathers prefer greeting cards that are not too sentimental. Most greeting cards are **whimsical** (异想天开的) so fathers laugh when they open them. Some give heartfelt thanks for being there whenever the child needed Dad.

11. Independence Day

Independence Day is the national holiday of the United States commemorating the signing of the *Declaration of Independence* by the Continental Congress on July 4, 1776, in Philadelphia, Pennsylvania. Independence Day is commonly associated with fireworks, parades, barbecues, carnivals, picnics, concerts, baseball games, political speeches and ceremonies, and various other public and private events celebrating the history, government, and traditions of the United States.

Independence Day, the only holiday that celebrates the United States, is a national holiday marked by patriotic displays. Similar to other summer-themed events, Fourth of July celebrations often take place outdoors. Independence Day is a federal holiday, so all non-essential federal institutions are closed on that day. Many politicians make it a point on this day to appear at a public event to praise the nation's heritage, society, and people. Speeches and editorials may invoke American Revolutionary themes such as the founding fathers (including John Adams, Thomas Jefferson, Patrick Henry, and George Washington), the *Constitution*, **the Liberty Bell**

(独立钟), and democratic principles such as liberty, freedom, equality under the law, inalienable rights, and representative government.

Independence Day Poster

12. Labor Day

Labor Day is a United States federal holiday observed on the first Monday in September. The holiday originated in 1882 as the **Central Labor Union** (中央劳工联盟) sought to create "a day off for the working citizens". Congress made Labor Day a federal holiday on June 28, 1894, two months after the May Day Riots of 1894. All 50 states have made Labor Day a state holiday. Traditionally, Labor Day is celebrated by most Americans as the symbolic end of the summer.

Today, Labor Day is often regarded as a day of rest and parades. Speeches or political demonstrations are more low-key than May 1 Labor Day celebrations in most countries, although events held by labor organizations often feature political themes and appearances by candidates for office, especially in election years. Forms of celebration include picnics, barbecues, fireworks displays, water sports, and public art events. Families with school-age children take it as the last chance to travel before the end of summer. Some teenagers and young adults view it as the last weekend for parties before returning to school. However, of later, schools have begun well before Labor Day, as early as July 24 in many urban districts. In addition, Labor Day marks the beginning of the season for the National Football League (NFL) and National Collegiate Athletic Association (NCAA) College Football. The NCAA usually plays their first games the week before Labor Day, with the NFL traditionally playing their first game the Thursday following Labor Day.

13. Veterans Day

Veterans Day is an annual American holiday honoring military veterans. Both a federal holiday and a state holiday in all states, it is usually observed on November 11. However, if it occurs on a Sunday then the following Monday is designated for holiday leave, and if it occurs Saturday then either Saturday or Friday may be so designated. It was first incorporated as by President Wilson as **Armistice Day** (停战日) in 1919. Other countries today also recognize November 11 as Armistice Day or **Remembrance Day** (荣军纪念日) in honor of the Armistice

Veterans Day 2008 Poster

treaty which ended World War I. It was in 1938 that Armistice Day was enacted as an official American holiday. But eventually after World War II, citizens felt that the veterans of all wars should be recognized, not only those of World War I. So in 1954 Congress changed the name from Armistice Day to Veterans Day. In America, the holiday now celebrates the approximate 2.9 million US veterans with parades and ceremonies among other events. Americans still give thanks for peace on Veterans Day. There are ceremonies and speeches at 11:00 in the morning, most Americans observe a moment of silence, remembering those who fought for peace.

14. Halloween

Halloween is a holiday celebrated on October 31. Since the 1800s, when Irish and Scottish immigrants brought their Halloween festivities to North America, the holiday has evolved considerably. The celebration's connection with All Saints' Day and All Souls' Day has mostly fallen by the wayside, and a number of new secular traditions have developed. Halloween is a big deal in the United Sates, for kids and adults alike.

For children, dressing up and trick-or-treating door to door is still the main event. Most households in the United States participate, and those who do not run the risk of petty **vandalism** (故意破坏公物的行为). Many adults dress up themselves, to go out with their children or to attend costume parties and contests.

Other Halloween activities fill the whole month of October. These traditions preserve Samhain's spirit of revelry in the face of frightening thoughts of death and the supernatural. Americans have added scary movies, community haunted houses, ghost stories and **Ouija boards** (显灵板) to the celebration. Greeting cards and festive decorations are also a big part of Halloween. The holiday is second only to Christmas in total revenue dollars for retailers.

15. Thanksgiving Day

Thanksgiving Day is a harvest festival. Traditionally, it is a time to give thanks to God for the harvest and express gratitude in general. It is celebrated on the fourth Thursday of November. Thanksgiving Day has a special significance for Americans because it is traced back to that group of people who were among the first to come to the New World in search of freedom.

The First Thanksgiving
Painting by Jean Louis Gerome Ferris

In 1620, 102 sea-weary Pilgrims landed on the **peninsula** (半岛) of Cape Cod. Their ship, the *Mayflower*, had intended to go to Virginia, but it made its landfall far to the north. After some weeks of exploring, the colonists decided not to make the trip to Virginia but to remain where they were. They chose the area near Plymouth harbour as a site for their colony. When they stepped ashore in this utterly alien world, they were totally isolated from any outside help and knew no means of livelihood. And the greater trouble is that in the woods lived Indians, some of whom were hostile. This added to the hardship of daily life. But the vast stretches of forest gave them a hope. In this way, the nation's forefathers not only survived the first severe winter, but also saw the first harvest of crops in the next autumn. In November of 1621, the settlers spent three days to celebrate and show thanks to God for a successful harvest. Their Indian friends were also invited to join their festival and feast.

Today, in America Thanksgiving Day is celebrated by many Americans whose roots do not stem from Britain. Now it is marked by families gathering together to enjoy a traditional dinner for roast turkey, and to speak to one another of the things for which they are thankful. Basically the dinner menu remains as it was in early times: roast turkey, **stuffing** (馅饼), **cranberry sauce** (越橘沙司), sweet potatoes, mashed white potatoes, and pumpkin. They understand that Thanksgiving is a kind of secular, nationalistic "mass" where people eat symbols of their folk history, thereby regaining some of the qualities they believe their ancestors possessed.

16. Christmas

Christmas Day, which is the most festive time in the United States, falls on December 25 on which Christian people believe Jesus Christ was born, although no one can tell the exact date of his birth. This is the biggest and best-loved holiday in the United States, which is full of joy and gaiety, love and laughter, hospitality and good will. People usually have two weeks for this holiday.

Americans begin to prepare Christmas long before the holiday comes. Small families and large business firms prepare the holiday differently. Stores are decorated with the traditional Christmas colors of green and red. Goods associated with Christmas become best sellers at this time. Many Americans take advantage of the time to earn extra money by selling Christmas cards, small gifts and ornaments.

Christmas food is special: peppermint-flavored red and white striped canes of sugar, bright colored hard sweets, chocolate bonbons, creamy homemade fudge and clusters of chocolate-covered **raisins** (葡萄干), **walnuts** (核桃) or **pecans** (山核桃), etc.; as for the Christmas dinner, Americans traditionally have turkey or ham, sweet potatoes, vegetables, and cranberry sauce.

Some of the most popular Christmas customs are as follows:

(1) Exchanging Gifts

This custom originated from the ancient religion of believing that the first Christmas gifts were given by the three Wise Men to the infant Jesus Christ. In the United States, it has been passed down and become very popular among friends, family, etc.

(2) Receiving Toys from Santa Claus

Santa Claus is believed by American children to be a fat jolly old man with a red suit, red hat and a long white beard. On Christmas Eve Santa Claus comes down through the chimney to bring them toys. Children try to lie away listening carefully because they are told that on Christmas Eve Santa Claus comes on a sleigh pulled by **reindeer** (驯鹿).

(3) Hanging a Stocking near the Chimney

On Christmas Eve, American children hang their stockings by the fireplace, hoping that Santa Claus will fill them with sweets and toys. This is said to be a custom from Britain.

Christmas Day in America

(4) Christmas Tree

The Christmas tree is now the center of interest at most Christmas celebrations. People like evergreens and they think that branches of **fir** (冷杉) will bring good luck and symbolize spring. The Christmas tree is usually covered with strings of colored lights, and a star fixed on top representing the star in the East which guided the three Wise Men to where Jesus was born.

(5) Singing Christmas Carols

Christmas songs, also called carols, are sung from house to house by Americans together with friends.

(6) Sending Christmas Cards

This custom first started in London in the 19th century. Today, most Americans send Christmas cards to their friends, relatives and colleagues, etc..

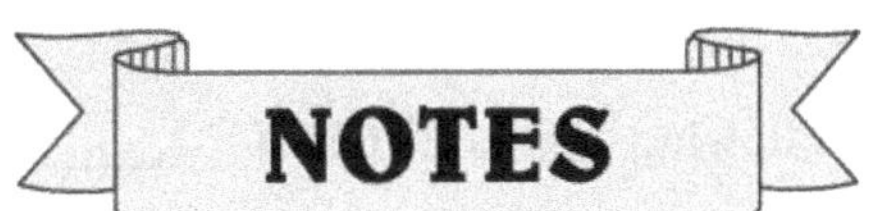

1. **irreconcilable differences**：无法协调的差异。
2. **Tex-Mex treats**：墨式德州小吃。
3. **Super Bowl**：超级碗是美国国家橄榄球大联盟冠军奖杯的名称，也代指总决赛。
4. **the Academy of Motion Picture Arts and Sciences**：电影艺术与科学学院，是一个由超过 6 000 位电影界的专业或资深人士组成的非营利组织，同时也是奥斯卡金像奖的主办单位，于 1927 年 5 月 11 日在美国加利福尼亚州建立。
5. **Academy Honorary Award**：奥斯卡荣誉奖，近年来又称奥斯卡终身成就奖，在奥斯卡奖设立之初由美国电影艺术与科学学院颁给奥斯卡奖项没有包括的领域的杰出人士或团体机构。后来随着奥斯卡奖项的增加和完善，奥斯卡荣誉奖逐渐演变成颁给终身为电影事业贡献的人士。
6. **Academy Special Achievement Award**：特别成就奖。
7. **Academy Scientific and Technical Award**：科技成果奖。
8. **The Irving G. Thalberg Memorial Award**：欧文·撒尔伯格纪念奖。
9. **Jean Hersholt Humanitarian Award**：吉恩·赫肖尔特人道主义奖。
10. **Gordon E. Sawyer Award**：戈登·E·索耶奖。
11. **The TKTS Booths**：是贩售纽约市百老汇音乐剧和伦敦音乐剧的售票厅，提供 25%至 50%之间的折扣，因此经常排长龙。
12. **Off-Broadway**：外百老汇音乐剧，简称外百老汇，指的是美国纽约市演出规模较百老汇音乐剧小型的剧场演出。外百老汇的剧场坐落于百老汇戏剧的剧场区，但是大部分都是位于离曼哈顿市中心较远的地方。

▶▶ I. Multiple Choice

1. Divorce may depend on the following factors EXCEPT _______.
   A) social class B) race
   C) education D) economic situations

2. All of the following sports are typical American sports EXCEPT _______.
   A) volleyball B) American football
   C) basketball D) baseball

3. The Academy Awards, widely known as the Oscars, are awards of merit presented annually by the _______.
   A) Nestor Company
   B) Academy Award of Merit
   C) Academy of Motion Picture Arts and Sciences
   D) Broadway Academy

4. Which of the following is thought to be impolite as one dines with others?
   A) When you finish your meal, place all used utensils onto your plate together, on the right side, pointed down.
   B) When you finish your meal, just leave the used napkin directly on your dinner plate.
   C) Keep your elbows off the table while dining.
   D) Eat soup noiselessly, from the side of the spoon.

5. If you appreciate the dinner you are invited to, you can do all of the following EXCEPT _______.
   A) send flowers to your hostess beforehand
   B) send flowers later as a thank-you for a very special evening
   C) give a phone call the next day to say how much you enjoyed the evening
   D) give a sweet smile to your hostess

▶▶ II. True or False

1. A nuclear family usually consists of a husband, a wife, their children and grandparents.
2. Millions of couples choose to live a DINK lifestyle, simply because of the economic burden.
3. As marriage is a big event in one's life, most parents in America will give suggestions and advice for their children to follow when it is time for them to make the decision.
4. Family values are based on happiness, economic support and the opportunity to have children.
5. Although it is quite common for the American people to get divorced, most children in such families still feel embarrassed.
6. It has been long since every American employee has received an annual vacation with pay, and it has become customary to use this time off for travel.
7. As American young people have a strong desire to be different, there are no traditions for them to follow when they get married.
8. Easter Bunny and Easter Eggs have become part of the Easter Day's celebrations.
9. Father's Day is celebrated on the third Sunday in June.

▶▶ III. Questions for Discussion

1. Which holiday do you think is the most important one to Americans?
2. What makes divorce rate increase in America and around the world?
3. Have you ever been to America? If yes, what impresses you most? If no, which city do you dream to visit?
4. Are table manners universal around the world?
5. Are there any differences between American music and Chinese music?
6. What are the family moralities in America? What about in China?

SUMMARY

All countries have their social customs and peculiarities, and the United States is no exception. The Americans have developed individual customs regarding family, food and drinks, leisure time, social manners and etiquettes, holidays and so on, in response to their own particular environments, social conditions and levels of economic development.

Americans view the family as a group whose primary purpose is to advance the happiness of individual members. Many homes are run like a democracy. Each family member can have a say. A sense of equality often exists in American homes. Instead of fearing Mom and Dad, children may consider them as good friends. Husbands and wives often share household chores. Often parents give children freedom to make their own decisions. Young adults generally make their own choices about what career to pursue and whom to marry.

Families in America, like those in every culture, face many problems. Social pressures are breaking apart more and more American homes. Over half of the United States marriages now end in divorce. More than one in four American children is growing up in single-parent homes. As a result, many people believe the American families are in trouble.

American food and drinks come from many different countries. When people moved to America, they bring their cooking styles with them. That is why you can find almost every kind of ethnic food in America.

Most American holidays are not religious, but commemorative in nature and origin. Because the nation is blessed with rich ethnic heritage, it is possible to trace some of the American holidays to diverse cultural sources and traditions, but all holidays have taken on a distinctively American flavor.

Chapter 8

Who's Who

HIGHLIGHTS

George Washington — Abraham Lincoln — Franklin Delano Roosevelt — John Fitzgerald Kennedy — Richard Milhous Nixon—George Walker Bush — Barack Hussein Obama — Benjamin Franklin — Martin Luther King — Washington Irving — Walt Whitman — Emily Dickinson — Mark Twain — Ernest Miller Hemingway — Edgar Parks Snow — Thomas Alva Edison — Henry Ford — Wilbur and Orville Wright — Albert Einstein — Neil Armstrong and Edwin Aldrin — John Davison Rockefeller — Ray Kroc — Walt Disney — Marilyn Monroe — Elvis Aaron Presley — Steven Allan Spielberg — William Henry Bill Gates — Michael Jeffrey Jordan — Michael Phelps

I. Politicians

Every nation has its heroes. In the passage of time, certain political leaders have become better known than others. Their contributions at national and international levels have placed them above thousands of others who have made a career in politics.

1. George Washington

Statue in the George Washington Museum

George Washington (1732–1799), the "Father of America", was the first President of the United States of America. He was born on February 22, 1732, in Westmoreland County, Virginia. His father died when George was 11 and his half brother, Lawrence, took over his care.

He did not attend school regularly, but by age 11 he acquired basic reading, writing, and mathematics skills. Math was his best subject. He did not attend university. When he was 16, George moved to Lawrence's estate, Mount Vernon, and learned to be a surveyor. He inherited Mount Vernon on Lawrence's death, where he lived for the remainder of his life. At 26, he married a young widow, Martha, and adopted her two children. They joined him at Mount Vernon. George had no children of his own.

George received his first military appointment as a major in the militia during the French and Indian War. In 1758 Washington was elected to the **House of Burgesses** (城镇自治议会) and expressed his opposition to Britain's unfair taxes and land laws. He was active in resisting British rule. When the Revolutionary War began, the Continental Congress asked George Washington to be the commander in chief of the Continental army.

With a force of about 10,000 men, he faced a difficult winter at Valley Forge, Pennsylvania. They had little food and were poorly clothed. Those who survived until spring were pleased to learn that France had recognized America's independence. With aid from France, the troops were able to trap the main British force at Yorktown in 1781. After the war, Washington returned home to Mount Vernon.

George Washington was a member of the **Federalist Party** (联邦党), believing in a strong central American government. His popularity caused him to be elected President of the constitutional convention in 1787, and in 1789 he became the first President of the United States. He was elected to a second term, with John Adams serving as Vice President. He refused to run for a third term as president.

He died on December 14, 1799, of a throat infection brought on by several hours outside in a freezing rain. He was buried in the family tomb at Mount Vernon.

2. Abraham Lincoln

Although Americans admire George Washington, the greatest of all American heroes is certainly Abraham Lincoln (1809–1865). Why? Basic to the American philosophy is the idea that a person who is honest and hardworking can achieve success no matter how humble his or her beginnings are. Lincoln is a perfect example of a self-made man.

Lincoln was born on February 12, 1809 in a log cabin in Kentucky. His parents were uneducated and poor. Everyone worked hard just to obtain the necessities of life. Lincoln himself did manual labour on the family farm until he was a young man of 22 years old. When it was possible, the family sent young Abraham to a local school. During his whole life, however, he had less than one year of formal education. Nevertheless, through natural ability, determination, and study at home, he became one of the most learned men in the world of his time.

Lincoln, while still young, became a successful lawyer. He succeeded not only because of his knowledge of law but also because of his great skill in speaking. Throughout life he used words with great power and effectiveness, both in speaking and writing, to influence and persuade others.

Lincoln did have a brilliant mind and great moral strength. He had the courage to do what he felt was right, no matter what the sacrifice. In 1858 Lincoln failed a second time as a candidate to the United States Senate. Even though he failed, he became nationally famous and popular because of his position against slavery. In 1860 the Republican Party chose him as its nominee to the United States Presidency. He won the election, and was the first member of the young Republican Party — formed six years earlier in 1854 — to become President of the United States.

Statue in the Lincoln Memorial

Lincoln became President of the United States at the moment of the nation's greatest crisis since 1776, when 13 American colonies had declared their independence from Great Britain.

By the end of his Presidency slavery had been ended forever in the nation. The long, slow work began restoring unity among all the people and of rebuilding the country.

But for Lincoln that new and happier life did not last long. On April 14, 1865, he was shot by an **assassin** (暗杀者) while sitting in a theater in Washington, D.C. with his wife. The next day he died — only six days after the peace.

Lincoln's death brought great sorrow to the country. While millions mourned, a giant funeral ceremony was conducted in Washington, D.C.. At the end of the ceremony, his body was sent a third of the way across the continent by train for burial in the state of Illinois. At all hours of the day and night, in all kinds of weather, millions of Americans across the country stood along the railroad tracks, waiting for the funeral train — waiting to pay their last respects to the man who had led them so well, a man who would live forever in their hearts and in the hearts of every new generation of American.

People of the United States regard Abraham Lincoln as one of the greatest leaders in the history of their country. Every year many thousands of Americans visit the great white marble Lincoln Memorial in Washington, D.C.; they have put his likeness on their money and their stamps; and they have preserved the cabin where some people think he was born as a national shrine.

3. Franklin Delano Roosevelt

Franklin Delano Roosevelt (1882–1945) was the 32nd President of the United States. He was a central figure of the 20th century during a time of worldwide economic crisis and world war. Elected to four terms in office, he served from 1933 to 1945 and is the only US President to have served more than two terms.

Franklin D. Roosevelt, 1933

Franklin was born in New York. He attended Harvard University and Columbia Law School, two of the nation's finest educational institutions. In 1905, he married Eleanor Roosevelt, a distant cousin.

During the **Great Depression** (大萧条) of the 1930s, Roosevelt created the New Deal to provide relief for the unemployed, recovery of the economy, and reform of the economic and banking systems, through various agencies, such as the Works Project Administration, National Recovery Administration, and the Agricultural Adjustment Administration. Although recovery of the economy was incomplete until World War II, several programs he initiated, such as the Federal Deposit Insurance Corporation, Tennessee Valley Authority, and the United States Securities and Exchange Commission, continue to have instrumental roles in the nation's commerce. Some of his other legacies include the Social Security System and the National Labour Relations Board.

As Britain warred with Nazi Germany, Roosevelt provided Lend-Lease aid to Winston Churchill before America's entry into World War II in December, 1941. On the home front he introduced price controls and rationing, and relocation camps for 110,000 Japanese-Americans. Roosevelt led the United States as it became the "Arsenal of Democracy". Roosevelt, working closely with his aide Harry Hopkins, made the United States the principal arms supplier and financier of the Allies. As the Allies neared victory, Roosevelt played a critical role in shaping the post-war world, particularly through the **Yalta Conference** (雅尔塔会议) and the creation of the United Nations. Later, alongside the United States, the Allies defeated Germany, Italy and Japan.

Roosevelt's election to the presidency brought about realignment political scientists has called the Fifth Party System. His aggressive use of the federal government created a New Deal Coalition which dominated the Democratic Party until the late 1960s. Roosevelt introduced new taxes that affected all income groups. Conservatives vehemently fought back, but Roosevelt usually prevailed until he tried to pack the Supreme Court in 1937. He and his wife, Eleanor Roosevelt, have remained touchstones for modern American liberalism. Roosevelt's administration redefined American liberalism and realigned the Democratic Party based on his New Deal coalition of labor unions; farmers; ethnic, religious and racial minorities; intellectuals; the South; big city machines; and the poor and workers on relief. Roosevelt has been consistently ranked by scholars as one of the greatest US presidents.

4. John Fitzgerald Kennedy

On November 22, 1963, when he was hardly past his first thousand days in office, John Fitzgerald Kennedy (1917–1963) was killed by an assassin's bullets as his motorcade wound through Dallas, Texas. Kennedy was the youngest man elected President; he was the youngest to die.

35th President of the United States, John F. Kennedy

Of Irish descent, he was born in Brookline, Massachusetts, on May 29, 1917. Graduating from Harvard in 1940, he entered the Navy. In 1943, when his **PT boat** (鱼雷快艇) was rammed and sunk by a Japanese destroyer, Kennedy, despite grave injuries, led the survivors through perilous waters to safety.

Back from the war, he became a Democratic Congressman from the Boston area, advancing in 1953 to the Senate. He married Jacqueline Bouvier on September 12, 1953. In 1955, he wrote *Profiles in Courage*, which won the Pulitzer Prize in history.

In 1956 Kennedy almost gained the Democratic nomination for Vice President, and four years later was a first-ballot nominee for President. Millions watched his television debates with the Republican candidate, Richard M. Nixon. Winning by a narrow margin in the popular vote, Kennedy became the first **Roman Catholic** (天主教会的) President.

His Inaugural Address offered the memorable injunction, "Ask not what your country can do for you; ask what you can do for your country." As President, he set out to redeem his campaign pledge to get America moving again. His economic programs launched the country on its longest sustained expansion since World War II; before his death, he laid plans for a massive assault on persisting pockets of privation and poverty.

Responding to ever more urgent demands, he took vigorous action in the cause of equal rights, calling for new civil rights legislation. His vision of America extended to the quality of the national culture and the central role of the arts in a vital society.

He wished America resume its old mission as the first nation dedicated to the revolution of human rights. With the **Alliance for Progress** (进步联盟) and the **Peace Corps** (和平队), he brought American idealism to the aid of developing nations, but the hard reality of the Communist challenge remained.

Shortly after his inauguration, Kennedy permitted a band of Cuban exiles, already armed and trained, to invade their homeland. The attempt to overthrow the regime of Fidel Castro was a failure. Soon thereafter, the **Soviet Union** (苏联) renewed its campaign against West Berlin. Kennedy replied by reinforcing the Berlin garrison and increasing the Nation's military strength, including new efforts in **outer space** (外层空间). Confronted by this reaction, Moscow, after the erection of the Berlin Wall, relaxed its pressure in central Europe.

Instead, the Russians then sought to install nuclear missiles in Cuba. When this was discovered by air reconnaissance in October, 1962, Kennedy imposed quarantine on all offensive weapons bound for Cuba. While the world trembled on the brink of nuclear war, the Russians backed down and agreed to take the missiles away. The American response to the Cuban crisis evidently persuaded Moscow of the futility of nuclear blackmail.

Kennedy contended that both sides had a vital interest in stopping the spread of nuclear weapons and slowing the **arms race** (军备竞赛) — a contention which led to the test ban treaty of 1963. The months after the Cuban crisis showed significant progress toward his goal of "a world of law and free choice, banishing the world of war and coercion". His administration thus saw the beginning of new hope for both the equal rights of Americans and the peace of the world.

5. Richard Milhous Nixon

Reconciliation was the first goal set by President Richard M. Nixon (1913–1994). The Nation was painfully divided, with turbulence in the cities and war overseas. During his Presidency, Nixon succeeded in ending American fight in Viet Nam and improving relations with China. But the Watergate scandal brought fresh divisions to the country and ultimately led to his resignation.

37th President of the United States, Richard M. Nixon

His election in 1968 had climaxed a career unusual on two counts: his early success and his comeback after being defeated for President in 1960 and for Governor of California in 1962.

Born in California in 1913, Nixon had a brilliant record at Whittier College and Duke University Law School before beginning the practice of law. In 1940, he married Patricia Ryan; they had two daughters, Patricia and Julie. During World War II, Nixon served as a Navy

lieutenant (上尉) commander in the Pacific.

On leaving the service, he was elected to Congress from his California district. In 1950, he won a Senate seat. Two years later, General Eisenhower selected Nixon, aged 39, to be his **running mate** (竞选伙伴).

As Vice President, Nixon took on major duties in the Eisenhower Administration. Nominated for President by acclamation in 1960, he lost by a narrow margin to John F. Kennedy. In 1968, he again won his party's nomination, and went on to defeat Vice President Hubert H. Humphrey and third-party candidate George C. Wallace.

His accomplishments while in office included revenue sharing, the end of the draft, new anticrime laws, and a broad environmental program. As he had promised, he appointed Justices of conservative philosophy to the **Supreme Court** (最高法院). One of the most dramatic events of his first term occurred in 1969, when American astronauts made the first moon landing.

In his 1972 bid for office, Nixon defeated Democratic candidate George McGovern by one of the widest margins on record. Within a few months, his administration was embattled over the so-called "Watergate" scandal, stemming from a break-in at the offices of the Democratic National Committee during the 1972 campaign. The break-in was traced to officials of the Committee to re-elect the President. A number of administration officials resigned; some were later convicted of offenses connected with efforts to cover up the affair. Nixon denied any personal involvement, but the courts forced him to yield tape recordings which indicated that he had, in fact, tried to divert the investigation.

As a result of unrelated scandals in Maryland, Vice President Spiro T. Agnew resigned in 1973. Nixon nominated, and Congress approved, House Minority Leader Gerald R. Ford as Vice President.

Faced with what seemed almost certain **impeachment** (弹劾), Nixon announced on August 8, 1974, that he would resign the next day to begin "that process of healing which is so desperately needed in America".

In his last years, Nixon gained praise as an elder statesman. By the time of his death on April 22, 1994, he had written numerous books on his experiences in public life and on foreign policy.

6. George Walker Bush

George Walker Bush (1946–), the 43rd President of the United States, was sworn into office on January 20, 2001, re-elected on November 2, 2004, and sworn in for a second term on January 20, 2005. Prior to his Presidency, President Bush served for six years as the 46th Governor of the State of Texas, where he earned a reputation for **bipartisanship** (两党合作) and as a compassionate conservative who shaped public policy based on the principles of limited government, personal responsibility, strong families, and local control.

President Bush was born on July 6, 1946, in New Haven, Connecticut, and grew up in Midland and Houston, Texas. He received a bachelor's degree in history from Yale University in 1968, and then served as an F-102 fighter pilot in the Texas Air National Guard. President Bush received a Master of Business Administration from Harvard Business School in 1975. Following graduation, he moved back to Midland and began a career in the energy business. After working on his father's successful 1988 Presidential campaign, President Bush assembled the group of partners who purchased the Texas Rangers baseball franchise in 1989. On November 8, 1994, President Bush was elected Governor of Texas. He became the first Governor in Texas history to be elected to consecutive four-year terms when he was re-elected on November 3, 1998.

President Bush worked with the Congress to create an ownership society and build a future of security, prosperity, and opportunity for all Americans. He signed into law tax relief that helped workers keep more of their hard-earned money, as well as the most comprehensive education reforms in a generation, the *No Child Left Behind Act* of 2001. This legislation ushered in a new era of accountability, flexibility, local control, and more choices for parents, affirming America's fundamental belief in the promise of every child. President Bush also worked to improve healthcare and modernize Medicare, providing the first-ever prescription drug benefit for seniors; to increase homeownership, especially among minorities; to conserve their environment; and to increase military strength, pay, and benefits. Because President Bush believed the strength of America lies in the hearts and souls of their citizens, he supported programs that encourage individuals to help their neighbours in need.

On the morning of September 11, 2001, terrorists attacked the United States. President Bush took unprecedented steps to protect America and create a world free from terror. He was grateful for the service and sacrifice of brave men and women in uniform and their families. The President believed that by helping build free and prosperous societies, the United States and their friends and allies can succeed in making America more secure and the world more peaceful.

7. Barack Hussein Obama, Jr.

Barack H. Obama (1961–) is the 44th President of the United States.

His story is the American story — values from the heartland, a middle-class upbringing in a strong family, hard work and education as the means of getting ahead, and the conviction that a life so blessed should be lived in service to others.

With a father from Kenya and a mother from Kansas, President Obama was born in Hawaii on August 4, 1961. He was raised with help from his grandfather, who served in Patton's army, and his grandmother, who worked her way up from the secretarial pool to middle management at a bank.

The Inauguration of Barack Obama on January 20, 2009

After working his way through college with the help of scholarships and student loans, President Obama moved to Chicago, where he worked with a group of churches to help rebuild communities devastated by the closure of local steel plants.

He went on to attend law school, where he became the first African-American president of the *Harvard Law Review*. Upon graduation, he returned to Chicago to help lead a voter registration drive, teach constitutional law at the University of Chicago, and remain active in his community.

President Obama's years of public service are based around his **unwavering** (坚定的) belief in the ability to unite people around political purposes. In the Illinois State Senate, he passed the first major ethics reform in 25 years, cut taxes for working families, and expanded health care for children and their parents. As a United States Senator, he reached across the aisle to pass groundbreaking lobbying reform, lock up the world's most dangerous weapons, and bring transparency to government by putting federal spending online.

He was elected the 44th President of the United States on November 4, 2008, and sworn in on January 20, 2009. He and his wife, Michelle, are the proud parents of two daughters, Malia, 10, and Sasha, 7.

8. Benjamin Franklin

In a pious **Puritan** (清教徒) house in Boston, Massachusetts, a boy was born in 1706. The boy was named Benjamin Franklin (1706–1790) and he would use his intellect to pursue many professions. Perhaps he was a model for the national character of what an 18th century American should be.

He only had two years of schooling when his father put him to work in the family trade of candle-making and mechanics. He was such an avid reader that books became his teachers. He became an apprentice to his brother, James, who was the printer of the *New England Courant*. At age 16, Benjamin wrote articles for this newspaper. He wrote satirical essays about Boston society and signed the articles with the name, *Silence Dogood*.

In 1726 at age 20, he started his own newspaper called *the Philadelphia Gazette*. He was very successful as a publisher and he began to print *Poor Richard's Almanac*, which was filled with profound sayings like "Early to bed and early to rise makes a man healthy, wealthy, and wise."

In 1727, he became a civic leader by inviting businessmen to meet to plan for successful businesses. They called their business club "the Jun-to." This civic-minded group started a city library, a fire company, a learned society, an insurance company, a hospital, and a voluntary militia. They also started a college that later became the University of Pennsylvania. The group also made plans to pave, clean, and light the streets. All these plans occurred in a 24 year period from 1727 to 1751.

Franklin invented a stove to heat homes and businesses which was simply called the Franklin stove. It soon heated buildings all over America and Europe.

He read treatises on electricity which led to his flying a kite with a wire attached to a key. He was trying to prove that electricity produced in a laboratory was similar to electricity in nature, as found in lightning. This led to the use of lightning rods placed on buildings as a protection from lightning storms.

The **Royal Society** (皇家学会) in London published these discoveries and Franklin became famous throughout the world. Franklin joined the Royal Society in 1756 and also the **French Academy of Sciences** (法国科学院) in 1772.

Franklin also produced research on heat absorption, measurement of the **Gulf Stream** (墨西哥暖流), ship design, tracking violent storms, and the invention of bifocal lenses for glasses.

Franklin lived both in England and France, representing the interests of the United States. He was in Pennsylvania for a few years where he served in Congress in 1775 and 1776. During this time, at the age of 70, he signed the *Declaration of Independence*.

Franklin's careers included printer, moralist, essayist, civic leader, scientist, inventor, statesman, diplomat and philosopher. Few Americans have had significant success in so many vocations.

9. Martin Luther King, Jr.

Only three persons in American history have been honoured by Congress by declaring a national holiday to remember their contributions. Former presidents Abraham Lincoln and George Washington are honoured on their birthdays. Martin Luther King, Jr. (1929–1968) was never a president but his work to bring equality to black Americans was so profound in its historical significance that Congress declared a national holiday in January to remember his life.

Rosa Parks is considered the mother of Civil Rights movement. In December, 1955, she refused to give her seat to a white male passenger on a Montgomery, Alabama bus. Her arrest and the bus boycott which followed became national news. Black residents started the **Montgomery Improvement Association** (蒙哥马利改进协会) and they elected Martin Luther King as their president. Within one year, Alabama's racial segregation was declared unconstitutional (unlawful because of the *Constitution*) by the United States Congress.

Martin Luther King, 1964

The success in Alabama led to a movement throughout the Southern states to start the **Southern Christian Leadership Conference** (南方基督教领袖会议). Their choice for president was Martin Luther King. It was on August 28, 1963, that 250,000 marchers came to Washington, D.C. to hear Martin Luther King give his speech, *I Have a Dream*. King spoke in front of the famous Lincoln Memorial. It was 100 years after Lincoln signed the ***Emancipation Proclamation*** (解放奴隶宣言) which freed all black persons from slavery.

This speech and King's growing national influence caused *Time* magazine to declare him "the Man of the Year" for 1963. This award is annually given to the most significant person from throughout the world. The next year, the Nobel Peace Prize was given to him. Thus, he had been recognized both in his own country and internationally for his work in the civil rights movement.

In 1965, the *Voting Rights Act* was approved. The success of King's work toward equality was finally written into law. He continued to travel to Southern states to help black people. He went to Memphis, Tennessee to help garbage workers receive adequate pay for their work. It was there he was assassinated on April 4, 1968.

The legacy of Martin Luther King lies in his success to bring equality to black Americans through non-violent means. His challenge has always been for Americans to treat all men equally regardless of the color of their skin. As American minorities become active in all aspects of American life, they will be indebted to Martin Luther King who opened the way for all persons to participate fully and equally in achieving their individual American dream.

II. Writers and Scientists

America is a young country so all the scientists, inventors, novelists, poets, and non-fiction writers have appeared only in the last 200 years. When the country was young, they were involved in politics or in expanding the frontiers of their new country. Inventors use research to make products that change the way people travel, communicate, and live. They rely on their ability to test theories, make mistakes, but finally find success.

1. Washington Irving

Washington Irving (1783–1859) was America's first man of letters, devoting much of his career to literature. He was born into a wealthy New York merchant family. From a very early age he began to read widely and write juvenile poems, essays, and plays. Later, he studied law and led for a time the leisurely life of a gentleman lawyer, but he loved writing more. His first book *A History of New York from the Beginning of the World to the End of the Dutch Dynasty* (1809), written under the name of Diedrich Knickerbocker, was a great success and won him wide popularity. In 1815 he went to England to take care of his family business there, and when it failed, he had to write to support himself. With the publication of *The Sketch Book of Geoffrey Crayon, Gent.* (1819–1820), he won a measure of international recognition. In 1826 as an American diplomatic attaché, he was sent to Spain where he gathered material for his *The History of the Life and Voyages of Christopher Columbus* (1828), *A Chronicle of the Conquest of Granada* (1829) and *The Alhambra* (1832). From 1829 to 1932 he was Secretary of the United States Legation in London. When he was about 50, after an absence of 17 years, he returned to America and bought Sunnyside, his famous home on the Hudson River at Tarrytown. There he spent the rest of his life, except for a period of four years (1842–1846) when he was away from home as Minister to Spain, living a life of leisure and comfort, and writing the *Life of Goldsmith* and a five-volume *Life of Washington* and a miscellany of other works. He did not get married, until he died in 1859.

Irving's contribution to American literature is unique in more ways than one. He did a number of things that have been regarded as the first of their kind in America. He was the first American writer of imaginative literature to gain international fame: when he returned home in 1832, he was acclaimed as the one American author whom people in Europe knew about, and this American took as a sign that American literature was emerging as an independent entity. To say that he was father of American literature is not much exaggeration. The short story as a genre in American literature probably began with Irving's *The Sketch Book*, a collection of essays, sketches, and tales, of which the most famous and frequently anthologized are *Rip Van Winkle* (1809) and *The Legend of Sleepy Hollow* (1820). The book touched the American imagination and foreshadowed the coming of Hawthorne, Melville, and Poe, in whose hands the short story attained a degree of perfection as a literary tradition. It also marked the beginning of American romanticism. The Gothic, the supernatural, and the longing for the good old days which some of its pieces clearly exhibit, are romantic enough in subject if not exactly in style, as Irving wrote in the neoclassical tradition of Joseph Addison and Oliver Goldsmith.

2. Walt Whitman

Whitman (1819–1892) was one of the great innovators in American literature. In the cluster of poems he called *Leaves of Grass* (1855) he gave America its first genuine epic poem. The poetic style he devised is now called free verse. Whitman thought that the voice of democracy should not be haltered by traditional forms of verse. His influence on the poetic technique of other writers was small during the time he was writing *Leaves of Grass* but today elements of his style are apparent in the work of many poets.

Whitman grew up in Brooklyn, New York, and worked there as a schoolteacher, as an apprentice to a printer, and as the editor of various newspapers. He had very little schooling but read a great deal on his own. He was especially intrigued by the works of Shakespeare and Milton. Strangely enough, his only contact with the Eastern religions or with German **Transcendentalists** (超验主义), whose ideas he frequently used in his poetry, was what he had read of them in the writings of Emerson.

In the 1840s Whitman supported Jackson's Democratic Party; he also favored the exclusion of slavery from new states in his newspaper writing and because of this, in 1848, he was dismissed from his job. He then worked **sporadically** (偶尔) at carpentry and odd jobs, and had some of his writing — which was conventional and undistinguished — printed in newspaper.

In 1848 he visited New Orleans, Chicago, and the Western frontier; the latter impressed him greatly. There is speculation that some of his experiences on this trip marked a turning point in his career, though it is more likely that he was gradually developing as an artist. At any rate, soon after this period he began to write in a new style — the "free verse" for which he became famous. He published the first edition of *Leaves of Grass* in 1855, setting the type for the book himself, and writing favorable reviews of it in the papers, anonymously. He continued to add new poems to the collection, and to rearrange and revise them, until his death in 1892. His best work is usually considered to have been done before 1871.

Most of the poems in *Leaves of Grass* are about man and nature. However, a small number of very good poems deal with New York, the city that fascinated Whitman, and with the Civil War, in which he served as a volunteer male nurse. In his poetry, Whitman combined the ideal of the democratic common man and that of the rugged individual. He envisioned the poet as a hero, a savior and a prophet, one who leads the community by his expressions of the truth.

With the publication of *Leaves of Grass* Whitman was praised by Ralph Waldo Emerson and a few other **literati** (文人学士) but was attacked by the majority of critics because of his unconventional style. He wanted his poetry to be for the common people.

3. Emily Dickinson

Emily Dickinson (1830–1886) wrote her whimsical, darting verse with sublime indifference to any notion of being a democratic or popular poet. Her work, far different from that of either Whitman or Longfellow, illustrated the fact that one could take a single household and an inactive life, and make enchanting poetry out of it.

Black and white daguerreotype of Emily Dickinson, early 1847.

Miss Dickinson was born in Amherst, Massachusetts, where her father was a prominent lawyer and politician and where her grandfather had established an academy and college. Emily's father was very **closely knit** (关系紧密) and she and her sister remained at home and did not marry. Emily seldom left Amherst; she attended college in a nearby town for one year, and later made one trip as far as Washington and two or three trips to Boston. After 1862 she became a total recluse, not leaving her house nor seeing even close friends. Her early letters and descriptions of herself in her youth reveal an attractive girl with a lively wit. Her later retirement from the world, though perhaps affected by an unhappy love affair, seems mainly to have resulted from her own personality, from a desire to separate herself from the world. The range of her poetry suggests not her limited experiences but the power of her creativity and imagination.

When she began writing poetry Emily had relatively little formal education. She did know Shakespeare and classical mythology and was especially interested in women authors such as Elizabeth Browning and the Brontë sisters. She was also acquainted with the works of Emerson, Thoreau and Hawthorne. Though she did not believe in the conventional religion of her family, she had studied the *Bible*, and many of her poems resemble hymns in form.

There were several men who, at different times in her life, acted as teacher or master to Emily. The first was Benjamin Newton, a young lawyer in her father's law office who improved her literary and cultural tastes and influenced her ideas on religion. She refers to him as "a friend, who taught me Immortality".

Emily's next teacher was Charles Wadsworth, a married, middle-aged minister who provided her with intellectual challenge and contact with the outside world. It appears that she felt affection for him that he could not return, and when he moved to San Francisco in 1862, she removed herself from society even more than she had before. Wadsworth may have been the model for the lover in her poems, though it is just as likely that the literary figure is purely imaginary.

Miss Dickinson's greatest outpouring of poems occurred in the early 1860s, and because she was so isolated, the Civil War affected her thinking very little. At this time she sent some of her work to Thomas Higginson, a prominent critic and author. He was impressed by her poetry, but suggested that she use a more conventional grammar. Emily, however, refused to revise her poems to fit the standards of others and took no interest in having them published; in fact she had only seven poems published during her lifetime. In Higginson she did, nevertheless, gain an intelligent and sympathetic critic with whom to discuss her work.

In the last years of her life Emily seldom saw visitors, but kept in touch with her friends through letters, short poems and small gifts. After her death in 1886, her sister found nearly 1,800 poems that she had written. Many of the poems were finally published in the 1890s, and Emily Dickinson, like Melville, was rediscovered by the literary world in the 1920s.

Emily Dickinson's poetry comes out in bursts. The poems are short, many of them being based on a single image or symbol. But within her little lyrics Miss Dickinson writes about some of the most important things in life. She writes about love and a lover, whom she either never really found or else gave up. She writes about nature. She writes about mortality and immortality. She writes about success, which she thought she never achieved, and about failure, which she considered her constant companion. She writes of these things so brilliantly that she is now ranked as one of America's great poets.

Her poetry is read today throughout much of the world and yet its exact wording has not been completely determined, nor has its arrangement and punctuation. Since Emily never prepared her poems for publication, one of the bitterest battles in American literary history has been fought over who should publish and edit what she wrote. However, regardless of details or conflicts, there is no doubt that the solitary Miss Dickinson of Amherst, Massachusetts, is a writer of great power and beauty.

4. Mark Twain

Mark Twain (1835–1910) is the pen name of Samuel Langhorne Clemens, who the writer H. L. Mencken called "the true father of our national literature". This title may be justified, for Twain made a more extensive combination of American folk humour and serious literature than previous writers had done.

Twain was born in the backwoods of Missouri, but while he was yet a small boy the family moved to Hannibal on the Mississippi River. There Twain developed a passion for the river and a

Mark Twain

desire to become the pilot on a riverboat. This was the dream of all the boys along the river, and Twain was very proud of himself when, later on, he actually became a pilot.

Twain's father had wanted to be a lawyer, and did actually serve as a justice of the peace and judge, but had to make his living as a farmer and storekeeper. He was a popular man in Hannibal, but remained poor, and when he died Twain was apprenticed to a printer. Thus at age 11 Twain's formal schooling ended, though he continued to read extensively. As was the case with many 19th century writers, the print shop and journalism served as preparation for his literary career.

After working on his brother's newspaper for a while, in 1854 Twain set out on his own, working as a printer in various Eastern and Midwestern towns. In 1856 he fulfilled his boyhood dream by becoming a riverboat pilot. When the boats stopped operating during the Civil War, Twain served for a time as a volunteer soldier and then, in 1862, he went West.

Twain first wrote for a newspaper in Nevada and then moved to San Francisco. During this period he wrote mainly humorous sketches, the most famous being *The Celebrated Jumping Frog of Calaveras County* (1865). Between 1865 and 1870, Twain went on tours of Hawaii, Europe, and the Middle East as a correspondent; later his adventures served as the subject of several books. His newspaper accounts of his travels spread his popularity, so that on his return he also became a successful humorous lecturer.

In 1870, Twain married a wealthy and rather aristocratic girl and settled in the East, first in Buffalo and then permanently in Hartford, Connecticut. When he moved to Hartford, Twain gave up journalism to make fiction writing his career. His writing was popular and sold well, although he sometimes found lecture tours necessary to supplement his income.

In Hartford, Twain was surrounded by a wealthy, genteel society including several other popular authors of the time, and it has been assumed that this influence modified the **boisterous** (活跃的) writer of newspaper days, **curbing** (约束) his wit and social criticism. *A Connecticut Yankee in King Arthur's Court* (1889), *The Man That Corrupted Hadleyburg* (1900), *The Mysterious Stranger* (1916), and his *Autobiography* (1924) all contain bitter attacks on the human race. Twain's work does not suffer from being over **genteel** (上流社会的), and his satirical writing is a sharp attack on society. In his last year, Twain became increasingly bitter; some of his writing of this period is so pessimistic that he withheld it from publication.

5. Ernest Miller Hemingway

Ernest Hemingway in Kenya, 1953

Ernest M. Hemingway (1899–1961) was born in Illinois. His family took him, as a boy, on frequent hunting and fishing trips and so acquainted him early with the kinds of virtues, such as courage and endurance, which were later reflected in his fiction. After high school, he worked as a newspaper reporter and then went overseas to take part in World War I. After the war he lived for several years in Paris, where he became part of a group of Americans who felt alienated from their country. They considered themselves a lost generation. It was not long before he began publishing remarkable and completely individual short stories. The year he left Paris he published the powerful novel, *The Sun Also Rises* (1926). His subjects were often war and its effects on people, or contests, such as hunting or bullfighting, which demand **stamina** (毅力) and courage.

Hemingway's style of writing is striking. His sentences are short, his words simple, yet they are often filled with emotion. A careful reading can show us, furthermore, that he is a master of the pause. He perfected the art of conveying emotion with few words.

The book that appeared in 1925, *In Our Time*, is interesting precisely because, for the first time, a Hemingway hero appears on the scene to learn to live in grace under pressure. *A Farewell to Arms* (1928), his next important novel, can be read as a footnote to *The Sun Also Rises* in that it explains how people like Jack Barnes come to behave the way they do. The break of the Hemingway hero with society becomes extreme in his next two books, *Death in the Afternoon* (1932), and *Green Hills of Africa* (1935). Between 1940 and 1950 when his next novel, *Across the River and into the Trees* appeared, Hemingway is silent from a literary point of view. *Across the River and into the Trees* is such a poor performance that critics all agreed that Hemingway's talent is dead. But not for long, *The Old Man and the Sea* (1952) helps toward restoring his literary image, so that he wins the Nobel Prize in 1954.

In contrast to the romantic writers, who often emphasize abundance and even excess, Hemingway is a Classicist in his restraint and understatement. He believes, with many other Classicists that the strongest effect comes with an economy of means.

6. Thomas Alva Edison

When Thomas Alva Edison (1847–1931) was born in the small town of Milan, Ohio, in

Thomas A. Edison, 1932

1847, America was just beginning its great industrial development. In his lifetime of 84 years, Edison shared in the excitement of America's growth into a modern nation. The story of his life takes us back to that "heroic age of invention" as the last of the 19th century has been called. It was a time filled with human and scientific adventures, and Edison became the hero of that age.

In 1869, when he was only 22 years old, Edison invented an improved stock market ticket-tape machine which could better report the prices on the New York Stock Market. The ticket-tape machine was successful, and Edison decided to concentrate wholly on inventing.

Edison formed his own "invention factory" in Newark, New Jersey. Over the next few years, he invented and produced many new items, including the **mimeograph machine** (油印机), wax wrapping paper, and improvements of the telegraph.

On August 12, 1877, Edison began experimenting with an apparatus which he had designed and ordered to be built. It was a **cylinder** (圆柱形), wrapped in **tinfoil** (锡纸), turned by a handle, and as it revolved, a needle made a groove in the foil. So Edison had just invented the phonograph, a completely new concept: a talking machine.

No one but Edison knew how hard and long he had worked to achieve his great victory with the light bulb. Nor did he stop there. He not only developed an improved **dynamo** (直流发电机) to provide the power for electric lighting, but he also perfected other electric power equipment such as the generator, conductors, and underground power cables.

As a result of this electrical revolution begun by Edison, masses of people throughout the world were released from their dependence on oil and gas lamps for light. The enormous steam engines long used for power in factories now could be replaced by a more practical power turned on with a switch.

For 60 years Thomas Alva Edison was the world's leading inventor. He patented over 1,000 inventions which changed the way people live. He designed the central power station which became the model for the first public electric plant in New York City, providing electric power for thousands of homes and businesses. Edison was one of the earliest inventors of the motion-picture machines. His invention of the phonograph was joined with photography to produce talking pictures. He also perfected the electric motor which made streetcars and electric trains possible.

Therefore, it is no wonder that Edison received many honours during his life for his contributions to the progress of mankind. America bestowed on him its highest award, a special Congressional Medal of Honour. Yet, amid all his fame, Edison remained a modest man. He preferred to continue his work rather than rest on his achievements. His motto was, "I find what the world needs; then I go ahead and try to invent it." He never considered himself a brilliant man and once remarked that genius was "2% inspiration and 98% perspiration". He never stopped trying to learn more about science and what it could do for man. His discoveries probably increased the wealth of the world more than those of any other single man in history.

On October 18, 1931, Edison died at the age of 84 at his home in Orange, New Jersey. Several days later, the whole United States turned off its electric lights for one minute, in honour of the man whose discoveries had so changed and improved the life of people everywhere.

7. Henry Ford

Henry Ford (1863—1947) was the American founder of the Ford Motor Company and father of modern assembly lines used in mass production. The Ford family came from Ireland to the United States in 1847. Their child Henry was born in 1863. He had an interest in mechanics. He invented a car called the quadric-cycle which had four wheels. It essentially had four bicycle tires and no cab.

Henry Ford, 1914

Henry built race cars in the 1890s and even became a race car driver. But he wanted to build cars for everyone to use, so he began the Ford Motor Company in 1903. He had formulated a business motto which would be the reason for his success, "The way to make automobiles is to make one automobile like another automobile, to make them all alike." His company declared that they could make automobiles in any color, as long as it was black.

Henry gave much credit to his wife whom he called "The Believer". From the earliest days of their relationship she was the one who encouraged him to build a horseless carriage. Her belief in him was a constant encouragement to produce what would become the primary mode of transportation in the future.

Henry's greatest task was to produce a gasoline engine that would be the power for his cars. He finally produced one in the kitchen sink in his house. He worked so many hours each day that his friends called him crazy Henry. He was inspired to work until his invention would work effectively.

When he designed the Model T, he decided he could build it cheaply for what he called "the great multitude". To do this he had to design an assembly line where many cars could be built in a single day. Each worker would have only his individual parts to put on each car. Then he could limit himself to the few tools needed for the task. The Model T was introduced in 1908 and began to be produced on an assembly line in 1913. Henry Ford was the major figure in the auto industry for the next 15 years.

On May 26, 1927, Henry watched the 15 millionth Model T Ford roll off the assembly line. He had become the richest man in America. He was able to bring the price low enough so that most Americans could buy his car. This gave every family much independence for they could move about freely without the aid of others transporting them.

Because he did not change his Model T, others began experimenting with different types of cars. However, the Ford Motor Company still exists and all car owners are indebted to the creation of the automobile by Henry Ford.

8. Wilbur and Orville Wright

The Wright brothers, Orville (1871–1948) and Wilbur (1867–1912), were two Americans who are generally credited with inventing and building the world's first successful airplane and making the first controlled, powered and sustained heavier-than-air human flight on December 17, 1903.

The Wright brothers were business partners in a bicycle repair shop in Dayton, Ohio, in 1901. They were fascinated with the sport of flying in the air with gliders. Soon, they decided that if they could attach a motor that weighed only a few pounds, they might keep a glider in the air for a longer period of time.

In October of 1902, they tested their first motor driven plane, flying it for 3.5 seconds. This was a great satisfaction to them. They decided that flying an airplane powered by a motor was a real possibility.

The next year, they improved the design of the airplane and tried again. Wilbur wrote a description of the flight by saying, "The flight lasted only 12 seconds, but it was nevertheless the first in the history of the world in which a machine carrying a man had raised itself by its own power into the air in full flight, had sailed forward without reduction of speed and had finally landed at a point as high as that from which it started." The date was December 17, 1903, and the location was the city of Kitty Hawk, North Carolina.

They tried three more flights that day and on the last one, the plane stayed in the air for 54 seconds. It flew a distance of 852 feet, more than the length of two football fields.

While they were discussing the success of the last flight, a strong gust of wind picked the plane up and began to turn it over. The wings were very wide and the plane was very light. Wilbur and Orville rushed to the plane and took hold of it. One of the assistants, named Mr. Daniels, refused to release his grip and when the plane rolled over, he found himself inside the wings. He was thrown head over heels but he was not seriously injured. The damage to the plane ended the flight experiment for the rest of the year.

Two years later on October 5, 1905, Wilbur flew a plane for 38 minutes over a circular course of 24 miles. The Wright brothers now felt they had a plane that could be developed for practical usefulness. They began to seek buyers for their invention. They also went to Europe and they flew their plane in LeMans, France, and Rome, Italy. This caused them to become world famous. They received many medals in Europe and America for their ingenuity and skill in building the first airplane.

9. Albert Einstein

Albert Einstein (1879—1955) was born at Ulm, in Württemberg, Germany, on March 14, 1879. Six weeks later the family moved to Munich, where he later on began his schooling at the Luitpold Gymnasium. Later, they moved to Italy and Albert continued his education at Aarau, Switzerland and in 1896 he entered the Swiss Federal Polytechnic School in Zurich to be trained as a teacher in physics and mathematics. In 1901, the year he gained his diploma, he acquired Swiss citizenship and, as he was unable to find a teaching post, he accepted a position as technical assistant in the Swiss Patent Office. In 1905 he obtained his doctor's degree.

During his stay at the Patent Office, and in his spare time, he produced much of his remarkable work and in 1908 he was appointed **privatdozent** (无薪大学教师) in Berne. In 1909 he became Professor Extraordinary at Zurich, in 1911 Professor of Theoretical Physics at Prague, returning to Zurich in the following year to fill a similar post. In 1914 he was appointed Director of the Kaiser Wilhelm Physical Institute and Professor in the University of Berlin. He became a German citizen in 1914 and remained in Berlin until 1933 when he renounced his citizenship for political reasons and emigrated to America to take the position of Professor of Theoretical Physics at Princeton. He became a United States citizen in 1940 and retired from his post in 1945.

Albert Einstein, 1921

Einstein always appeared to have a clear view of the problems of physics and the determination to solve them. He had a strategy of his own and was able to visualize the main stages on the way to his goal. He regarded his major achievements as mere stepping-stones for the next advance.

At the start of his scientific work, Einstein realized the inadequacies of Newtonian mechanics and his special theory of relativity stemmed from an attempt to **reconcile** (使一致) the laws of mechanics with the laws of the **electromagnetic field** (电磁场). He dealt with classical problems of statistical mechanics and problems in which they were merged with **quantum theory** (量子论), which led to an explanation of the Brownian movement of **molecules** (分子). He investigated the **thermal properties** (热性质) of light with a low radiation density and his observations laid the foundation of the photon theory of light.

Einstein's researches are, of course, well chronicled and his more important works include *Special Theory of Relativity* (1905), *Relativity* (1920), *General Theory of Relativity* (1916), *Investigations on Theory of Brownian Movement* (1926), and *The Evolution of Physics* (1938). Among his non-scientific works, *About Zionism* (1930), *Why War?* (1933), *My Philosophy* (1934), and *Out of My Later Years* (1950) are perhaps the most important.

Albert Einstein received honorary doctorate degrees in science, medicine and philosophy from many European and American universities. During the 1920s he lectured in Europe, America and the Far East and he was awarded Fellowships or Memberships of all the leading scientific academies throughout the world. He gained numerous awards in recognition of his work, including the Copley Medal of the Royal Society of London in 1925, and the Franklin Medal of the Franklin Institute in 1935.

Einstein's gifts inevitably resulted in his dwelling much in intellectual solitude, and for relaxation, music played an important part in his life. He married Mileva Maric in 1903 and they had a daughter and two sons; their marriage was dissolved in 1919 and in the same year he married his cousin, Elsa Löwenthal, who died in 1936. He died on April 18, 1955 at Princeton, New Jersey.

10. Neil Armstrong and Edwin Aldrin

On July 16, 1969, the Apollo 11 spacecraft was sent into the sky by powerful rockets. Three astronauts were inside: Neil Armstrong (1930–), Edwin Aldrin (1930–) and Michael Collins (1930–). Three days later, they arrived at the moon. The men went to sleep as they orbited the moon 10 times.

On July 20, Neil and Edwin got into the lunar module called "the Eagle" and began to descend to the surface of the moon. Michael stayed in the command ship and continued to circle the moon.

As the Eagle descended, Neil saw that they were going to land on rocks so he maneuvered the lunar module to a flat space called the **Sea of Tranquility** (静海). Moments later, he told the millions of viewers who were watching on television, "Houston…The Eagle has landed." It was 4:17 p.m. at Cape Kennedy in the Eastern time zone of the United States.

Neil Armstrong on the Moon, on July 20, 1969

Neil Armstrong, 1969

Six hours later, Neil and Edwin left the lunar module and stepped on the moon. Neil looked at the camera and said, "That is one small step for man, one giant leap for mankind."

The two men set up a television camera, planted an American flag, collected soil and rock samples and set up scientific instruments. They could move around easily as the gravity pull on the moon was only one-sixth of the gravity on the earth. This means they could jump easily. Walking was more like hopping.

President Richard Nixon was able to talk to them by a special telephone transmission. He said the call was one of the most historic phone calls ever made.

The cameras were quite clear so everyone in the world could watch the men do their work. The television audience was estimated at more than 600 million people throughout the world. The two men stayed on the moon for two hours and 21 minutes. They described the moon as being barren with only dust and rocks. When they walked, their feet pressed into the ground slightly as they were walking through dust.

Neil Armstrong unveiled a **plaque** (匾) with the inscription, "Here, man from the planet earth first set foot upon the moon, July, 1969 A.D.. We came in peace for all mankind." The response from persons on the earth was that this might have been the greatest human achievement of all time. Certainly, the calculation of the distance, the critical landing and return to the command ship in a foreign environment was commendable.

All three astronauts will be remembered for traveling so far to land on the moon. This was one of the most interesting events of the last century.

III. Celebrities in Social Life

There is no resting place for an enterprise in a competitive economy. Businessmen use research to create wealth and jobs for many people.

Most people see sport as an unscripted event pitting two opposing entities against each other, resulting in a victor and a loser. In a few sports, athletes can become professionals where their sport activity is their job. Athletes must be in top condition both mentally and physically.

The development of art is actually the history of how artists, pop stars develop and create themselves. This was a long process of development, during which artists and pop stars used their creativity, ability, and capacity for struggle to gradually gain the understanding of society and the public. They eventually won the respect of society.

1. John Davison Rockefeller and Family

The birth of John (1839–1937), occurred in New York. He and his family provided such leadership that the name Rockefeller has been institutionalized as one of the greatest American families.

John made his money in the oil business in Cleveland, Ohio. He founded a business in 1870 which was called the Standard Oil Company of Ohio. It became the world's largest oil company in the last part of the 19th century. The company was divided into 30 corporations in 1899. By 1911, it had grown to 39 separate companies. This was the year Rockefeller decided to retire and think about what he should do in the future.

Due to his great personal wealth, he decided to give one half of his money away to various organizations which caused him to start the Rockefeller Foundation and the Rockefeller Institute for Medical Research. He started the University of Chicago and gave gifts to many colleges and churches.

His son, continued his father's **philanthropic** (慈善的) interests. The huge Rockefeller Center in New York has become a major center of business activity. There is a large church called Riverside Church that has received support. The Rockefellers donated the land where the United Nations headquarters are located.

The grandsons of John D. Rockefeller have held significant positions in American society. John D. Rockefeller III continued to operate the philanthropies of the family as well as other businesses. Nelson Rockefeller became Governor of New York State. Laurance Rockefeller became a significant conservationist with a world-wide reputation. Winthrop Rockefeller became the Governor of the state of Arkansas. David Rockefeller became the leader of New York's Chase Manhattan Bank.

In the next generation, Jay Rockefeller IV was born in New York in 1937. He was elected the Governor of West Virginia in 1976 and was re-elected in 1980. He became a United States Senator in 1984 and was re-elected in 1990 and 1996.

The desire to be active in American society has brought a certain distinction to these families. They are greatly admired for their service to the country, especially when they share their wealth as widely as the Rockefellers did.

2. Ray Kroc

Ray Kroc (1902–1984) was born on October 5, 1902 in Illinois. When he was 15 years old, he told a little white lie so that he can become qualified as an ambulance driver in the war. The war, however, ended on the last day of his training, so he had to find some other employment.

He worked in various jobs and in 1922 he was selling paper cups. It was during these "menial" jobs, he learned the vital skill of selling. He ended up settling for selling milk shake mixers for Prince Multi-mixers.

It was on one of his outings selling milkshake mixers in San Bernardino that he came across McDonald's famous hamburgers. Through his experience crisscrossing the country to sell his mixers, he saw that they had an unusual operation, especially since they wanted eight of his mixers. Their mass-production of food intrigued him and the next day he asked them if he could market their concept.

Ray Kroc opened his first McDonald's in 1955 in Des Plaines, Illinois. Though the concept caught on quickly and sold several franchises, he ran into some financial problems that nearly bankrupted him early on. He recovered and in 1961 bought out Dick and Mac McDonald for $2.7 million. Kroc was now free to run the business as he thought best and by 1963 McDonald's had sold a billion hamburgers. Ronald McDonald made his first appearance later that year. A study in 1965 determined that more children knew who Ronald McDonald was than who the President of the United States was.

In 1965 McDonald's went public and Ray Kroc's wealth shot up into the hundreds of millions — making the earlier deal with the McDonald's stand out as one of the great business deals of the century. By 1967 McDonald's decided to branch out — first to Canada, then to Europe, then to Asia and the rest of the world. McDonald's remained successful through their focus on quality, service, cleanliness and value.

His wealth, however, did not **go to his head** (冲昏他的头脑) and he stayed actively involved in McDonald's until his death on January 14, 1984. After Ray Kroc's death, McDonald's lost some of its sparkle in America, but it continues to flourish in the rest of the world. Ray Kroc is remembered as the man that introduced the assembly line to food and leveraging it on a massive scale.

3. Walt Disney

Walt Disney (1901–1966) was a multiple Academy Award winning American film producer, director, screenwriter, voice actor, animator, entrepreneur and philanthropist. Disney is famous for his influence in the field of entertainment during the 20th century.

Disney was born on December 5, 1901 in Chicago Illinois, to his father Elias Disney, and mother Flora Call Disney. Walt was one of five children, four boys and a girl. After Walt's birth, the Disney family moved to Marceline, Missouri, Walt lived most of his childhood there.

Walt had very early interests in art. He would often sell drawings to neighbours to make extra money. He pursued his art career, by studying art and photography by going to McKinley High School in Chicago.

Walt began to love, and appreciate nature and wildlife, and family and community, which were a large part of agrarian living. Though his father could be quite stern, and often there was little money, Walt was encouraged by his mother and older brother to pursue his talents.

During the autumn of 1918, Disney attempted to enlist for military service. He was rejected because he was under age, only 16 years old at the time. Instead, Walt joined the Red Cross and was sent overseas to France, where he spent a year driving an ambulance and **chauffeuring** (为……开车) Red Cross officials. His ambulance was covered **from stem to stern** (从头到尾，完全), not with stock camouflage, but with Disney cartoons.

Once Walt returned from France, he began to pursue a career in commercial art. He started a small company called Laugh-O-Grams, which eventually fell bankrupt. With his suitcase, and 20 dollars, Walt headed to Hollywood to start anew.

Walt Disney and Mickey Statue at Disney World

After making a success of his *Alice Comedies*, Walt became a recognized Hollywood figure. On July 13, 1925, Walt married one of his first employees, Lillian Bounds, in Lewiston, Idaho. Later on they would be blessed with two daughters, Diane and Sharon.

In 1932, the production entitled *Flowers and Trees* (the first colour cartoon) won Walt the first of his studio's Academy Awards. In 1937, he released ***The Old Mill*** (老磨坊), the first short subject to utilize the multi-plane camera technique.

On December 21, 1937, *Snow White and the Seven Dwarfs*, the first full-length animated musical feature, premiered at the Carthay Theater in Los Angeles. The film produced at the unheard cost of $1,499,000 during the depths of the Depression. The film is still considered one of the great feats and imperishable monuments of the motion picture industry. During the next five years, Walt Disney Studios completed other full-length animated classics such as *Pinocchio*, *Fantasia*, *Dumbo*, and *Bambi*.

Walt Disney's dream of a clean and organized amusement park came true, as Disneyland Park opened in 1955. Walt also became a television pioneer. Disney began television production in 1954, and was among the first to present full-colour programming with his *Wonderful World of Colour* in 1961.

Walt Disney is a legend, a folk hero of the 20th century. His worldwide popularity was based upon the ideals which his name represents: imagination, optimism, creation, and self-made success in the American tradition.

4. Marilyn Monroe

Marilyn Monroe (1926–1962), Hollywood legend, famous even among the famous, began life as plain or not so plain Norma Jean Baker. Already at 16, something of a **stunner** (绝代佳人), she was soon spotted by a photographer who gave her name to a model agency. Norma Jean was in the fast lane to the cinema. Some acting lessons, a few small parts in B movie films and within no time at all, Marilyn Monroe, as she had now been named, was mixing it with Hollywood greats. Her first big break came alongside Jane Russell in *Gentleman Prefer Blondes*. It was enough of a success for her to join the stars whose hand-prints are set in concrete on Sunset Boulevard. In 1954, at the age of 27, Marilyn Monroe married another American superstar, the baseball player Joe Demagio. It seemed a perfect match. He came from a large family, where it seemed it was the security she had lacked as a child, but it was not to be. Marilyn Monroe was a prisoner of her public. In Korea, entertaining the troops, one song she always performed in particular seemed to say it all. In fact her heart belonged to the playwright Arthur Miller. "The intellectual and show girl" was how the press was putting it.

Marilyn Monroe was really then at the height of her fame. She had traveled a road from a lonely obscure teenager to a glamorous, self-assured celebrity, and all in the space of less than 10 years. But the price she had paid was enormous. She had friends in the very high social status. In America she was dating the President of the United States, and his brother Bobby, the **attorney general** (司法部长). She was **feted** (吹捧) by writers, artists, playwrights as well as the world of entertainment. Behind all the adulation though, something a good deal more sinister was developing in her life. It was the time of the **Cuban Missile Crisis** (古巴导弹危机), when the political atmosphere was almost as intense as the public pressure on the stars. The FBI opened a file on her as a possible **subversive** (颠覆分子). Then, suddenly in August 1962 she died, appa-

Marilyn Monroe

rently from an overdose of **barbiturates** (安眠药).

From the day of her funeral onward, there were many unanswered questions. It was ironic that for someone who lived in the glare of publicity, the death should have taken place in such shadowy circumstances. Was it murder, accident or suicide? No one really knows. But whatever the answer to that, there is no doubt that Marilyn Monroe was a Hollywood giant who gave delight to millions during her short, glamorous life. If she was a victim, if anyone is to take the blame of her death, then the one certain candidate is fame itself.

5. Elvis Aaron Presley

Elvis A. Presley (1935–1977) was an American singer, actor, and musician. A cultural icon, he is commonly known simply as "Elvis", and is also sometimes referred to as "the King of Rock and Roll" or "the King".

The Southern state of Mississippi was the birthplace of Elvis Presley in 1935. He began singing as a child and he won $5 when he entered a local song contest at the age of eight. He sang a ballad about a dog entitled, "**Old Shep** (老牧师)".

His musical influence came from his church where he learned hymns and gospel songs. He also loved country music and the blues. When he was only 13 years old, he began to wear sideburns with his long hair. He began to wear clothes of bright colours in order to make an image of himself as a **nonconformist** (不墨守成规的人). When he left school, he took a job as a truck driver where he had the independence to do whatever he desired with his clothes and hairstyle.

Elvis meets President Richard Nixon in the White House Oval Office, December 21, 1970.

He produced a recording of a blue song in the 1950s and the recording manager realized Elvis had some talent. He talked to the owner of the company, called Sun Records. His name was Sam Phillips. After he heard Elvis sing, he decided to take a special interest in him. He trained Elvis for nearly a year. Then he brought in some of the best music talent of the time, including guitarist Scotty Moor and bass guitarist Bill Black.

When they provided a professional backup to Elvis' singing, Sam realized Elvis would be a star.

Elvis began a singing career that led him to a performance on *The Grand Old Opry*, probably the best country music radio program. As he became known, he began to sing at county fairs. Sometimes there would be thousands in the audience, due to his popularity.

Elvis' greatest hits were "Hound Dog", "Do not Be Cruel", "Love Me Tender" and "All Shook Up". He could sing softly with great compassion or wildly with great energy. He truly became a teenage idol.

Hollywood producers realized he could be successful in films. He made 33 pictures altogether. Teenagers flocked to the theaters but his acting was only average. It was the music that teenagers came to hear.

In the United States, his music was more popular than any other popular music singer or group. The only competition came from the Beatles, a rock music phenomenon from England.

His home in Memphis, Tennessee, is also where he was buried. Though he lived to be only 42 years of age, his music lives on through singers who are Elvis impersonators. His home is like a shrine for those who love his music.

6. Steven Allan Spielberg

Steven A. Spielberg (1946–) is one of the most critically acclaimed, successful and influential film directors in international filmdom. Despite numerous critics' attacks on his directing style and several of his films, he has 24 films under his belt, including some major blockbuster hits.

He has accumulated six Academy Award nominations for Best Director, and won two for *Schindler's List* and *Saving Private Ryan*. He also won the Irving G. Thalberg Memorial Award, received an honorary degree from Brown University and another from the University of Southern California's School of Cinema Television and was presented the honour of Knight Commander of the British Empire by Queen Elizabeth II in 2001.

Steven Spielberg (left), winner of the Cecil B. Demille Lifetime Achievement award at the 66th Annual Golden Globe Awards.

Steven Spielberg was born on December 18, 1946 in Cincinnati, Ohio to a Jewish family and was later raised in both New Jersey and Arizona.

He has been passionate about movie-making since he was young, shooting amateur videos with his friends as a kid and teen. In 1968 he created his first short film for theatre release, *Amblin* — after which his first production company, Amblin Entertainment, was named. Spielberg attended California State University after high school to major in English and dropped out in the late 1960s to take a position as television director at Universal Studios. 35 years later Steven Spielberg finished his degree and was granted a Bachelor of Arts (BA) in film production and electronic arts.

Spielberg's first official feature film for theatrical release was *The Sugarland Express* in 1974. Despite good reviews, it never took off at the **box office** (票房). Then producers Richard Zanuck and David Brown offered him the chance to direct *Jaws*, a horror flick about killer sharks starring actor Roy Scheider, what Spielberg maintains was his most difficult-to-direct film. *Jaws* won three Academy Awards and grossed more than $100 million at the box office — giving Steven Spielberg the jumpstart he needed. He later rejected offers to direct both *Jaws II* and *Superman* to work with actor Richard Dreyfus to direct a movie about UFOs — *Close Encounters of the Third Kind*.

Steven Spielberg then joined forces with director, producer and friend George Lucas to create *Raiders of the Lost Ark*, the first of the Indiana Jones series starring Harrison Ford, in the early 1980s, which was a huge hit and garnered several Oscar nominations. In 1982, Spielberg directed *E.T. (The Extra-Terrestrial)*, Spielberg's personal favorite, which became the top-grossing movie of all time for many years.

Steven Spielberg was off to a great start, and he went on to direct a plethora of other films, including *The Colour Purple* (1985), *Hook* (1991), *Schindler's List* (1993), *Saving Private Ryan* (1998), *Catch Me If You Can* (2002), and *War of the Worlds* (2005).

If film-making and directing do not keep him busy enough, his family certainly will. Spielberg has seven children: four biological, two adopted and one stepdaughter. Steven Spielberg married actress Amy Irving in 1985, only to divorce her four years later after they had one child together, Max. He married actress Kate Capshaw in 1991, who has a daughter, and has three children with Kate.

7. William Henry Bill Gates

William Henry Bill Gates (1955–) is an American **business magnate** (商业巨头), philanthropist, author, the world's third richest person (as of February 8, 2008) and chairman of Microsoft, the software company he founded with Paul Allen. Gates was the richest person in the world for 15 consecutive years. During his career at Microsoft, Gates held the positions of CEO (Chief Executive Officer) and chief software architect, and remains the largest individual shareholder with more than 8% of the common stock. He has also authored or co-authored several books.

Gates was born in Seattle, Washington. At age 13, he began programming computers. He went to the prestigious Harvard University only to drop out his junior year when he was age 20. He had just started a company with Paul Allen called Microsoft.

Bill Gates and his wife watched the swimming events during the Beijing 2008 Olympic.

Gates is one of the best-known entrepreneurs of the personal computer revolution. He oversaw the invention and marketing of the MS-DOS operating system, the Windows operating interface, the Internet Explorer **browser** (浏览器), and a multitude of other popular computer products. Along the way he gained a reputation for fierce competitiveness and aggressive **business savvy** (商业头脑). During the 1990s rising Microsoft stock prices made Gates the world's wealthiest man; his wealth has at times exceeded $75 billion, making Gates a popular symbol of the ascendant computer **geek** (奇客) of the late 20th century. Although he is admired by many, a large number of industry insiders criticize his business tactics, which they consider anticompetitive, an opinion which has in some cases been upheld by the courts. In the later stages of his career, Gates has pursued a number of philanthropic endeavors, donating large amounts of money to various charitable organizations and scientific research programs through the Bill & Melinda Gates Foundation, established in 2000.

Bill Gates stepped down as chief executive officer of Microsoft in January, 2000. He remained as chairman and created the position of chief software architect. In June, 2006, Gates announced that he would be transitioning from full-time work at Microsoft to part-time work, but full-time work at the Bill & Melinda Gates Foundation. He gradually transferred his duties to Ray Ozzie, chief software architect and Craig Mundie, chief research and strategy officer. Gates' last full-time day at Microsoft was June 27, 2008. He remains at Microsoft as non-executive chairman.

8. Michael Jeffrey Jordan

Michael Jeffrey Jordan (1963–) is a retired American professional basketball player and active businessman. Michael Jordan is the greatest basketball player of all time. Jordan was one of the most effectively marketed athletes of his generation and was instrumental in popularizing the NBA around the world in the 1980s and 1990s.

Jordan was born in Brooklyn, New York, the third son of James and Delores Jordan, who moved the family to Wilmington, North Carolina when Michael was young. Jordan attended Ogden Elementary School and then Trask Junior High School. At Laney High School he became a better student and a three-sport star in football, baseball, and basketball. He was cut from the varsity basketball team during his sophomore year because at five feet nine inches he was deemed underdeveloped, but over the summer he grew four inches and practiced even harder. Over his next two seasons, he averaged 25 points per game. He began focusing on basketball, practicing every morning before school with his high school varsity coach. In his senior season at Laney High, Jordan averaged a **triple-double** (三双): 29.2 **points** (得分), 11.6 **rebounds** (篮板), and 10.1 **assists** (助攻). He was selected to the McDonald's All-American Team as a senior.

Jordan going in for a slam dunk with his signature exposed tongue.

Jordan earned a basketball scholarship to the University of North Carolina at Chapel Hill, where he majored in geography. As a freshman in Coach Dean Smith's team-oriented system, Jordan was named ACC (Atlantic Coast Conference) Freshman of the Year. He was an exciting if not dominant player, but the Tar Heels were led by All-American and future Hall of Famer James Worthy. Nonetheless, Jordan made the game-winning shot in the 1982 NCAA (National Collegiate Athletic Association) Basketball Championship game against Georgetown, which was led by future NBA rival Patrick Ewing. After winning the Naismith College Player of the Year Award in 1984, he left school early to enter the NBA **Draft** (选秀), and was selected by the Chicago Bulls in the first round as the third pick overall, after Houston Rockets centers Hakeem Olajuwon and Sam Bowie of the **Portland Trail Blazers** (波特兰开拓者队). Jordan returned to UNC (University of North Carolina) to complete his degree in 1986.

Jordan played 13 seasons for the Bulls and two seasons with the **Washington Wizards** (华盛顿奇才). Generally used as a shooting guard, his height of six feet six inches, skills, and physical conditioning also made him a versatile threat at **point guard** (控球后卫) and **small forward** (小前锋). He won six NBA Championships (1991–1993, 1996–1998) and was league Most Valuable Player (MVP) five times (1988, 1991, 1992, 1996 and 1998). He was also named Rookie of the Year (1985) and Defensive Player of the Year (1988), and won the Finals MVP award every year the Bulls reached the Finals. He also earned the elusive MVP triple crown (regular season, Finals, and All-Star Game) twice, in 1996 and 1998. Only Willis Reed and Shaquille O'Neal have won all three MVP awards in the same season. In 1997, he also recorded the only triple-double in an All-Star Game. Jordan retired for a second time in 1999, but he returned for two more NBA seasons in 2001 as a member of the Washington Wizards. He will be eligible for induction into the **Basketball Hall of Fame** (篮球名人堂) in 2009.

NOTES

1. **Mount Vernon**：维农山庄，又译为弗农山庄，是乔治·华盛顿的故居，位于美国维吉尼亚州北部的费尔法克斯郡。
2. ***Lend-Lease***：1941年美国国会通过的租借法案。
3. **The New Deal included Works Project Administration, National Recovery Administration, the Agricultural Adjustment Administration, Federal Deposit Insurance Corporation, Tennessee Valley Authority, the United States Securities and Exchange Commission, the Social Security system and the National Labour Relations Board**：在19世纪30年代经济大萧条期间，富兰克林·罗斯福推行新政，目的是为了供失业救济与复苏经济，并成立一些机构，如公共事业振兴署（WPA）、国家复兴管理局（NRA）、农业调整管理局（AAA）来改革经济和银行体系。同时，他还发起了一系列的计划，如美国联邦存款保险公司（FDIC）、田纳西河谷管理局 （TVA）以及美国证券交易委员会（SEC）。此外，他还设立了一些制度，包括社会安全系统和全国劳资关系委员会（NLRB）等等。
4. **Rosa Parks**：罗莎·帕克思（1913—2005），美国黑人民权行动主义者，美国国会称她为“现代民权运动之母”。
5. **Civil Rights movement**：民权运动。
6. **the Man of the Year**：年度人物。
7. **His company declared that they could make automobiles in any color, as long as it was black**：截至1913年底，美国有50%的汽车都是福特公司生产的。然而至1918年底，美国的汽车有一半都是T型车。当时绝大部分T型车的颜色都是黑色的，基本没有其他颜色可供选择。据传亨利·福特有一句名言：“顾客可以选择他想要的任何一种颜色，只要它是黑色。”意思就是顾客只能购买黑色的T型车。亨利·福特并不是对黑色有特殊癖好，其坚持黑色的真正原因在于黑色油漆干燥快，可以使汽车在落地的第一时间被卖出去。这也算是亨利·福特追求生产效率的极端表现之一。
8. **Copley Medal**：科普利奖章是英国皇家学院所颁发的科学奖章，起始于乔菲利·科普利爵士在1709年捐赠100英镑作为实验研究的基金，于1731年开始颁发，也是当时科学界的最高荣誉之一。
9. **the Rockefeller Foundation**：洛克菲勒基金会。

10. **the Rockefeller Institute for Medical Research**：洛克菲勒医学研究院。
11. **Rockefeller Center**：洛克菲勒中心，是位于美国纽约州纽约市第五大道的一个由数个摩天大楼组成的复合设施。
12. **B movie**：B 级片即拍摄时间短且制作预算低的影片，所以布景简陋、道具粗糙，影片缺乏质感，剧情也趋于公式化，没有良好的品质。另一方面，因为制作预算的限制，通常 B 级片并没有大明星参与演出，但都挑选大众喜欢的电影类型，例如与牛仔、情欲、黑帮、恐怖、神怪、科幻有关的剧情题材，偶尔也会抄袭当下所流行的剧情模式。
13. **Knight Commander**：爵士勋衔。
14. **geek**：极客，又译为技客、奇客，是 geek 的音译。这个词在美国俚语中意指智力超群、善于钻研但不懂与人交往的学者或知识分子，或是指过分沉迷于某事的人、令人讨厌的人。但近年来，随着互联网文化的兴起，通常被用于形容对计算机或网络技术有狂热兴趣并投入大量时间钻研的人。俗称“发烧友”或“怪杰”，例如：computer geek、techno-geek、gamer geek 等。
15. **triple-double**：三双是篮球的术语，指一场比赛中球员的个人表现在以下任何三项中达到两位数：得分、篮板、助攻、抢断和盖帽。
16. **Tar Heels**：柏油脚跟是对北卡罗来纳州和北卡罗来纳州人的昵称，它也是北卡罗莱纳大学教堂山分校运动队统一的名称。
17. **Rookie of the Year**：年度最佳新秀。
18. **Defensive Player of the Year**：年度最佳防守球员。

I. Multiple Choice

1. Abraham Lincoln was a successful lawyer because of his _______.
   A) great skill in speaking
   B) high education
   C) personality
   D) social status

2. Franklin Delano Roosevelt did all of the followings EXCEPT _______.
   A) provide *Lend-Lease* aid to Winston Churchill before America's entry into World War II
   B) play a critical role in shaping the post-war world, particularly through the Yalta Conference and the creation of the United Nations
   C) work closely with his aide Harry Hopkins, making the United States the principal arms supplier and financier of the Allies
   D) bring American idealism to the aid of developing nations

3. Winning by a narrow margin in the popular vote, _______ became the first Roman Catholic President.
   A) Abraham Lincoln
   B) Richard Nixon
   C) John Fitzgerald Kennedy
   D) Franklin Delano Roosevelt

4. The Watergate Scandal brought fresh divisions to the country and ultimately led to _______ resignation.
   A) Abraham Lincoln's
   B) Richard Nixon's
   C) John Fitzgerald Kennedy's
   D) Franklin Delano Roosevelt's

5. _______ ever gave the profound sayings like "Early to bed and early to rise makes a man healthy, wealthy, and wise."
   A) Abraham Lincoln
   B) Benjamin Franklin
   C) John Fitzgerald Kennedy
   D) Barack Hussein Obama

6. All of the following Americans have been honoured by Congress by declaring a national holiday to remember their contributions EXCEPT _______.
   A) Martin Luther King, Jr.
   B) Abraham Lincoln
   C) John Fitzgerald Kennedy
   D) George Washington

7. _______ has accumulated six Academy Award nominations for Best Director, and won two for *Schindler's List* and *Saving Private Ryan*.
   A) Anthony Minghella
   B) Steven Spielberg
   C) Ron Howard
   D) Mel Gibson

8. _______ is the greatest basketball player of all time.
   A) Michael Jeffrey Jordan　　B) Kobe Bean Bryant Cox
   C) Yao Ming　　D) Joe Dumars

9. H. L. Mencken called _______ as "the true father of American national literature".
   A) Emily Dickinson　　B) Ernest Hemingway
   C) Mark Twain　　D) Saul Bellow

10. _______ had invented the phonograph, a completely new concept: a talking machine.
   A) Henry Ford　　B) Wilbur and Orville Wright
   C) Albert Einstein　　D) Thomas Alva Edison

▶▶ II. Sentence Completion

1. __________ is the first President of the United States of America.
2. Franklin Delano Roosevelt created __________ to provide relief for the unemployed, recovery of the economy, and reform of the economic and banking systems during the Great Depression of the 1930s.
3. __________ inaugural address offered the memorable injunction, "Ask not what your country can do for you; ask what you can do for your country."
4. __________ signed into law tax relief that helped workers keep more of their hard-earned money, as well as the most comprehensive education reforms in a generation, the *No Child Left behind Act* of 2001.
5. __________ became the first African-American president of the *Harvard Law Review*.
6. The legacy of __________ lies in his success to bring equality to black Americans through non-violent means.
7. __________ opened his first McDonald's in 1955 in Des Plaines, Illinois.
8. Walt Disney's dream of a clean and organized amusement park came true, as __________ opened in 1955.
9. __________ is the chairman of Microsoft.
10. The short story as a genre in American literature probably began with Irving's __________, a collection of essays, sketches, and tales.

▶▶ III. Questions for Discussion

1. Who, do you think, can be honoured as the most important president in American history? Why?
2. Of all these celebrities mentioned in this chapter, who do you dream to be? Why?

SUMMARY

George Washington was the Commanding General of the War of Independence. Without his success, America would have become part of England. Due to his leadership, the country elected him the first President. Abraham Lincoln refused to let the Southern states leave the United States at the time of the Civil War. His kindness to all soldiers of the South and North caused him to give his Gettysburg Address. Franklin Roosevelt was the most important President in the 20th century because of his leadership in World War II and the Great Depression. John F. Kennedy and his family were significant leaders in American politics for 40 years and many Kennedys are currently in politics. Richard Nixon was a true friend to China and he assisted in improving its relations with Western countries. On November 4, 2008, Barack Obama won the campaign. He became the first African-American President. Everybody knows that change is coming to America.

The Rockefeller Family created many businesses and they shared their wealth broadly. Roy Kroc created a world business with fast food. Walt Disney may be the greatest entertainer of all with his movies and theme parks. Marilyn Monroe was the beautiful actress everyone wanted to see. Elvis Presley was America's "Rock and Roll" teen idol. Stephen Spielberg has created the best movies which draw the most attention from audiences in many countries. Bill Gates created Microsoft. Michael Jordan won so many basketball awards that he is considered the best athlete of the 20th century.

Washington Irving was a very gifted writer with an extensive vocabulary. He is called, "the Father of American Literature". Ernest Hemingway's novels became movies and reflect the adventures he had in many countries. Thomas Edison lit up the world with his light bulb. Henry Ford also had to design a motor to push a four wheel carriage which became an automobile. Wilbur and Orville Wright put a motor on a glider to create an airplane. Albert Einstein used physics to find new sources of energy. Perhaps the greatest journey was the trip from the earth to the moon. Only two people have ever walked on the moon. They are Neil Armstrong and Edwin Aldrin. They proved that people can be space explorers.

Appendices

1. States of America

	Chinese Name	English Name	Abbreviation	Capital
1	亚拉巴马	Alabama	AL	Montgomery
2	阿拉斯加	Alaska	AK	Juneau
3	亚利桑那	Arizona	AZ	Phoenix
4	阿肯色	Arkansas	AR	Little Rock
5	加利福尼亚	California	CA	Sacramento
6	科罗拉多	Colorado	CO	Denver
7	康涅狄格	Connecticut	CT	Hartford
8	特拉华	Delaware	DE	Dover
9	佛罗里达	Florida	FL	Tallahassee
10	乔治亚	Georgia	GA	Atlanta
11	夏威夷	Hawaii	HI	Honolulu
12	爱达荷	Idaho	ID	Boise
13	伊利诺斯	Illinois	IL	Springfield
14	印第安纳	Indiana	IN	Indianapolis
15	爱荷华	Iowa	IA	Des Moines
16	堪萨斯	Kansas	KS	Topeka
17	肯塔基	Kentucky	KY	Frankfort
18	路易斯安那	Louisiana	LA	Baton Rouge
19	缅因	Maine	ME	Augusta
20	马里兰	Maryland	MD	Annapolis
21	马萨诸塞	Massachusetts	MA	Boston

Continue

	Chinese Name	English Name	Abbreviation	Capital
22	密歇根	Michigan	MI	Lansing
23	明尼苏达	Minnesota	MN	St. Paul
24	密西西比	Mississippi	MS	Jackson
25	密苏里	Missouri	MO	Jefferson City
26	蒙大拿	Montana	MT	Helena
27	内布拉斯加	Nebraska	NE	Lincoln
28	内华达	Nevada	NV	Carson City
29	新罕布什尔	New Hampshire	NH	Concord
30	新泽西	New Jersey	NJ	Trenton
31	新墨西哥	New Mexico	NM	Santa Fe
32	纽约	New York	NY	Albany
33	北卡罗来纳	North Carolina	NC	Raleigh
34	北达科他	North Dakota	ND	Bismarck
35	俄亥俄	Ohio	OH	Columbus
36	俄克拉何马	Oklahoma	OK	Oklahoma City
37	俄勒冈	Oregon	OR	Salem
38	宾夕法尼亚	Pennsylvania	PA	Harrisburg
39	罗得岛	Rhode Island	RL	Providence
40	南卡罗来纳	South Carolina	SC	Columbia
41	南达科他	South Dakota	SD	Pierre
42	田纳西	Tennessee	TN	Nashville
43	得克萨斯	Texas	TX	Austin
44	犹他	Utah	UT	Salt Lake City
45	佛蒙特	Vermont	VT	Montpelier
46	弗吉尼亚	Virginia	VA	Richmond
47	华盛顿	Washington	WA	Olympia
48	西弗吉尼亚	West Virginia	WV	Charleston
49	威斯康星	Wisconsin	WI	Madison
50	怀俄明	Wyoming	WY	Cheyenne

2. American Presidents

	English Name	Chinese Name	B & D	Term
1	George Washington	乔治·华盛顿	1732–1799	1789–1797
2	John Adams	约翰·亚当斯	1735–1826	1797–1801
3	Thomas Jefferson	托马斯·杰斐逊	1743–1826	1801–1809
4	James Madison	詹姆斯·麦迪逊	1751–1836	1809–1817
5	James Monroe	詹姆斯·门罗	1758–1831	1817–1825
6	John Quincy Adams	约翰·昆西·亚当斯	1767–1848	1825–1829
7	Andrew Jackson	安德鲁·杰克逊	1767–1845	1829–1837
8	Martin van Buren	马丁·范·布伦	1782–1862	1837–1841
9	William Henry Harrison	威廉·亨利·哈里森	1773–1841	1841
10	John Tyler	约翰·泰勒	1790–1862	1841–1845
11	James Knox Polk	詹姆斯·诺克斯·波尔克	1795–1849	1845–1849
12	Zachary Taylor	扎卡里·泰勒	1784–1850	1849–1850
13	Millard Fillmore	米勒德·菲尔莫尔	1800–1874	1850–1853
14	Franklin Pierce	富兰克林·皮尔斯	1804–1869	1853–1857
15	James Buchanan	詹姆斯·布坎南	1791–1868	1857–1861
16	Abraham Lincoln	亚伯拉罕·林肯	1809–1865	1861–1865
17	Andrew Johnson	安德鲁·约翰逊	1808–1875	1865–1869
18	Ulysses Simpson Grant	尤利塞斯·辛普森·格兰特	1822–1885	1869–1877
19	Rutherford Hayes	拉瑟福德·海斯	1822–1893	1877–1881
20	James Garfield	詹姆斯·加菲尔德	1831–1881	1881
21	Chester Alan Arthur	切斯特·艾伦·阿瑟	1829–1886	1881–1885
22	Grover Cleveland	格罗弗·克利夫兰	1837–1908	1885–1889

Continue

	English Name	Chinese Name	B & D	Term
23	Benjamin Harrison	本杰明・哈里森	1833–1901	1889–1893
24	Grover Cleveland	格罗弗・克利夫兰	1837–1908	1893–1897
25	William McKinley	威廉・麦金利	1843–1901	1897–1901
26	Theodore Roosevelt	西里奥・罗斯福	1858–1919	1901–1909
27	William Howard Taft	威廉・霍华德・塔夫脱	1857–1930	1909–1913
28	Woodrow Wilson	伍德罗・威尔逊	1856–1924	1913–1921
29	Warren Harding	沃伦・哈定	1865–1923	1921–1923
30	Calvin Coolidge	卡尔文・柯立芝	1872–1933	1923–1929
31	Herbert Hoover	赫伯特・胡佛	1874–1964	1929–1933
32	Franklin Delano Roosevelt	富兰克林・德拉诺・罗斯福	1882–1945	1933–1945
33	Harry Truman	哈里・杜鲁门	1884–1972	1945–1953
34	Dwight Eisenhower	德怀特・艾森豪威尔	1890–1969	1953–1961
35	John Fitzgerald Kennedy	约翰・菲茨杰拉德・肯尼迪	1917–1963	1961–1963
36	Lyndon Johnson	林登・约翰逊	1908–1973	1963–1969
37	Richard Nixon	理査德・尼克松	1913–1994	1969–1974
38	Gerald Ford	杰拉尔德・福特	1913–2006	1974–1977
39	Jimmy Carter	吉米・卡特	1924–	1977–1981
40	Ronald Reagan	罗纳德・里根	1911–2004	1981–1989
41	George Bush	乔治・布什	1924–	1989–1993
42	William Jefferson Clinton	威廉・杰斐逊・克林顿	1946–	1993–2001
43	George Walker Bush	乔治・沃克・布什	1946–	2001–2009
44	Barack Hussein Obama	巴拉克・胡赛因・奥巴马	1961–	2009–

3. Major Events in History

1492	哥伦布（Columbus）发现新大陆。
1607	英国殖民建立詹姆斯镇（Jamestown）。
1620.11.11	《“五月花号”公约》（*Mayflower Compact*）签署。签署人立誓创立一个自治团体，这个团体是基于被管理者的同意而成立的，而且将依法而治。这是美国历史上第一份重要的政治文献。
1756	英法七年战争爆发。
1774	召开“第一届大陆会议”（*First Continental Congress*）：大会通过决议向英王呈递请愿书，要求英国取消对殖民地的高压政策；同时，大会通过了与英国断绝一切贸易关系的决议，继而通过了“关于殖民地权利和怨恨的宣言”，并建立大陆协会。
1775	英军奔袭康科德的民兵武器库，遭到列克星敦（Lexington）和康科德（Concord）民兵的抵抗。独立战争（War of Independence）揭开序幕。
1776.7.4	通过杰斐逊起草的《独立宣言》（*Declaration of Independence*），美国正式成立。
1777.11.15	通过《联邦条例》（*Articles of Confederation*），并于 1781 年获各州批准生效。据此成立的联邦国会代替大陆会议，成为直到 1789 年 3 月为止的美国立法机构。
1783.9	英美签署《巴黎条约》（*Treaty of Paris*），英国正式承认美国独立。
1786—1787	马萨诸塞州爆发农民起义——史称“谢斯起义”（Shays's Rebellion），震动了政府当局，决心加强中央政权。1787 年，在费城秘密召开制宪会议。并于 1788 年 6 月在 9 个州批准生效。然而，广大群众对宪法不满，掀起抗议运动，由此增加了宪法前 10 条修正案，于 1791 年 12 月，经 11 个州批准生效。
1789	首任总统华盛顿（George Washington）就任。
1794.11	英美签订《杰伊条约》（*Jay Treaty*），因损害了美国利益，遭到反对。同年，镇压宾夕法尼亚农民起义。
1803	从法国手中购买了路易斯安那州（Louisiana）。
1812—1814	第二次对英战争（War of 1812），1814 年 12 月美英签订《根特条约》（*Treaty of Ghent*），自此美国完全脱离了英国的政治控制和经济渗透。
1820	为了缓解南北双方的矛盾，签订了“密苏里妥协案”（*Missouri Compromise*）。这个协议表明，北部的资产阶级向南部的种植奴隶主做了让步。

1823　《门罗宣言》(*Monroe Doctrine*)：美国将不干涉欧洲的事务和内部战争，欧洲也不得干预美洲的内部事务。

1831　由特纳领导的反奴隶制起义（Nat Turner's Rebellion）在美国弗吉尼亚州爆发。这次起义导致南部奴隶主在立法上加强对黑人奴隶的压迫。他们颁布了一系列禁止黑人受教育、不准黑人集会等新禁令。

1837　美国产业革命开始。

1844　胁迫中国清政府签订《望厦条约》(*Sino-American Treaty of Wangxia*)，提出“利益均沾”原则。

1846—1848　发动对墨西哥战争（War against Mexico），把得克萨斯、新墨西哥、加利福尼亚并入美国领土。

1848　淘金热开始。

1851—1864　参加镇压中国太平天国运动（Taiping Rebellion），并胁迫日本开放门户（Open Door Policy）。

1857　美国最高法院作出德莱特·斯科特判决案（*Dred Scott Decision*），其法律含义是使奴隶制的范围推向全国。

1861—1865　美国南北战争（Civil War）。

1862　宅地法（*Homestead Act*）颁布，孤立了南部同盟。

1863　解放宣言（*Emancipation Proclamation*）颁布，短期内即有 18.6 万黑人参加联邦军队作战。

1865.4.15　亚伯拉罕·林肯（Abraham Lincoln）在华盛顿的福特剧院遇刺身亡。

1865.11　密西西比州首先颁布黑人法典，对黑人残酷迫害。

1866　三 K 党（Ku Klux Klan，缩写为 KKK）成立，对黑人施以私刑。三 K 党是美国历史上和现在的一个奉行白人至上主义的民间组织，也是美国种族主义的代表性组织。

1867　从俄罗斯购入阿拉斯加州（Alaska）。

1867.3　国会通过重新建设南部法案，对南部实行军管。

1867—1877　南部进行民主重建。

1869　横贯铁路完成。

1877.7　西弗吉尼亚和宾夕法尼亚铁路工人举行罢工，随后波及全国铁路工人罢工。

1877.12.15　爱迪生为他的留声机申请专利。

1879　爱迪生发明了电灯泡。

1886.5.1　35 万工人争取 8 小时工作制举行示威游行。5 月 3 日晚，发生芝加哥干草市场惨案（Haymarket Massacre）。1889 年第二国际（The Second International）巴黎大会上，通过决议，规定 5 月 1 日为国际劳动节。

1898　发动美西战争（War on Spain），夺取了加勒比海的古巴和波多黎各、太平洋的关岛和菲律宾群岛，合并了夏威夷群岛。

1898　对中国提出“门户开放”政策（Open Door Policy）。即在承认各国在中国的“势力范围”基础上，提出“机会均等”，把最初的“势力范围”和租借地政策（*Lend-Lease Program*）应用到整个中国。

1900　美国参加八国联军（Eight-Power Allied Forces）入侵中国。

1901.9　美国总统威廉·麦金利（William McKinley）在出席布法罗泛美博览会时，被一名无政府主义者射伤，不久便去世身亡。麦金利是美国立国后被刺身亡的第三位总统。

1902　美国从古巴撤军，承认古巴独立。

1903　莱特兄弟（Wright Brothers）发明飞机。

1904　罗斯福提出“罗斯福推论”，进一步补充了门罗主义。他指出：拉美国家一旦“闹事”，美国可以干涉其内部事务。

1906　美国历史上最严重的地震 4 月 18 日在旧金山爆发了，此次地震共死亡 750 人，财产损失达 5 亿美元。

1907　美国出现 1907 大恐慌（The Panic of 1907/the 1907 Bankers' Panic）：当时的美国股市一泻千里，券商和知名企业纷纷倒闭，市场流动性陷入困境，银行挤兑风潮席卷全美。为了稳定市场，增加市场流动性，摩根联手另外一家兄弟公司共同出资 25 亿美元注资市场。直到 1909 年，道琼斯指数才恢复到恐慌发生前的水平。

1908　美国联邦调查局（Federal Bureau of Investigation [FBI]）成立。

1909　罗伯特·培利（Robert Peary）成为第一个到达北极的人。

1909.3　芝加哥女工为争取同工同酬，举行罢工游行。博得全世界妇女的同情和响应。次年，国际妇女代表大会决定将 3 月 8 日定为国际劳动妇女节（International Working Women's Day）。

1912　新墨西哥州（New Mexico）成为美国的第 47 个州，亚利桑那州（Arizona）成为美国第 48 个州。

1914　经过 10 年的努力，花费了 3.66 亿元，巴拿马运河（Panama Canal）终于修建成功。

1914.6.28　第一次世界大战爆发（World War I）。

1920　国会通过宪法第 19 条修正案（*The 19th Amendment to the Constitution*），给予妇女选举权。

1924　美国国会通过了《约翰逊·里德移民法案》（*Johnson-Reed Immigration Act*），开始全面控制每年入境的移民数量。结果，随后 40 年里的新移民构成基本反映了美国已有的族裔结构，即绝大多数是欧洲人和北美人。

1929—1933	华尔街金融风暴（Wallstreet Financial Crisis）引发全球经济危机。
1938	实施公平劳动标准法（*Labor Standard Act*），提出工资下限和工时上限。
1939—1945	第二次世界大战（World War II）。美参加对德、意、日的反法西斯战斗（Anti-Fascist War）。为反法西斯各国提供武器物资，成为盟国的兵工厂，战时经济繁荣，确立了美元作为世界货币的地位。利用参战的机会，控制了世界许多战略据点，建立了军事基地。推行冷战政策（Cold War Policy），提出杜鲁门主义（*Truman Doctrine*）、马歇尔计划（*Marshall Plan*），筹划成立北大西洋公约组织（North Atlantic Treaty Organization）。
1941.8	与英国发表大西洋宪章（*Atlantic Charter*），奠定了美、英、苏战时合作的基础。
1941.12.7	日本偷袭珍珠港（Pearl Harbour），美国对日宣战。
1945.8.15	日本无条件投降，第二次世界大战结束。
1945	联合国成立（the United Nations）。 美军进驻日本，实现了美国独家控制日本的局面。
1946	第一台计算机在美国发明。
1950—1953	朝鲜战争（Korean War）。
1954—1965	美国民权运动（Civil Rights Movement），反对种族隔离和歧视。
1963.11.22	约翰·肯尼迪（John Kennedy）在达拉斯遇刺。
1964.1	美军直接干涉巴拿马。
1965	美国出兵多米尼加镇压起义。
1968.4.4	马丁·路德·金（Martin Luther King）遇刺。
1969.7.20	阿波罗（Apollo）登月。
1969	互联网诞生。
1969	尼克松总统以“伙伴关系、实力加谈判”作为美国对外政策的新战略。
1972.5	尼克松访苏，签署了限制战略武器条约。
1972	尼克松访华，发表了中美上海公报（*Shanghai Communiqué*）。
1974.8.9	尼克松因水门事件（The Watergate Scandal）被迫辞职，副总统杰拉尔德·福特（Gerald Ford）就任第 38 届总统。
1975.5	正式宣布越南战争结束。
1983	美国组织“多国部队”出兵格林纳达。
1985	美国成为债务国。
1988.6.1	美苏两国领导人在莫斯科交换了中程导弹条约的批准书。美苏关系进一步趋向缓和。
1998	克林顿总统遭弹劾。
1999	美国干预科索沃战争。

2000	美国在线服务公司（AOL：American on Line）收购华纳兄弟娱乐公司（Time Warner）。
2001.9.11	“9・11”恐怖袭击，是发生在美国本土，通过劫持多架民航飞机冲撞摩天高楼的自杀式恐怖袭击。在事件中共有 2 998 人死亡，包括美国纽约地标性建筑世界贸易中心双塔（World Trade Center Towers）在内的六座建筑被完全摧毁，美国国防部总部（U.S. Department of Defense）所在地五角大楼（Pentagon）也受到袭击。
2003.8.14	美国东北部和加拿大部分地区发生大面积停电（blackout），这是北美历史上最大规模的断电事故，波及美、加两国的许多城市，给当地交通、通信和居民的生活造成严重影响。
2005	飓风卡特里娜（Hurricane Katrina）摧毁了美国从路易斯安那到佛罗里达、西弗吉尼亚的大部分墨西哥湾沿岸地区，造成逾 1836 人遇难，灾难损失超过 1 150 亿美元。
2008	巴拉克・胡赛因・奥巴马（Barack Hussein Obama Jr.）当选总统，这是美国历史上第一次黑人（African-American）当选总统。

4. *Declaration of Independence*

When in the Course of human events, it becomes necessary for one People to dissolve the Political Bands which have connected them with another, and to assume among the Powers of the Earth, the separate and equal Station to which the Laws of Nature and of Nature's God entitle them, a decent Respect to the Opinions of Mankind requires that they should declare the causes which impel them to the Separation.

We hold these Truths to be self-evident, that all Men are created equal, that they are endowed by their Creator with certain unalienable Rights, that among these are Life, Liberty and the Pursuit of Happiness — That to secure these Rights, Governments are instituted among Men, deriving their just Powers from the Consent of the Governed, That whenever any Form of Government becomes destructive of these Ends, it is the Right of the People to alter or to abolish it, and to institute new Government, laying its Foundation on such Principles and organizing its Powers in such Form, as to them shall seem most likely to effect their Safety and Happiness. Prudence, indeed, will dictate that Governments long established should not be changed for light and transient Causes; and accordingly all Experience hath shewn, that Mankind are more disposed to suffer, while Evils are sufferable, than to right themselves by abolishing the Forms to which they are accustomed. But when a long Train of Abuses and Usurpations, pursuing invariably the same Object, evinces a

Design to reduce them under absolute Despotism, it is their Right, it is their Duty, to throw off such Government, and to provide new Guards for their future Security. Such has been the patient Sufferance of these Colonies; and such is now the Necessity which constrains them to alter their former Systems of Government. The History of the present King of Great Britain is a history of repeated Injuries and Usurpations, all having in direct Object the Establishment of an absolute Tyranny over these States. To prove this, let Facts be submitted to a candid World.

He has refused his Assent to Laws, the most wholesome and necessary for the public Good.

He has forbidden his Governors to pass Laws of immediate and pressing Importance, unless suspended in their Operation till his Assent should be obtained; and when so suspended, he has utterly neglected to attend to them

He has refused to pass other Laws for the Accommodation of large Districts of People, unless those People would relinquish the Right of Representation in the Legislature, a Right inestimable to them and formidable to Tyrants only.

He has called together Legislative Bodies at Places unusual, uncomfortable, and distant from the Depository or their public Records, for the sole Purpose of fatiguing them into Compliance with his Measures.

He has dissolved Representative Houses repeatedly, for opposing with manly Firmness his Invasions on the Rights of the people.

He has refused for a long time, after such Dissolutions, to cause others to be elected; whereby the Legislative Powers, incapable of Annihilation, have returned to the People at large for their exercise; the State remaining in the mean time exposed to all the Dangers of Invasion from without, and Convulsions within.

He has endeavored to prevent the Population of these States; for that Purpose obstructing the Laws for Naturalization of Foreigners; refusing to pass others to encourage their Migration hither, and raising the Conditions of new Appropriations of Lands.

He has obstructed the Administration of Justice, by refusing his Assent to Laws for establishing Judiciary Powers.

He has made Judges dependent on his Will alone, for the Tenure of their Offices, and the Amount and Payment of their Salaries.

He has erected a Multitude of new Offices, and sent hither Swarms of Officers to harass our People, and eat out their Substance.

He has kept among us, in Times of Peace, Standing Armies, without the consent of our Legislatures.

He has affected to render the Military independent of and superior to the Civil Power;

He has combined with others to subject us to a Jurisdiction foreign to our Constitution, and unacknowledged by our laws; giving his Assent to their Acts of pretended Legislation;

For quartering large Bodies of Armed Troops among us;

For protecting them, by a mock Trial, from Punishment for any Murders which they should commit on the Inhabitants of these States;

For cutting off our Trade with all Parts of the World;

For imposing Taxes on us without our Consent;

For depriving us, in many Cases, of the Benefits of Trial by Jury;

For transporting us beyond Seas to be tried for pretended Offences;

For abolishing the free System of English Laws in a neighbouring Province, establishing therein an arbitrary Government, and enlarging its Boundaries so as to render it at once an Example and fit Instrument for introducing the same absolute Rule into these Colonies;

For taking away our Charters, abolishing our most valuable Laws, and altering fundamentally the Forms of our Governments;

For suspending our own Legislatures, and declaring themselves invested with Power to legislate for us in all Cases whatsoever.

He has abdicated Government here, by declaring us out of his Protection and waging War against us.

He has plundered our Seas, ravaged our Coasts, burnt our Towns, and destroyed the Lives of our People.

He is at this Time transporting large Armies of foreign Mercenaries to compleat the Works of Death, Desolation and Tyranny, already begun with circumstances of Cruelty and perfidy, scarcely paralleled in the most barbarous Ages, and totally unworthy the Head of a civilized Nation.

He has constrained our fellow Citizens taken Captive on the high Seas to bear Arms against their Country, to become the Executioners of their Friends and Brethren, or to fall themselves by their Hands.

He has excited domestic Insurrections amongst us, and has endeavored to bring on the Inhabitants of our Frontiers, the merciless Indian Savages, whose known Rule of Warfare, is an undistinguished Destruction of all Ages, Sexes and Conditions.

In every state of these Oppressions we have Petitioned for Redress in the most humble Terms: Our repeated Petitions have been answered only by repeated Injury. A Prince, whose character is thus marked by every act which may define a Tyrant, is unfit to be the Ruler of a free People.

Nor have we been wanting in Attentions to our British Brethren. We have warned them from Time to Time of Attempts by their Legislature to extend an unwarrantable Jurisdiction over us. We have reminded them of the Circumstances of our Emigration and Settlement here. We have appealed to their native Justice and Magnanimity, and we have conjured them by the Ties of our common Kindred to disavow these Usurpations, which would inevitably interrupt our Connections and Correspondence. They too have been deaf to the Voice of Justice and of Consanguinity. We must, therefore, acquiesce in the Necessity, which denounces our Separation, and hold them, as we hold the rest of Mankind, Enemies in War, in Peace, Friends.

WE, therefore, the Representatives of the UNITED STATES OF AMERICA, in General Congress, Assembled, appealing to the Supreme Judge of the World for the Rectitude of our Intentions, do, in the Name, and by Authority of the good People of these Colonies, solemnly Publish and Declare, That these United Colonies are, and of Right ought to be FREE AND INDEPENDENT STATES; that they are Absolved from all Allegiance to the British Crown, and that all political connection between them and the State of Great Britain, is and ought to be totally dissolved; and that as Free and Independent States, they have full Power to levy War, conclude Peace, contract Alliances, establish Commerce, and to do all other Acts and Things which INDEPENDENT STATES may of right do. And for the support of this Declaration, with a firm Reliance on the Protection of divine Providence, we mutually pledge to each other our Lives, our Fortunes and our sacred Honor.

Key

Chapter 1 Geography

▶▶ I. Multiple Choice

1. C 2. A 3. D 4. A 5. A 6. B 7. C 8. B 9. A 10. B

▶▶ II. Sentence Completion

1. Canada; Mexico; Russia
2. 1783
3. Russia; Canada; China
4. north-central; four
5. tropical; volcanic islands
6. "Father of Waters"; "Old Man River", the Rockies; the Gulf of Mexico
7. the Mississippi River; the Columbia River
8. the Great Lakes; Lake Superior; Lake Michigan; Lake Huron; Lake Erie; Lake Ontario; Lake Michigan; Canada
9. the west; the USA; Mexico; Canada
10. hurricanes

Chapter 2 History

▶▶ I. Multiple Choice

1. B 2. D 3. A 4. B 5. A 6. D 7. C 8. B 9. C 10. B

▶▶ II. Sentence Completion

1. Puritans; religious; *Mayflower*
2. Thomas Jefferson; *Declaration of Independence*; National Day

3. *Monroe Doctrine*; colonize; interfere
4. agrarian; industrial; Andrew Jackson
5. Harriet Beecher Stowe; *Uncle Tom's Cabin*; slavery
6. 1932; recovery; *New Deal*

▶▶ III. Term Explanation

1. In September 1774, 55 representatives from all the colonies except Georgia held a meeting in Philadelphia to talk about their troubles with their mother country. The meeting was called the First Continental Congress. At the meeting the majority of representatives still thought they could settle their quarrel with the British by peaceful means. They agreed to refuse to buy British goods, hoping in this way to force the British Government to give in to their demands. They also agreed to raise a volunteer army to protect the colonies if Britain used force to break the boycott.
2. The most glorious achievement of Jefferson as President was the Louisiana Purchase. The Louisiana Purchase, in 1803, gave Western farmers use of the important Mississippi River waterway, removed the French presence from the western border of US, provided US farmers with vast expanses of land, and furthered American leaders' vision of creating a "Great Nation".
3. The US-Spanish War broke out in April, 1898, lasted for only 70 days and ended with US as the victor. A peace treaty was signed in December 1898 in Paris. As a result of the war, Spain was forced to cede her former colonies Cuba, Puerto Rico, Guam and the Philippines to US; US agreed to pay 20 million dollars for them in an attempt to put a good face on its foreign expansion. Cuba remained a US "protectorate" for some years, while the Philippines were not granted its independence until after the end of WW I. US seized Hawaii from Spain after the US-Spanish War. The US-Spanish War was the first imperialist war for redividing the world. It marked a new stage in which US transformed into an imperialist power. From that time the US began its modern history.
4. The expression of "roaring twenties" is often used to describe the period of American life. The roaring twenties ushered in an exciting time of social change and economic prosperity, as the recession at the end of WW II was quickly replaced by an unprecedented period of financial growth. The stock market soared to unimaginable heights because of the so-called Second Industrial Revolution at the turn of the 20th century, which saw the development of new inventions and machines that changed American society drastically.
5. In the presidential election year 1972, five men of the Committee for the Reelection of the President broke into the Democratic national headquarters at the Watergate Hotel, Washington, D.C., where they planted bugs in order to get information for the Committee. But unfor-

tunately they were arrested. Although it was never approved that Nixon planned the Watergate break-in or that he ever knew about it beforehand, he was eventually forced out of office because he was found guilty for his effect to avoid the investigation and disclosures.

Chapter 3 Government and Politics

▶▶ I. Sentence Completion

1. supreme law
2. the *Articles of Confederation*
3. republic; state; president
4. ratification
5. *Bill of Rights*; amendments
6. executive; checks and balances
7. bicameral; the Senate; the House of Representatives
8. President; Constitutional Amendment; two
9. Supreme Court
10. Democratic; Republican
11. the Electoral College

▶▶ II. Term Explanation

1. *The Constitution of the United States of America* is the supreme law of the United States. It provides the framework for the organization of the United States Government. The document defines the three main branches of the government: the legislative, the executive branch, and a judicial branch headed by the Supreme Court. Besides providing for the organization of these branches, the Constitution carefully outlines which powers each branch may exercise. It also reserves numerous rights for the individual states. It is the shortest and oldest written Constitution of any major sovereign state.
2. Many of the recommendations of the states ratifying conventions were considered later by James Madison as he drafted what became the *Bill of the Rights*. It is commonly viewed as consisting of the first 10 articles of *Amendments to the Constitution*. These amendments give all Americans rights to believe in any religion; to speak, write and publish as they like; to gather together peaceably and to petition the government; to be secure in their homes without

fear of unreasonable searches and seizure of persons and property; and to receive fair and just treatment in courts of law. The *Bill of Rights* was added in 1791.

3. Jurisdiction is the authority to hear and decide cases. According to the *Constitution*, the federal courts exercise jurisdiction over cases in which the subject involves either the U.S. *Constitution*, statutes, or treaties; maritime law; or cases in which the litigants include either the U.S. government, more than one state government, one state government and a citizen of another state, citizens of more than one state, or a foreign government or citizen. The state courts exercise jurisdiction over the remaining cases. These include most criminal cases.
4. It is a body that elects the president and vice-president. Each state is represented by the same number of members as in its congressional delegation. In another word, each has as many electors as the total representation in Congress (House plus Senate). The voters vote for electors who will cast their ballots in the Electoral College. Because of the winner-take-all feature of the Electoral College, the system gives an advantage to large states and their urban populations.
5. The 19th century journalist John O'Sullivan coined the phrase "manifest destiny" in an 1839 article. It conveyed the belief in the divinely conferred right of the republic to expand westward and bring more of the continent into "the great experiment of Liberty and Federated self-government".

▶▶ III. True or False

1. T 2. F 3. T 4. F 5. F 6. T 7. F 8. F 9. T 10. T

▶▶ IV. Questions for Discussion

1. *The Articles of Confederation* was the first governing *Constitution* of the United States of America. Although serving a crucial role in the victory in the American Revolutionary War, a group of reformers felt that the Articles lacked the necessary provisions for a sufficiently effective government. Another problem is that the government lacked taxing authority; it had to request funds from the states. Another criticism of the Articles was that they did not strike the right balance between large and small states in the legislative decision making process.
2. Legislature is a type of representative assembly with the power to create and change laws. The President has the authority to appoint federal judges as vacancies occur. Under the *Constitution*, the President is responsible for foreign relations with other nations. He also has the right to veto or sign any bills passed by Congress. He can call into service of the National Guard. The judicial

4. It stands for Nation's Gross Product.
5. It is mainly for the following five reasons:
   - over-production;
   - less-competitive ability problems of farms;
   - the poverty problems of the black and urban poor;
   - increasing military spending;
   - soaring federal deficits and trade deficit.
6. The farm population has decreased over the years for the following tow reasons: one is the high farming costs, and the other is low product prices, hence small farmers could hardly make any profits.
7. It refers to industry in America.

Chapter 6 Education

▶▶ I. True or False

1. F　2. F　3. T　4. F　5. F　6. F　7. T

▶▶ II. Short Answer Questions

1. *No Child Left Behind Act* was passed to mandate *Adequate Yearly Progress*, which helped, to some extent, set some national learning standards.
2. Because the individual state has the law-endowed rights to make its own educational decisions.
3. American universities select their students up to their GPA and SAT mainly, at the same time, they may also take into consideration some subjective factors such as a commitment to extracurricular activities, a personal essay, and possibly an interview.
4. GPA stands for Grade Point Average; SAT stands for Scholastic Aptitude Test.
5. Charter schools receive public money but have been freed from some of the rules, regulations, and statutes that apply to other public schools in exchange for some type of accountability for producing certain results, which are set forth in each school's charter.

   School vouchers, or education vouchers are a certificate issued by the government by which parents can pay for the education of their children at a school of their choice, rather than the public school to which they are assigned.

Chapter 7 Social Life and Customs

▶▶ I. Multiple Choice

1. D 2. A 3. C 4. B 5. D

▶▶ II. True or False

1. F 2. T 3. F 4. F 5. F 6. F 7. T 8. F 9. T 10. T

▶▶ III. Questions for Discussion

[Open]

Chapter 8 Who's Who

▶▶ I. Multiple Choice

1. A 2. D 3. C 4. B 5. A 6. C 7. B 8. A 9. C 10. D

▶▶ II. Sentence Completion

1. George Washington
2. New Deal
3. John Fitzgerald Kennedy
4. George Walker Bush
5. Barack Hussein Obama
6. Martin Luther King
7. Ray Kroc
8. Disneyland Park
9. William Henry Bill Gates
10. *The Sketch Book*

▶▶ III. Questions for Discussion

[Open]